ISLAM INFLAMED

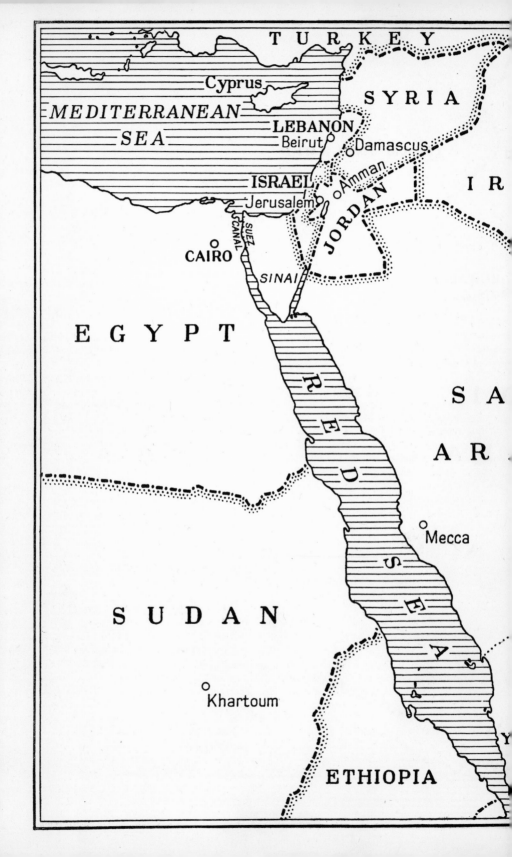

By the Same Author:

As I Saw the U.S.A.

Sultan in Oman

ISLAM INFLAMED

A MIDDLE EAST PICTURE

BY *James Morris*

PANTHEON BOOKS

© 1957 by Pantheon Books Inc.
333 Sixth Avenue, New York 14, N.Y.
Library of Congress Catalog Card Number: 57-11758
Manufactured in the U.S.A.

CONTENTS

ISLAM INFLAMED

INTRODUCTORY

THIS IS an impression of the Muslim Middle East as it was at a decisive moment of its history.

One day in November, 1956, I stood beside a road in the Sinai desert with a colonel of the Israel army. A troop of French-built tanks had stopped nearby, and the young Israeli tank crews were sprawled on their turrets or eating sandwiches in the sand. There were Yemenis, Poles, Hungarians, Germans, and a solitary fair-haired South African, and they were in uproarious spirits, their laughter swirling all about us and their white teeth flashing as they talked. Overhead there sometimes swept a Mystère jet fighter or a lumbering transport aircraft; in the distance a platoon of infantry was marching in jaunty silhouette along a ridge.

All around us, as we stood there talking that afternoon, there lay the debris of a defeated army. There were smoking and blackened trucks; burnt-out tanks; guns destroyed in their emplacements; boots and tents and rifles and ammunition boxes; and a multitude of papers, paybooks, and orders and letters home, littered among the tentage or blowing fitful and forlorn across the desert. Up the road from the south came a succession of lorries. They were piled high with the booty of war, from bedspreads to gasoline drums, and as they rumbled northwards their drivers leaned out and waved to the tank men, or whistled jubilantly in their cabs. Sometimes captured tanks came past on transporters; once a column of prisoners marched despondently by, their hands behind their heads. There was success in the air, and the smell of blood, and the Sinai that day was both sinister and stimulating.

This was the aftermath of a cataclysmic battle. The Israelis, hurling themselves upon their Egyptian enemies, had driven them helter-skelter out of Sinai to the banks of the Suez Canal; and at the same time, by collusion or by circumstance, the British and French armies had attacked Port Said. That afternoon the Tricolor and the Union Jack flew side by side over the Suez Canal, and the Israelis were masters of Sinai from Gaza in the north to Sharm es Sheikh at the southern tip. The world waited in an awed hush to see what would happen next. It was a crux of the twentieth century, in which the future of the world hung in balance, and more than one proud Power faced ignominy or disaster; and in particular it was a turning point for the Muslims of the Middle East, who stood breathless and aghast all around us.

"And what's going to happen now?" I asked the colonel, who was drinking warm orange juice out of a bottle. He wiped his mouth and smiled, not without a trace of satisfaction. "God knows," he said, "but I can promise you this: after this little lot, the face of the Middle East will never be the same again."

This book is a picture of the region as it was that day, frozen for a moment in all its varied attitudes, before the hot breath of history melted the tableau.

It was, as usual, a mess. Nine principal territories form the subject of our study, and there was tumult in them all, ranging from the trivial to the tragic. Egypt was in the throes of hysterical ambition; the Sudan was divided; Lebanon was bickering over oil rights; Syria seemed to be going Communist; Iraq was threatened by subversion; Jordan was riddled with intrigue; in Persia the fanatics were restless; in Saudi Arabia the King clung grimly to his privileges; in the other territories of the Arabian Peninsula nationalists of varying degrees of sincerity chafed against imperialism.

These separate derangements were linked by shared emotions. All the Arabs, whatever their flag or ruler, looked towards Israel with an implacable loathing, tinged with fear; no peace treaty had been signed with the Jews, there were frequent frontier clashes, a million Arab refugees were still homeless, and a rigid economic blockade of Israel was enforced by all the Arab Powers. Similarly in all these countries, monarchies or republics, sovereign states or dependencies, new social forces were seething and bubbling; many a king and many a rich landlord, still entrenched in feudalism, thought he saw the writing on the wall. At the same time there was encouched somewhere in the heart of the Arab world a yearning for unity, a nebulous longing for the revival of old glories and the reenactment of ancient triumphs; and coupled with these grand but fuzzy sentiments was a distrust of foreign influence so profound and unreasoning that it sometimes amounted to paranoia.

Within the ungainly framework of this triad—hatred of Israel, social fermentation, perfervid nationalism—powerful forces of political change were at work in the Middle East, sometimes in partnership, sometimes in enmity, some indigenous, some foreign. The strategic situation of these countries had always been recognized; immense oil deposits had brought them new international importance; and the chronic instability of the place had given impetus to perpetual struggles for its control. The decline of Britain had left a vacuum in the Middle East, and there were several applicants to fill it.

Of the indigenous forces, much the most virile and potent was the new Republic of Egypt, under its formidable President, Gamal Abdel Nasser. By overthrowing the feudal masters of Egypt, brazenly defying the West, and leading the vendetta against Israel, Nasser had made himself the Saladin of the time. Within a few years he had expelled a king, forced the withdrawal of British troops, nationalized the Suez Canal, armed the Egyptian army with weapons from Communist Europe, and given the Arab world a telling (if strident) voice in the counsels of Bandung and the United Nations. He had made Egypt supreme in the Middle East, and his influence was apparent among all the Arab peoples.

Inflamed by these successes, the insolence of Egypt was unbounded. Constant threats of annihilation were thrown at Israel. Abuse was screamed at the Western Powers and those allied to them—notably Iraq, Egypt's principal rival among the Arabs. Cairo radio, impelled by a variety of malicious motives, and one or two honorable ones, projected the creeds of subversion to the most improbable destinations, stirring up anti-Western feeling anywhere from Zanzibar to Kurdestan. All over the Middle East the agents of Egypt, often financed by the oil kingdom of Saudi Arabia, worked for the denigration of the West, the glorification of Egypt, and the attainment of Arab unity under the aegis of Cairo.

The other Arab Powers wavered before the dynamism of this new Egypt. Some—Saudi Arabia, Yemen, Syria—thought it best to ally themselves with Colonel Nasser. Some—Jordan and Lebanon—sat warily on the fence. One only, the oil-rich Kingdom of Iraq, remained obviously hostile, except in support of Egypt's anti-Israel passions. Not only logic guided the Arabs in these several policies.

Old rivalries still played their part in Middle East affairs, notably the perennial feud between the Hashemite dynasty, which ruled in Iraq and Jordan, and the Saudis, who dominated the Arabian Peninsula. The Saudis saw Egypt as an ally against the Hashemites; the Hashemites distrusted the power of an Egyptian-Saudi alliance; the Egyptians feared, as always, that the Hashemites would one day create a Greater Syria, a federation of Iraq, Syria, and Jordan which could become the dominant force among the Arabs.

The Great Powers did their best to exploit these fears and ferments, but did not always succeed. Their interest was primarily in oil, of which the Middle East held the greatest known reserves, and by 1956 the cold war between capitalism and Communism had spread southwards to Arabia and the Levant. The British, so recently masters of the Middle East, were reluctantly withdrawing their power, and the succession was contested (rather fitfully at first) by the Russians and the Americans. The Americans had great oil interests and had poured money and good will into the area, but they were tainted with Zionist sympathies and suspected of colonialist tendencies. The Russians were not linked with Israel, were seldom regarded as imperialists, offered convictions easily grasped by a people so generally poor and discontented, and had the advantage of being the devil that nobody knew.

In this developing struggle the West relied largely upon a semimilitary alliance, the Baghdad Pact, which was gravely weakened by the frenetic hostility of Egypt to any military association with the West. Persia and Iraq became members of the pact, together with Britain, Turkey, and Pakistan; and the Americans, fumbling and dilatory, gave it their economic support. The treaty offered some military advantages, at least on paper, because it welded the northern tier of the Middle East into defensive cohesion; and it was useful in countering subversion and as a channel for financial and technical help; but the Egyptians successfully tarred it with the imperialist brush, and it provided the Russians with an excuse for leapfrogging the northern tier and insinuating their influence farther south.

This they did with energy, thus becoming a Middle Eastern Power at last. They rearmed the Egyptian army, backed Colonel Nasser in his inflammatory policies, offered lavish economic help, and fostered flourishing trade relations. They made a potential Trojan camel of Syria, and they even managed to establish a tentative foothold in the Yemen. By the middle of 1956 the Russians had all but succeeded in identifying themselves with the cause of pan-Arabism. They supported the Arabs in their relentless blockade of Israel, and they sometimes gave the impression that they would willingly connive in a holy war to restore Palestine to the Muslims.

These were the bones of the situation when, in November, 1956, the Israelis, the British, and the French threw themselves upon Egypt and ended an era in the Middle East. There were several different cankers which, in Western eyes, urgently needed piercing. One was the Arab blockade of Israel, which threatened to erupt into another war. Another was the infiltration of militant Communism. A third was the mischief-making of Egypt. It was too much to hope that the eternal squabbles and backbitings of the Arab world could be calmed, or that its terrible social problems could be solved overnight; but these three principal perils could all be removed, it was thought, if only Egypt could be humbled.

The plan misfired. Victory it was in the Sinai that day, and the tank men had reason to celebrate; but it brought few immediate fruits to Israel, and obloquy (if only temporary) to Britain and France. This is a familiar phenomenon of the Middle East, where high intentions are nearly always blunted, where motives are insidiously perverted over the years, where precious buds blossom into thistles, where good and bad, noble and despicable, gay and sad are inextricably confused. When that Israeli colonel wiped his mouth, shrugged his shoulders, and waved a mocking hand towards the Muslim horizons all around us, he was thinking of these prickly and sometimes laughable paradoxes.

Nor can the impartial Englishman escape them. There are Persians in this book and Negroes, Britons, Kurds, and Copts; but most of the people who appear in it are Arabs, and they share the pungent characteristics of their race, at once delicate and vulgar, at once infinitely subtle and bafflingly obtuse. Doughty once said that they were like men sitting in a cloaca, but with their brows touch-

ing heaven. I think the flavor of their territories is even more hauntingly reflected in a poem by C. P. Cafavy, the great Greek poet
of Alexandria. It describes one of the gods, on a visit from the All-
Holy Mansions, making his way through the ancient market place
of Seleukia for an evening of debauchery. Nobility stalks among
talkative bystanders toward depravity; and that is what happens,
all too often, in the tumultuous market place of the Middle East.

PART ONE

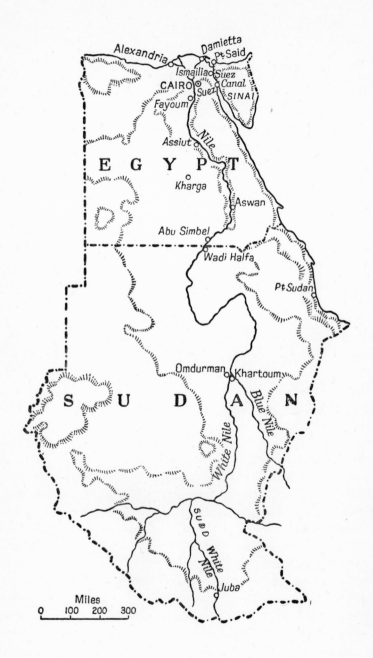

NEW EGYPT

NOT FAR TO THE EAST of Alexandria a small road leads between orchards to the Mediterranean Sea. It runs through neat gardens, well-watered by irrigation canals, and if it is early on a summer morning the old gardeners, their *gallabiyas* hitched up to their waists, will straighten themselves creaking from their work and wave to you as you pass. Presently blue water appears between the trees—the bay of Aboukir, where Nelson drove the French fleet ashore; and when you emerge from the shadows onto the golden beach there stands before you, a grotesque ornate fable, the palace of Montaza. Tall and fantastic are its towers and turrets. Its bridges and esplanades are encrusted with lamp standards, and around it a community of small elaborate outbuildings clusters and crouches like ornamental dogs beside some grand but gloomy master. A high wall surrounds the flower gardens of the palace; the Mediterranean laps its beaches and landing stages; and as the sun rises, and the hot Egyptian morning draws on, the whole thing shimmers in the sun as a back cloth flaps with the passing of the stage-hands.

This was the palace of King Farouk, a coarse but witty monarch, until in 1952 he was deposed by the Egyptian revolution and shipped away to Italy in the royal yacht. Sad speculations may cross your mind as you stand in the sunshine looking at Montaza; for this great silly palace is a symbol of a vanished Egypt, and thus of wasted years, of talents perverted, of corruption and greed and cruelty. There was a pungent feeling to that old Egypt, a country of laissez faire and belly-dancers, with the indolently hanging tassels of its red *tarbooshes*, and the avaricious pashas rolling from their cars to the tables of the Mohammed Ali Club. There was an easy-going, hubble-bubble, sleight-of-hand manner to society in those bad old days, when a discreet bank note would get you almost anything, and a Cabinet office was a passport to fortune, and the exiled aristocracy of Europe lived elegantly along the corniche at Alexandria. The rich were very rich and the poor were excruciatingly poor; you could walk with your lantern far and wide before you found a truly honest man; filth and disease and heartlessness stalked the land; and sometimes some terrible epidemic, sweeping down upon Cairo and the Delta, brought into the open all the medieval horrors of the Egyptian slums.

Yet in 1956 a sort of wry nostalgia is aroused by the sight of that misty palace, for the new Egypt is a hard military country, governed by beak-nosed incorruptibles, humorless and thrusting. The scent of cigar smoke and the clink of the roulette tables have almost gone. Instead all must be dedicated, and practical, and soldierly, and hotly nationalistic. To be sure, a strong sense of *plus ça change* lingers on, as you will discover when you apply for your exit visa among the moronic chaos of the Ministry of the Interior; but most of the old rococo pleasures represented by Montaza have gone with the revolutionary wind. The crenellated extravaganzas of the royal house—Montaza and Ras el-Tin, Abdin and Kubbra and Mataria—are tawdry museums; and the tourists move through them bemused, hoping to find some pornography.

Do not stand too long moralizing on the beach, or those old gardeners will seep around your car (garlic breath and broken teeth) smiling obsequiously and murmuring something about baksheesh. If you leave the sea and take the desert road to Cairo, in an hour or two the bold new Egypt will be all around you. You cannot escape its symptoms, for Colonel Nasser, President of the Egyptian Republic, has imposed his philosophies with a resolute and ubiquitous hand. Everywhere the eagle of the revolution, a governessy bird, sits primly between its stylized wings, and in the huge new offices of the government polite young officers with mustaches greet you with steely smiles. Fine new promenades run along the banks of the Nile. Expensive new hotels overlook it. Girls in gay blouses, proudly emancipated, drink fizzy lemonades beneath the sunshades of open-air cafes. Big new buses, from Germany or Czechoslovakia, roll out to Maadi or the pyramids. If you are lucky, Colonel Nasser himself may sweep by in the back of his black car, in a civilian suit with wide shoulders, while the citizenry stands and applauds (and round the corner, farther along his route, a mechanical street-sweeper hastens up and down the gutters).

This is a great capital, the largest city in Africa, and it is alive

with boisterous energy, dampened only by the dust and the tireless
sun. Perhaps it is a holiday, and a procession moves around the big
new fountain in Liberation Square. Girls in baggy uniforms, with
a fleshy hint of the harem clinging stubbornly to their figures;
boys with banners; workers shouting slogans; huge beflowered
floats on lorries, with plaster models and beauty queens symboliz-
ing Hope or Mother Egypt or The Egyptian Cement Industry.
In the evening there may be a festivity at the Officers' Club, headquarters of the new ruling class, and if you peer through its iron
gates with a wink at the policeman you can see the vast open-air
stage peopled with film stars, in jazzy dinner jackets and full-
skirted satin, while the band beneath plays some loud repetitive
Arabic melody, and the officers whistle and clap their approval.
Cairo is the Hollywood of the Muslim world, and its players are
familiar from Morocco to East Bengal.

It is also a city dedicated to politics. In the back-street coffee-
shops the radios blare their arrogant messages: revenge against
Israel, humiliation to the West, the renaissance of Arab glories, the
greatness of Nasser; this is a virile, restless, expansionist society,
and its present flavor is at once aggressive, petulant, and grandilo-
quent. The newspapers shout wild scurrilities in red banner head-
lines. The witty Egyptian cartoonists concentrate their spleen on
whatever target is politically fashionable (or discreet). Pictures of
Nasser decorate every shop and office. Guns, tanks, and airplanes
are daubed on the wall of every school. If you drive by the military college at Heliopolis some strapping cadet may thumb a lift,
and sit clean and well-behaved beside you with his weekend bag
on his lap, talking of the glories of the regime. Sometimes a solitary
jet fighter, made in Brno, screams out of the sun with a flash of
silver. Outside the railway station a colossal figure of Rameses II,
newly moved by tank transporter from the site of ancient Memphis,
stands magnificently above the crowd, gazing eastwards. There is
vigor and pride to Colonel Nasser's Egypt, and more than a hint
of latent power.

Into almost every activity of Egyptian life the mystique of the
new state has penetrated. This is partly because Nasser has suc-

ceeded in giving the Egyptians a new self-respect, and has made himself the most admired political leader they have ever had; and partly because this is a police state, and the tentacles of authority wriggle their way into every corner of society. The universities are well impregnated; the press is docile; the Muslim theorists are amenable; even Egyptology, most scholarly of sciences, is being recast in the revolutionary mould. Some of Nasser's principal advisers on publicity and propaganda (as on military matters) are Germans, and it is often easy to see the Goebbels touch in the presentation of affairs.

Inevitably there is an element of deceit and dishonesty to all this. The revolution gained power by force, but it can retain it only by keeping the people of Egypt in a state of patriotic excitement. Everything must be for the state, for the revolution, for the Arabs; and since this is a region addicted to violence, the rowdier and brassier things are, the more popular the regime will be. The original objectives of the revolution were modest and above reproach. Corruption was to be stifled, land ownership was to be thoroughly reformed, the country was to be made economically sound, social inequalities were to be levelled, international friendships were to be fostered. Alas, these aims have been replaced by wilder but more glamorous aspirations, and most of Egypt's energies are now directed towards foreign adventurings and the grasping of international power.

Still, the regime does its best to maintain its vanishing reputation for enlightenment, if only for the foreign market. I was once invited by the Ministry of National Guidance to be present at the opening of the sarcophagus of Princess Naferu-Ptah, a shadowy figure of the Middle Empire whose tomb had just been found beneath a vestigial pyramid in the Fayoum. It was hoped, said the man on the telephone breathily, that the sarcophagus would contain her mummy and all manner of golden and silver treasures—"like Tutenkhamon," he added, "and the Minister of Education himself will witness the opening!" So I drove down that hot May morning, across the desert from Cairo and into the strange, astringent farm land of the Fayoum. Flags, flowers, and bunting lined the way and children sang patriotic songs, for Major Kemal ed-Din

Hussein, one of the founder-revolutionaries, was on his way to
view the mummy.

The remains of the pyramid lay among green fields in bright
and peaceful countryside. Behind it a pair of blindfold buffaloes
labored around their water wheel, and from a nearby canal came
the shouts of naked bathing boys. All around that idyllic site,
though, the revolution had made its own arrangements. A big
marquee sheltered the privileged visitors. Four bright-red German
buses had brought representatives of the world's press. A military
band thumped away at a rousing air. A corps of photographers
waited; and when the Minister arrived with his cortège of cars,
the revolutionary anthem rang out and the flash bulbs sparkled
among the palm trees.

"This way, this way!" cried the bustling publicity men, distributing pamphlets, and the guests were ushered to the edge of the
tomb, where the lid of the sarcophagus was being slowly lifted with
a block and tackle. Scholars from the Department of Antiquities
stood self-consciously beside the sarcophagus, looking learned, and
the Minister stood at the head of it, looking well-groomed and
progressive. Inch by inch the lid was raised. The band was silenced,
for dramatic effect, and the crowd of journalists pressed and jostled
and prepared its cameras. "It is the new Egypt," remarked an
earnest young man as we clung together to the scaffolding—"the
new Egypt meeting the old!"

But it all went wrong. When at last the lid swung off, and the
laborers hauled the pulley away, all we could see in the gloom
of the sarcophagus was water. Upon its brownish surface there
floated a kind of scum, which the officials pushed with sticks into
jam jars; but in it there was nothing but a broken alabastar pot,
a few small jars, some wispy shreds of gold leaf, and a sediment
of Middle Empire muck. To be sure, one of the officials picked up
a desiccated white object and brandished it above his head, crying:
"It is a human thigh-bone!" but nobody seemed to believe him.
The day accordingly wilted. The band packed its instruments. The
press was whisked home grumbling. The Minister swept away
through the crowds of school children, still cheering and waving
their flags. Of the princess whose fragile and incongruous memory
haunted this event we had found not a lock of hair nor a breath of

lingering perfume; but the regime, faithful to the interests of culture, had done its best.

On another occasion I drove from Cairo into the countryside to the north to see this autocracy applied to the humanities. The regime had launched a big reclamation project, called Liberation Province, in the desert between Cairo and Alexandria. Water was to be conveyed there in canals, and large numbers of people were to be settled there to relieve the congestion of the Nile Delta. A start had already been made in irrigating and tilling this land, and gullible visitors, indeed, often left with the impression that the job was finished; for the project was elevated as symbolic of the new Egypt, and great pains were taken to publicize it accordingly. One morning the man from the Ministry rang me to say that candidates for resettlement in this Utopia were to be examined that day at a village in the Delta, and I was cordially invited to attend. "Major Magdi Hassanein will be going," said my informant respectfully, "for the revolution is especially conscious of its duty towards the country folk. It will be a strict examination, conducted according to the tenets of the new Egypt, and witnessed by Major Magdi Hassanein himself!"

Bai el Arab was a small higgledy-piggledy village beside a big canal. Great lateen-sailed boats lurched by on their passage through the Delta, and a few men with their clothes rolled up to their thighs were pumping water into fields with archaic mechanisms. Most of the inhabitants, though, were marshalled outside the school where the examination was to be held. The peddlers were selling sweetmeats, and four or five young men in turbans were brandishing staves in a slow and ungainly ballet. Arab horses, proudly caparisoned, were performing their famous dance—the *haute école* of country Egypt—with jerky movements of their hoofs and tossings of their heads, while a little band played a reedy melody. The bystanders greeted me with jokes and yellow smiles, for all the world like friendly country clowns; but soon there was a whisper from the cheer-leaders and a huge throaty roar arose from the assembled enthusiasts as the Major strode into the marquee. (There was little need for electioneering among such prudent peasants as these. When Colonel Nasser stood for the presidency—he was the only candidate—99.9 per cent of a compulsory electorate approved his distinguished candidacy: or so the man from the Ministry said.)

After the Major's speech, which was long, good-humored, and sprinkled with homespun jokes ("Look at the British! They occupied Egypt for seventy years just to get away from their mothers-in-law!"), we went into the school to see the candidates. A good house, new clothes, and secure, communal living were among the prizes for selection (not to be sniffed at in a country where the annual per capita income is less than $28.00), and the candidates seemed to be taking it very seriously. There they were, each in a spotless *gallabiya*, washed and well-shaven, like citizens of some new master race. "See how intelligent they look! They must all be under thirty, and literate, and of good appearance. They are very handsome! They will wear a fine new gabardine uniform in Liberation Province. They will be examined by doctors and by psychologists to see if they are suitable. Come and see them sitting for their examinations!"

They sat at their desks stiffly, those new Egyptians, each with a newly sharpened pencil, each with a virgin question sheet in front of him. When one of them sneezed, the others looked at him reproachfully. "Now they will begin. It is a very stringent test. Watch them preparing for it. Their *gallabiyas*, you will notice, are very clean, and each has a new pencil. Watch them preparing. No, no, my dear sir, certainly they have not been chosen already. This is their examination. They are about to begin. Wait!"

But suddenly the candidates arose as one man, clutching their pencils, to bawl: "Long live Gamal Abdel Nasser, our benefactor, and Major Magdi Hassanein, and our leaders of the Glorious Revolution!" before sitting down again, rather heavily, and resuming their academic duties. The Major smiled and nodded benevolently, and we filed out of the school into the dust (through which, as in a tapestry, the beautiful horses were still performing their gyrations). In a week or two those fortunate examinees had said goodbye to the peddlers, the reedy band, the stave-dancers and the horsemen, and had settled down in their gabardine uniforms among the concrete modernities of Liberation Province.

But not everything is sham or ludicrous. For a third glimpse of
the new order in Egypt, let me take you to one of the great military parades with which, from time to time, the government adds
fuel to the already flaming fervor of its populace. This is a military
state, with undertones of Nazi or Fascist manners; and its great
moments occur when the new Egyptian army marches by, proud
and warlike, with President Nasser ("The Chief") watching pater-
nally from the reviewing stand.

All Cairo seems to be present at such a parade. The ambassadors
and military attachés are there; many visiting journalists, guests of
the regime; celebrities from East and West; a stray foreign general
or two; and probably some distinguished political visitor, fêted
and pursued, from the Communist half of the world. The big
reviewing stand, with a picture of Colonel Nasser on its lintel, and
two or three eagles, is set up outside Abdin Palace (where, not so
long ago, British tanks forced King Farouk to dismiss one Egyptian government and appoint another). The great square in front
is already packed with static soldiers and bandsmen, and a shifting
multitude of citizens clings to the surrounding buildings, lining
their parapets with white draperies and waving flags. Republican
Guardsmen, in berets and riding breeches, usher you to your
place; the little man from the Ministry of National Guidance, with
a sickly smile, hands you an even sicklier lemonade. A blast of
trumpets, a stir around the assembly, a crescendo of sirens, and here
comes President Nasser, preceded by four stout motorcyclists, excessively stern and pompous, and accompanied in the back of his
big black car by the chief of the general staff, an able young man
who looks as if he needs more milk. In a trice the vast concourse
is on its feet. The cheer-groups, sprinkled unnecessarily around the
square, set up their plainsong. The bands play the national anthem.
The huge assembly of troops, packing the square to its farthest
corners, presents arms. The scores of thousands of spectators wave
their flags. The more enthusiastic newspapermen stand up on their
chairs and, especially if they are government guests from the
American interior, murmur some fatuous expression of admiration, such as: "My! It's like seeing the old historical Egypt come
to life, Mr. Ali!" The Communist guest, a big man with a round
face and hands that are constantly in uneasy motion, purrs from

his place of honor like a well-fed tabby cat. The Chief himself salutes and smiles; and, surrounded by his aides and courtiers, strides to his place.

The parade, you should be warned, will last for three or four hours, the last part of it in the blazing heat of an Egyptian noon-day. The German woman beside you, whose husband is an instructor at the military college, and who has been to several such functions before, wisely removes her shoes and places over her head a scarf with a picture of two tanks and a submarine upon it; but the soldiers and bandsmen in the square still stand doggedly to attention. Battalion after battalion marches by, each accorded its dutiful driblet of applause. There are National Guardsmen, drama-tized by bearded old men and very small boys; companies of plump grim-faced women, carrying rifles; parachutists prancing by at the double, shouting battle-cries; sailors in gaiters, like British landing-parties; officer cadets, swinging splendidly past in a modified goose-step ("Very good, no?" says the German lady with satisfaction). Sometimes the Allied Powers are represented—Lebanese ski-troops, big Sudanese, Saudi Arabians and Yemenis, Libyans, Syrians, and Jordanians—each reflecting, in the swing of an arm, the cut of a jacket, the make of a rifle, whatever sphere of influence recently oppressed them, and each, too, giving a flicker of reality to the distant prospect of Arab unity. Then come the mechanized units—guns, armored cars, troop-carriers—creeping by, hour after hour, regiment after regiment, until the eye dazes and the brain swims and the crowd droops and the jet fighters, swooping overhead, can scarcely induce us to levy a contribution upon our neck muscles (as Peacock would say). The honored guest's smile has a frozen look to it; Colonel Nasser's mustache twitches; the poor bandsmen, puffing away indefatigably at their tubas in the sunshine, are kept on their feet by the incessant application of smelling-salts, passed around from nose to nose by eager first-aid men.

But the *pièce de résistance* is yet to come. The stars of these shows are always the great Joseph Stalin tanks acquired by the regime from the Communists: the most powerful weapons in the Middle East, the very rumble of whose tracks is a patriotic stimu-lant. So, when the turrets of these ominous machines appear in the distance over the heads of the mounted policemen, a thrill of expectation revives that vast assembly. Even the bandsmen, blowing away, manage to peer up the road from the corners of their blood-shot eyes; and when at last the first tank enters the square, with a pulsing of engines and a clanking of tracks, the whole crowd roars. Here is the essence of the new Egypt—the monstrous sand-colored tanks, their guns turning in salute, with the head of the young Egyptian driver just to be seen through his open hatch, and the slim commander saluting in the turret; and the crowd seething with pride and the sense of power; and the Communist grandee smug in his chair; and the officers of the regime, only a little corpulent after their years of office, smiling in double-breasted rows; and the Chief himself in his peaked cap, basking in it all, the focal point of all that adoring assembly, like some strong idol brought to life.

What would King Farouk think, if he could smuggle himself back to Abdin Palace to peer at such a parade from his black marble bathroom? Never were two figureheads more different than these, the dissolute monarch and the dedicated dictator, the one playing with his instruments of salacity, the other with his Stalin tanks. It is a long step indeed from Montaza to this blazing parade ground. When the march past is over, and the long day's adulation is done, the President of Egypt returns to no be-draped boudoirs or gilded salons. His modest house up the road is plain to the point of ugliness, and he lives there blamelessly with his buxom wife and five children.

If you chance to call on him, no rude or ranting orator will greet you behind some big officious desk. This is the apogee of Nasser's career, and he is still both calm and unpretentious. In Egypt all opposition to his rule now seems to be silenced. The Communist party and the fanatical Muslim Brotherhood are squashed. The old politicians are dispersed and discredited. What immediate danger there is to the President seems to be from ambitious members of his own junta: and so complete is the ascendancy he has established over the people of Egypt, chiefly by policies at once arrogant and inflammatory, that it would be a brave man indeed who would dare defy him now.

So, in the autumn of 1956, he is relaxed and friendly. He is in his shirtsleeves, his vest showing between the buttons, and he gives you coffee and talks pleasantly and intelligently for as long as you like. No armored cars rumble past outside; no insolent sentry hinders you; the idol at home can be very agreeable. He is a big man, even off the saluting stand, with an air of persuasive decency. He likes to call himself the first indigenous ruler of Egypt since the Pharaohs, and there is something inspiring to the claim. Nasser is a genuine through-and-through Egyptian, born of peasant stock. His education is limited, his political philosophies muddled, his abilities more instinctive than intellectual; but he is a person of stature and significance, much more than a mere vulgar opportunist. "What a reasonable sort of man!" you will probably say to yourself as you chat with him across the plain deal table, sipping black coffee from cups edged with blue roses and gilt. "How very different from his public appearances! How grossly I have misjudged him till now, and how foolish the West has been to incur his hostility, and—oh, *thank* you, Mr. President, you certainly have a good coffee-maker!" But do not be deceived. For many long years Nasser led an underground movement within the Egyptian army, at a period when Farouk's secret police were all-powerful. He has charm, intelligence, great ability; but also talents of deception and conspiracy of a very high order.

He will no doubt tell you, with all sweet reasonableness, how much he desires the prosperity of his people and the friendship of the West; but what he really wants is power—not perhaps power for himself (not yet, anyway) but for Egypt, for the Arabs, for Asia, for all the backward, underdeveloped, downtrodden, powerless, black, brown, and yellow countries. His horizons are limitless, and his visions are given force by overriding ambition. Sometimes his conceptions are alarmingly misty—he thinks in terms of circles of power, of a unified Islam, of national destinies, of the interventions of fate. Sometimes they are disagreeably precise, and he contrives the expulsion of the British from some last imperial toehold, the nationalization of a canal or the Arabization of Middle East oil.

Around this contradictory man concentric circles of influence eddy. Here in Cairo are his colleagues of the revolution: a strange company, soldiers all, some plodding, some fanatical, some honest, some shady, some charming, some extremist to the point of eccentricity—that stiff row of youngish men whom we saw behind the Chief at the saluting stand. Then in the coffee-shops and back rooms of the capital are the devotees from other countries, a slatternly cominform of exiles and plotters; the shifty old Mufti of Jerusalem, in a high-crowned turban at garden parties, whose hand of intrigue has been apparent in the Middle East for decades; revolutionaries from French North Africa; malcontents from Iraq and Jordan; big Sudanese, draped in white or uncomfortable in gray flannel; troublemakers from the Persian Gulf, brooding refugees from Palestine. This is the dubious high court of Nasserism.

Farther away, beyond the frontiers of Egypt, are his myriad agents, the progressives and intellectuals of the Arab countries. Encouraged, in particular, by the schoolmasters who go out from Egypt to the ends of the Arab world, they look towards Egypt as steadfastly as ever an Ealing starlet glued her eyes on Sunset Boulevard: liberals and Communists, nationalists and muzzy-heads, officers and schoolteachers, who foresee the end of feudalism in the seizure of their own Montazas, and who look to the Egyptian revolutionaries as their leaders and exemplars. These are the envoys of Nasserism.

Finally there are the sweaty masses of the Middle East, the underfed and underprivileged inhabitants of a demi-continent. A million of them are homeless refugees; most of the rest are, in effect, serfs; some are even slaves. Just what they want of the future they are not quite sure. The ideologies of the world are blarney to them. Moscow and Washington are almost equally remote. They only know that something is wrong with their affairs, that some cruel destiny has cheated them, and that they are entitled to something better—more money, perhaps, better health, opportunity for self-respect; and from the dankness of their cloaca, through the screen of corruption and self-interest, they think they see the President of Egypt as their new prophet. They are Nasser's cannon fodder.

So by the latter months of 1956, with the baleful help of Russia, Nasser has made Cairo the capital of the Arab world as never before, and Egypt its undisputed leader. To be sure, he does not often promise his disciples happiness or prosperity: the words rarely

occur in the vocabulary of his ambitions. But he excites their loyalties by promising and giving them power. They will take their
place in the sun, he tells them. The power of oil will be theirs, and
they will stand like giants upon the crossroads of the world. Already they are masters of the Suez Canal, and there is almost nothing their united will cannot achieve. The balance of the continents
is shifting; the old mighty are in their dotage; the progress of the
new Egypt is only a beginning.

Few such controversial subjects, though, will jar the pleasant
course of your conversation with the President. The hours slip
smoothly by as he expounds his theories, compounded of understandable patriotism ("Sure, sure, we had a revolution too, that's
perfectly correct") and kindly reproach ("Oh, of course, nobody
can deny you *that*, Colonel. We British don't pretend to be perfect!"). The coffee cups come and go, and presently the President
rises from the table, his sandals flip-flopping across the linoleum,
to see you to the door in his shirtsleeves and wave you goodbye
into the night. As you return glowing to your room beside the Nile
you may notice, lining the hotel corridors, the glass cases in which
the ghastly remnants of Farouk's collection of jewelry are offered
for sale to the tourists.

CONSTANCIES

COLONEL NASSER, though, has been a power in Egypt only since 1952 and it takes more than a few years and a determined leader to change the character of a nation that has existed, more or less within its present boundaries, for more than four thousand years. A veneer of militarization has been imposed upon the Egyptians; a new concrete-and-brass-band civilization has been fostered; there has been a social levelling, symbolized by the abolition of titles; the new world importance of the state has certainly had its effect upon the psychology of the people. On the surface the new philosophies are everywhere apparent, and the middle class (the instrument of revolution in the Middle East) is ever more influential. During 1956 a national committee, as if to set its seal upon such social progress, resolved that the wearing of trousers by Egyptian males should be "officially encouraged."

Nevertheless, even Cairo, the greatest city of Africa, remains in many ways an archaic and changeless capital, haunted more by memories of the past than by visions of the glittering future. It is still a city of historical layers, in which the sediments of the centuries lie thickly. High above it there stands a plateau called the Mokattam Hills, from which Napoleon bombarded the city before the Battle of the Pyramids, and where the new regime has founded a pleasant housing estate. From this sparkling vantage point, littered with the ruins of mosques and fortresses, and crowned with an anti-aircraft battery, you can well see how history still imposes its patterns upon the capital. It is a noble view, a prospect of great power and character, from the immense rambling necropolis called the City of the Dead, at the foot of the hill, to the sand of the Libyan desert in the far distance. Across the Nile the pyramids of Giza stand in splendor, still the most magnificent of Egyptian monuments; but later civilizations built their memorials on the east side of the river. The Romans had a fortress upon its eastern bank, and in successive centuries the rulers of Cairo withdrew, step by step, inland from the Nile until the pressures of space and population forced the city back again.

All these generations of capitals have left their traces. A dead sandy mound in the distance is the site of Fostat, the first Arab settlement of Cairo, now so haunted by jealous spirits that nothing remains upon it but some small stone structures like pimples, said to be antique ammunition stores. A little nearer the hills is the ninth-century capital of Al Katai, with the famous twisted minaret of Ibn Tulun, gaunt and quixotic. Closer still, the Islamic university of Al Azhar survives among the relics of Fatimide Cairo, and if you strain your eyes from your hilltop you may just see the stream of its students, Arab and Indonesian, Moroccan and Pakistani, Burmese and East African, passing through the archway of the Barber's Gate. Saladin stormed in, and built his citadel at the very foot of the hill, massive walls and barbicans, mosques and barracks and cluttered palaces, with the dust of the centuries now yellowing its ramparts. The slave dynasty of the Mamelukes took Cairo back towards the river; below you, among the wilderness of jumbled mud-brown streets, there stand the minarets of their incomparable mosques, one for each day of the year, slender and ornate, some single, some double, some like pepper pots, some like lupins, at once austere and phallic, sprinkled across the city like air shafts from some vast subterranean storehouse. The Turks arrived, and built their houses and drinking fountains; the British came and built their bridges; and modern Cairo, with its skyscrapers and broad highways, leaps across the river again to Giza, completing the cycle and filling in, like putty, all the gaps between those several ancient capitals.

Thus from the Mokattam you can see the dynasties and the cultures spread out before you, rings on the shell of a tortoise; and the result is an impression of extraordinary historical continuity, linking the Pharaohs with the new regime. In everyday affairs, too, you will constantly be reminded of this chain of history, for some facets of Cairo life are astonishingly resilient and resistant to change. There are, for instance, no figures of contemporary life more incorrigibly changeless than the dragomen who hover like subservient vultures around those Pharaonic monuments across the river. From time to time the government conducts a purge among them, and the more shamelessly dishonest are whisked away to

oblivion; now and then a crisis disperses them, or some fluctuation
in the national fortune attracts them elsewhere. Somehow, though,
the corps always returns to strength sooner or later, and as you
sit sipping your coffee at Mena House the inevitable shuffling of
footsteps soon disturbs your meditations, and a deep, fruity voice
echoes through the garden, and there stands before you some
corpulent rogue in a cummerbund, a *tarboosh* on his head, a stout
stick in his hand, with an air of swaggering but obscurely injured
self-satisfaction, and a hint of an Oxford accent to his ingratiating
inquiry: "You want to see the sphinkis, Sir?"

Wild are the statistics he hurls at you as he drags you around
that suffering monument, and confused indeed the generations of
his Pharaohs; but it is worth while, for the sphinx and the pyramids
in the tourist season are like the dragoman himself, among the
perennial delights of Egypt. The air is crisp and clear, but thick
with suspicions of roguery. It has always been so. When M. Ingardin visited the pyramids in the eighteenth-century *Travels of
Orlando*, the dragomen of his time employed a phrase that might
well be an occupational slogan for the fraternity. The perspicacious
Frenchman was anxious to see a catacomb opened, but he had
haggled so effectively with the Egyptians that they had lowered
their demanded price from twenty piastres to six. Even then M.
Ingardin was preparing a haughty departure, but the dragomen
hastened after him with a memorable *cri de cœur*. "Stop, stop!"
said they. "Give us only five! *It is impossible to open a catacomb
cheaper!*"

Echoes of this glorious appeal still swirl around the sphinx two
centuries later, and upon the faces of the circling tourists there is
generally an expression of wary apprehension. Nevertheless, it is
a gay and lively scene. The sphinx stands as ever it did, with the
piles of the pyramids above, and the trains of caparisoned camels
walk round and round, up and down, now sitting, now standing
still for photographs, with the Iowa businessmen clutching their
white, waterproofed hats, and the bosomy German matron uncomfortably cross-legged on her hump, and the American girls in
their bright jeans, and the French flirt showing off her petticoats;
the two grave young priests in their black suits, and the Englishman
as correct as ever he is at his Whitehall desk; the children solemn

or screaming stickily; the splendid Australians, rejoining their ship at Port Said tomorrow; the old lady from Aberdeen with a flower in her hat; and, clashing across the sands, the incessant, dreary monotones of the dragomen, thick and rich: "And it is according to the legend, ladies and gen'lemen, that the Pharaoh Cheops married his lovely young bride here, where, according to a very old tradition, there was once a clear, lovely spring of fresh water coming straight up from Father Nile. The face of the sphinkis, ladies and gen'lemen, is fifteen feet four-and-a-half inches from ear to ear, and the weight of one of its legs, according to a very, very old tradition, is equal to. . . ." Sometimes youths in hand-me-downs canter precariously by on hired horses; and sometimes there comes clattering before the monument, creaking and smelling of leather, an old black garry with two emaciated horses, from which one expects to emerge, with an ivory-headed cane and a Baedeker, some well-fed English milord. Such is the atmosphere of the place of the sphinx, with its eternal pyramids and timeless rogues, and the shifting kaleidoscope of its visitors, that all the centuries and all the civilizations become a little confused.

Despite Colonel Nasser's worthy programs of slum clearance and replanning, another layer of Cairo life remains darkly medieval. In the city of the Mamelukes, east of the skyscrapers, there are alleyways and slums in which the Middle Ages are still robustly alive; where the evil eye is still a threat to be shunned, where women are still veiled or closeted, where the superstitions of pre-Islamic thought are still more potent by far than the certainties of science. Your trim and personable nursemaid, feeding the children their cornflakes, goes home at night, as likely as not, to the fourteenth century; and if you wander about the city at nighttime it is sometimes horribly easy to imagine the Egyptian famine of 1069, when the unsuspecting pedestrian, making his way down a side street, would find himself grappled with hooks and hauled upstairs to be eaten.

I was taken one night to a secluded corner of this old Cairo to attend a festival that must have existed unchanged since the earliest days of semi-pagan Islam. The center of the festivities was a small mosque squeezed among tumbled tenements; and the setting was a confusion of bright lanterns, clamorous shouting, the smell of incense and sweat, thin Arabic music, and fly-like hordes of beggars. The feast was to celebrate the birthday of a local holy man of antiquity, and it was in this mosque that he lay immured in a big cage-like tomb. Through the surrounding meshwork of streets, beneath the traceries of high harem windows, a dense mass of citizens moved cheerfully, in long robes or turbans, veiled or painted, sheepish or resplendent, precisely like the crowds that mill so vividly through prints of eighteenth-century Cairo (and probably not at all unlike the citizenry of London at the time of the Black Death). Traders had set up their ramshackle stalls, or spread their wares upon the thick layer of dirt that lined those murky thoroughfares. There were balloons for sale, small, crude dolls, wooden flutes, black coffee, and trays of sickly, squashy foods. A man with a clipped beard was selling sherbet, with a long-spouted silver urn slung about his shoulder and the metal cups clinking rhythmically in his hand like castanets. In one shadowy corner a group of veiled women gossiped loudly, while an old lady rapped casually upon a tambourine. From a window high above came the breathy strains of an unaccompanied flute. Outside the mosque, like unkempt barber-surgeons, the circumsisers had laid their instruments in front of them, for no day could be more pro-pitious for the operation. Some of the small boys passing down the street had, I fancied, a pallid look upon their peaked and grimy faces.

A high wall surrounded the mosque, illuminated by fairy lights upon the minaret, and beside its stout wooden gate we found a crowd of boys, dancing and shouting. A dervish of eccentric man-nerisms was entertaining them. His head was shaven, like a Buddhist priest's, and he wore a smock of ragged, grayish linen, ending at his knees. From the stave in his hand there flapped a bundle of strips of material, black and yellow and green; and he waved this tattered talisman wildly as he danced and bounded up the steps of the mosque, laughing shrilly, shouting alternate ribaldry and abuse, and sometimes leaping out of the dark shadows with a barbaric scream. He bowed to us, like a jester; and we passed through the gate into the courtyard. Its walls were lined with groups of ragged

men, squatting silently in circles holding sticks, and through it
there swirled a dense, jostling mass of Muslims, motley and dirty,
swarming incessantly in and out of the mosque. We groped our
way through this crowd in the half-light, and there came to meet
us a handsome man in a gray *gallabiya* and a white turban, exuding
an air of benevolent, if astute, prosperity. This rich merchant was
claiming indulgences from Allah by giving free meals that night
to the poor people of his neighborhood. Tonight any destitute
Muslim might claim a meal from him; and with a wave of his mani-
cured hand and a glittering of the ring upon his forefinger he
welcomed us to the feast.

In the kitchen, a small, smoky structure at the corner of the
courtyard, huge pans of beaten metal were steaming over open
fires, full of chunks of meat, rice, and rich, fatty gravies. The
smoke was so thick, as we viewed the arrangements, that we could
hardly open our eyes; but the merchant's wife, in discreet black
like a greasy deaconess, presided over this charitable inferno with
rectitude and decision. "Welcome!" said the merchant, leading us
into the eating place, and added thunderingly, with a clap of his
hands and a flourish: "Eat!" In a moment our food was there, spread
vastly before us: platters of mutton, to be seized with the fingers
and dipped in gravy; rice wrapped in vine leaves; piles of maca-
roni; pastes and sweetmeats and unleavened bread; and a multitude
of Egyptian familiars beyond my powers of analysis. If water was
needed, an old man limped around with a glass jug; if food, a procession of servants stumbled from the kitchen, until at last the
meal ended with a ceremonial washing of hands, with a white basin,
a handsome brass pitcher, and a large cake of kitchen soap.

Now there came signs of impatience from the indigent in the
courtyard. A few gruff shouts and a rumble of complaint seeped
through to us, and once or twice the big wooden doors which
separated us from the courtyard bulged ominously as a few of the
more resolute poor tried to force a way in. Presently, though, the
doors were swung open from the inside, and the big trays of food
were distributed. Lip-smackings and the noise of eagerly rended
meat could be heard from dark corners, and there was a low
rumble of animal satisfaction. I saw the dervish gnawing a leg of
mutton by the gate, his stave on the ground beside him.

We thanked the cooks and entered the mosque. Its huge unfurnished hall was alive with a shifting mass of worshippers, bearded and barefooted, some vacant of eye, some ecstatic, in queer and lavishly variegated costume. Around the tomb of the divine a stream of supplicants moved ceaselessly, their bedraggled clothes atrail, touching the bars softly with their fingers, peering through the grill of the latticework, stroking the woodwork sensuously, kissing the marble, whispering words of entreaty or appeasement into the tomb, or pausing to sniff the scent of dying roses that emerged heavily from its recesses. On the floor all around them, heaving in prayer, was a clutter of draped and jumbled forms. Some old men held copies of the Koran close to their eyes, chanting verses in unison; some stared devoutly at the decorated ceiling; many reached out their gnarled hands for baksheesh, in the name of Allah; and some stared at me with fanatical hostility, with an expression of hissing on their faces. An albino acolyte moved eerily through this throng. His beard was white and straggling, his hair tangled, his skin very fair, his eyes a creepy pink; and he stalked through the mosque aloofly, like a prophet or a reincarnation, praying and meditating. His pale, intellectual face contained, I thought, a hint of sublimity; but behind the tomb there was a manifestation of frenzied mindlessness. There thirty dervishes, in two quivering rows, had worked themselves into a trance of devotion; their faces blank and their eyes rolling, they were swaying backwards and forwards in somber rhythm across the stone flaggings of the floor. Strange and dreamlike were their gestures, and their limp bodies whirled and swayed, bent and straightened, twisted and twirled, like the branches of dark trees thrashed in a wind at night.

I found all this a chilling sight, and turned to leave the building, followed by the imprecations of the fanatics; but when I reached the door the beggars waiting there fell upon me savagely, pulling at my clothes, shouting, clutching my wrist with their sharp fingernails, whining and threatening; until I managed to shake them off angrily and escaped into the courtyard. There the albino took my head between his hands and blessed me; the merchant remarked that the evening would remain doubly precious to him because of my sweet presence; and the dotty dervish at the gate pirouetted and curtsied with a swish of the ribbons on his stave. It was midnight, and the festivities would continue until morning; the air was still loud with the cries of the peddlers, the beating of tambourines, the throbbing of holy chants, and the squeaking of children's perilous swings; but in a few minutes the Cairo of the Mamelukes was behind me, and I was among the department stores.

Such, at least on a feast day, is medieval Cairo. By comparison memories of the Turkish era are drab and motheaten, not at all like the echoes of holocausts and depravities that linger in the palaces of Istanbul. Sometimes, though, there is a mellow flavor to them that contrasts pleasantly with the usual harsh vivacity of this cruel city. Tucked away in one dusty backstreet, for example, is a little upstairs factory in which is woven, year after year, the vast and splendid carpet that covers the sacred shrine of the Kaaba in Mecca. It has long been the privilege of the ruler of Egypt to provide this carpet, the Kiswa, which is draped over the structure annually; and the new textile is taken to Mecca every year with pride and pomp, escorted by soldiers of the Egyptian army. During the first century of Islam the carpet was never removed, the new one being placed annually on top of the old; but there came a time when the shrine threatened to collapse beneath the weight of the accumulation, and now each year the carpet becomes the property of the guardians of the Kaaba, who promptly divide it into small sections and put it up for auction. Such is the spiritual value of the carpet, after so many months of holy elevation, that its material price is very high.

Forty men make this carpet every year. Even in 1956 they are nearly all Turkish by origin, and nearly all related to one another, and nearly all very old, and sometimes represent the third or fourth generation of their family to share in the work. They sit at trestle tables in a long, rickety room, and they stitch away there through the months like the tailors of fairy tales. The carpet is lavishly embroidered with gold thread. Verses from the Koran, in stylized script, surround the name of the princely giver—Gamal Abdel Nasser, President of the Egyptian Republic. By an agreeable paradox, much of the design of the carpet is the work of an English-

man, who produced it in the early years of the century; but it is
being changed, for those shrewd guardians at Mecca want something that can more conveniently be divided into small sections
for the auction. The tailors hold their eyes very close to their work,
and some of them wear, as you might expect, little steel-rimmed
spectacles on the ends of their noses. There is a delightfully family
flavor to the place. When I visited it the director, a portly and
paternal official who enjoyed a salary from the state, sauntered up
and down the tables with me, and the tailors, working away with
their reels of gold thread, threw pleasantries at us as we passed. I
asked one sage how old he was. "As old as the hills," he answered
bafflingly. "He is nearly one hundred years old," said the director
with pride, "and so," he added, peering round the room and indi-
cating another benevolent worthy, "and so is the one in the corner,
the one with the hat on." The old men grinned and nodded as we
inspected them, and showed me their work with interest; and
when we left them stitching there I heard from a distant corner
what sounded like a cracked but cheerful chuckle.

As we climbed down the staircase into the street outside, criss-
crossed with shadows, I noticed an elderly Egyptian sitting on a
stool outside the door, like a disconsolate watchman, with a white
scarf around his head and a string of beads in his lap. Who was he?
I wondered. "Well," they said, "until a few years ago the carpet
was taken to Mecca in the company of a camel, splendidly equipped
with a caparison we used to make in this very factory. It was an
emblem of royalty, you see. The revolution ended the custom,
for of course it was not in keeping with the new Egypt, as you
will understand, and this man here"—pointing him out, as he
shifted his big feet uneasily, rather as one suggests a criminal in an
identity parade—"was the camel driver. He never leaves the factory, poor fellow! He's dreaming of the *Mahmal!*"

All over the city, Nasser or no Nasser, there are scenes that
smack of the past in this beguiling way, and which suddenly bring
into focus some aspect of Egypt's involved and often sanguinary
history. Though the Egyptian state is the most restless, least serene
of political organisms, plunging perpetually from crisis to crisis,
there can be few capitals in the world with quite such a sense of
continuity: from the pyramids themselves, through the ceremonials

of Christianity and Islam, past the fusty relics of Turkish rule, to the young intellectuals of today, who sometimes manage to preserve, despite the distractions of the time, some of that cynical independence that has made Cairo a traditional center of thought and progress. Wherever you are, you may feel this underlying, ceaseless rhythm; and almost anywhere you may expect to hear some hoarse, conciliatory voice, speaking down the generations, insisting that it is impossible, perfectly impossible, my dear Sir, to open a catacomb for less.

THE DELTA

In the countryside, too, there is no less potent a sense of constancy. It is true that the revolution is "especially conscious of its duty towards the country folk." A limited start has been made in land reform. Minimum agricultural wages have been raised, and rents reduced. Dozens of social and medical centers have been erected, and stand gleaming—if a little forlorn, for there is generally no staff to run them properly—among the palm trees. There are new schools here and there, one or two new roads, an occasional hospital. The fabulous landowners of the past have been dispossessed, and many an eager farmer has been introduced to the pleasures of taxation and bureaucracy. A minor agricultural revolution has been launched; the peasant is, theoretically, emancipated, and cooperative farming is the hope of the future.

All this is true; and yet in general the Egyptian countryside has changed not a jot since the bad old days of the pashas, and indeed is very much the same now, both in spirit and in appearance, as it was in Pharaonic times. This is chiefly because the nature of the Egyptian fellah, for all the political whirligig in Cairo, remains astonishingly stable. He remains, as always, a warm-blooded, jovial, hard-working, humorous kind of person, much better at brawling than at plotting, and as ready for a belly-laugh as he is for a riot. The transformation of the town Egyptian continues apace; but the country fellow remains much the same as ever, filthy but persevering, at once grasping and generous, and blessed, thanks be to Allah, with a fresh and all-pervading sense of humor, which, encountered in the rubbish-blown alleys of some unutterable rural slum, springs like a fountain of clear water in a cesspool.

Perhaps it is partly geography that fosters this sense of continuity. The shape of Egypt is simple and functional—a great river flowing through a desert—and through all the vicissitudes of its history the country has rarely been disunited. It is all big and logical, an enormous palm tree with its roots in Africa and its spreading fronds shading the Mediterranean; and it seems only natural that life in the veins and branches of this ageless tree should move with a regular heart-like beat. I have often felt physically oppressed, no less, by the primeval feeling of the Nile Delta, the big triangle that stands between Cairo and the sea. Just as the tombs and monuments of ancient Egypt often feel haunted by cruel or debased memories, so the Delta has always seemed to me impregnated with taboos and timeless horrors. The peasants and their animals live there, teeming and hugger-mugger, wedded to the soil, prey to fears and primitive prejudices innumerable; and the canals stand brown and fetid, with water buffalo lazing in the mud; and the old water wheels turn slowly round, pulled by plodding, blindfold animals; and so rich is the foliage of the place, so violently green its fields, so thickly and anciently cultivated its every inch, that there is something almost obscene about its fecundity. It is mile after mile of productive manure, enriched by the thick ooze of the Nile, and so crowded that you are almost never out of sight of habitation.

Nevertheless, it has a pungent fascination. The villages look, at first sight, like heaps of solidified mud, riddled with alleyways, with shapeless piles of muck or maize heaped upon their roofs; as if some huge, burrowing creature has thrown up a mole-heap from the soil, and covered it with droppings and the remains of its food. Inside them, though, life is lived more variously and more intensely than you might suppose. The fellah is a man of infinite patience and his vitality is often sapped by disease, but he has flashes of sudden passion (ninety percent of the crimes of the Delta are crimes of revenge) and often these hovels are racked by feuds or enlivened by savage vendettas. Sometimes you can observe a sudden flaring of anger in a coffee-shop assembly, when some swarthy peasant, in a skullcap and a striped shirt, suddenly tautens and grins in fury and springs to his feet, clutching his stick and shouting insults; only to relax suddenly, like a man in a fit, and sink limply back on his stool among the restraining arms of his companions, back to that mood of hopeless resignation in which nothing can be done, nothing bettered, nothing altered, except by the will of God.

Not all the fellahin are Muslims. Side by side with Islam lives a primitive form of Christianity, often a confused mumbo-jumbo. In Egypt there are still some two million Copts, honoring a degenerate form of their religion, who are descended from the original

Egyptians. Sometimes in a Delta village you will therefore see the crude emblem of the Christians and the black veils of Islam side by side amid the squalor; and the children, if you ask them their religion, may pull up their sleeves and hold up their arms to show the Coptic cross tattooed on their wrists. In a hamlet deep in the country near Tanta I once stumbled within a few moments upon homely manifestations of both religions. First I walked through the doorway of the Coptic church, an endearing little structure with a tiny, toppling tower. It was dark inside, the only illumination being a few shafts of dusty sunshine entering through the roof; but when my eyes accustomed themselves to the gloom I found that, although it was eleven o'clock on a weekday morning, a service was in progress. A thin, elderly man in a brown *gallabiya* stood at a lectern declaiming an arabesque plainsong in the Coptic language; and sitting on a bench behind him were five very old, very bearded men. They had long sticks in their hands, and as they chanted their replies in an approximate unison, they closed their eyes in rapture and rocked themselves upon their bench, with the hint of a resemblance to the movement of those hypnotized dervishes in the Cairo mosque. When they caught sight of me, peering around a pillar, one of them arose and came across. I would be very welcome to join them, he said kindly, for we were all Christians, and today was, of course, the Festival. Desperately I ran my memory through the forgotten rubrics of the Anglican calendar—All Souls Day? St. Chrysostom? St. Simon and St. Jude?—but none of them fitted, and I felt ill-qualified to contribute very effectively to the responses; so I thanked him for his kindness; waved, perhaps a little irreverently, to the man at the lectern, who waved back boisterously; and withdrew cautiously into the sunshine.

At once there burst upon my ears a very different kind of noise. In the Muslim part of the village, beyond the crumbling church wall, a funeral had just taken place. A man had died ("A good enough man," my informant told me casually, "though he was as fat as a water buffalo") and his wife was mourning her loss, helped by many female sympathizers. They crouched there in the narrow village street, bundles of dirty black. The rubbish lay all about them, tins and old papers and bones, and a multitude of flies buzzed about the scene. The women had tucked their voluminous dresses beneath their knees and were squatting there grotesquely, black scarfs around their heads, thick black veils stifling most of their faces; and they were wailing, screeching, and clutching their clothes. Sometimes, like wolverines, they threw their heads back and screamed; sometimes they bent forward to grovel in the dust and wrench (but not too hard) at their horrid draperies. Occasionally the widow, purple in the face, would undertake a convulsion so extreme that the others would rush to soothe her; and for a brief moment, as I passed warily by, the Babel was silenced and the fluttering movement stilled as these impassioned ladies looked up to inspect me.

One of them even smiled; for if there is horror, squalor, and primitive passion in the Delta, there is also charm. Here and there, in such a village as this, there are pathetic traces of aesthetic yearnings—a door knocker carved curiously in the shape of a hand, some childish, colorful woodcarving, an ornamental tray, or a trinket of beaten brass. (A few years ago there was discovered in one of these villages a little Coptic boy, aged eight, with a virtuoso's gift for textile design. His enchanting tapestries, so the experts said, were comparable to the work of the greatest contemporary artist-weavers; but he was drowned while bathing in the Nile, still little more than a child.) The villagers are also graced with an instinctive courtesy. "*Fadl!*" some giant voice will boom at you peremptorily, as if threatening catastrophe; but when you turn to defend yourself there will stand a big, friendly peasant with a drooping mustache, his arm outstretched, welcoming you to his home. It will be a poor enough place in all conscience—a cave of mud, littered with rubbish indescribable, with the dogs, the goats, the chickens, the geese, the turkeys, the donkey, and even the cattle sharing living quarters with the family, and a stink of excrement and dirt, and a miasma of dust and insects. But the peasant and his wife will treat you with kindness, the children will be paraded before you bashfully, and the coffee in its little brass jug will be thick and stimulating.

There is a certain heavy, unhealthy beauty, too, to the Delta scene. The colors are so loudly smeared across the landscape; the big boats sail so ponderously up the canals, loaded with cotton bales or big yellow gourds; and the little country trains, like old-fashioned toys, potter along their narrow lines with such dainty, pastry-like puffs of smoke. If it is high summer, there may be rows of children searching for worms in the cotton, with a pompous overseer at the end of the line scratching his stomach and twiddling a white umbrella. If it is picking time the laborers will be chanting, not without gaiety. "We are going to be eaten by camels!" they sing, "We are frightened! We are frightened!" before sweeping irresistibly forward in their ranks, plucking the cotton as they go, as if in some elaborate symbolic rite. Sometimes the women place piles of corn in the middle of the road, so that your car's wheels will crush them as you pass, and they will run out with brooms when you have gone by to sweep the corn into position for the next vehicle. Sometimes a crooked bus, bent in the middle, will rattle down the road, or a tin car piled high with bundles; or a big American limousine will emerge from one of the drab, ornate manor houses which stand like foremen among the miseries. Everywhere farmers are threshing the corn with camel-drawn sledges; and once I saw, walking delicately along a country lane, a young woman balancing upon her head a large white goose in a basket.

Imposed upon the pattern of filth and fertility there is even a measure of variety. At Damietta, in the north, fine diesel fishing-boats stream out to the sea, while schooners stand handsomely in the roadstead; and outside a fishmonger's shop in the old town two portly pelicans stand sentinel, comfortably surveying the passers-by. At Rosetta, along the coast, nice white ducks wash themselves in the salt water, while a man in a yellow waistcoat shows you where the Rosetta Stone was found by a French soldier digging foundations for a fort. Mansura has an agreeable promenade along the Nile, Parisian in flavor, where the waiter from a restaurant across the street will serve you *arak* and *kebab*. At Mehalla el Kubra there stands a cotton plant as magnificent as any European factory, with its own clubs, swimming pools, mosques, hospital, gardens, vast halls of machinery, and a tall campanile above it all. In many a little town there are pleasant dilapidated gardens beside the river; and only once or twice, as you travel about the Delta, will you come across a city so filthy and decrepit, so ridden with flies and drugs and brutality, so undeviatingly hideous that you close your eyes and nostrils as you pass through it, and sigh for Shropshire or Wyoming.

But fertile monotony and fatalism dominate the Delta. At its extremities, to be sure, there are regions of totally different character: to the east is the queer salt lake of Manzala, in which I once spent the eeriest day of my life looking for a crashed aircraft among the marshes and bleak salt flats: a shimmering, empty, shuddery place, with a scattered fishing community of little-known customs. To the west is the battleground of the western desert; there the Bedouin are still collecting barbed wire, flowers creep over the war memorials, and the oil prospectors, before they begin work, still have to inspect the land with mine detectors. But the Delta proper offers neither romantic memory nor austere seclusion; it stands there impregnated with the uninterrupted harvests, the unchanged processes, the unresolved fears and squalors of forty centuries. An air of passivity, replete but diseased, hangs over it still. When God made the world, says an Egyptian fable, the qualities arranged themselves in pairs. "I will go to Syria," said Reason. "I will go with you," said Rebellion. "I will go to the desert," said Misery. "I will accompany you," said Health.

Two qualities came together, hand in hand, to the Delta. One was Abundance; the other was Resignation.

THREE TRADITIONS

ANOTHER REMARKABLE THING about Egypt, even under the materialist weight of a military government, is its guild or fraternity feeling. Certain places have always been noted for particular skills or characteristics, and they retain them with extraordinary persistence through the centuries. Certain families have always had monopolies of trades or products, and even in an age of industrialization they are generally left inviolate in their possession. Egyptian cities cling with extraordinary tenacity to their purposes and reputations. The advent of the revolutionary government in Egypt has inevitably done something to weaken these local or regional traditions—racial minorities have been discouraged (to put it kindly); the economic balance of the country has been shifted; Cairo is more than ever the center of all thought and development. But the guild feeling lingers, nonetheless, and it is instructive to visit a few of the places whose peculiar character has managed to survive the whirlwind, as a reminder of the depth and strength of Egyptian tradition.

One such place is Kharga. Most of the mysteries and eccentricities of Egypt lie on the west bank of the Nile, where the Pharaonic Sun-God set. "Steer to the west, the land of the justified!" the helmsman was told in the funerary boat. "In peace, in peace, to the west, thou praised one, come in peace!" The west is the land of the dead, and the land of hope; its lure is hazily conceived but eternal. All the sixty pyramids of Egypt are on the west bank, and most of the great monuments. It is true that occasionally the *Guide Bleu* will tell you *en passant* that, to the east of Beni Mazar for example, there lies a hill full of mummified dogs; but in general the queer things, the exceptions of Egypt lean towards the sunset. Thus well to the west of the river, and in ancient times veiled in legend and superstition, lie the oases: five small, isolated settlements, inhabited since time immemorial, which lie like outriders along the flank of Egypt. One is Siwa, where Alexander went to consult the oracle of Amon. Another is Farafra, famous for its wheat. A third

is Kharga, to the south, which has always been notorious as a place
of exile for criminals, political, religious, or merely social. Nestorius
was banished there, after propounding his revolutionary doctrines,
and Athanasius, it is said, also suffered in Kharga for his creed.
Nowadays political offenders are immured there, and one fine day
—but then, all the days are fine in Egypt—I paid a visit to the oasis,
hoping to meet some of the prisoners.

It is the perfect place for exile. It lies in a wide declivity in the
western desert, about one hundred and forty miles west of the
Nile, overlooked by burning bluffs and surrounded on every side
by waterless sands. (The country is so empty that the map even
marks the wreckage of a British aircraft that crashed near Kharga
in 1916 after bombing a village held by the Senussi.) So unfriendly
is the desert, so brooding of appearance, that one feels as though
at any moment the sands may reach some momentous decision and
engulf the whole oasis, palm groves, villages, detention camp, and
all. A rough road, once the route of slave caravans from the Sudan,
runs away northeast to the Nile; but the easiest way to get to
Kharga is to take a diesel railcar, made in England, from a place
on the river called Nag Hamadi. This endearing little vehicle (the
locals say its father was a steam train and its mother a bus) starts
very early in the morning and arrives in the shallow bowl of the
oasis just as the terrible heat of the sun is at its most blistering. The
passenger thus disembarks feeling rather as though he too has been
fostering schisms.

I spent a couple of days learning something of Kharga's curious
character. It had a hushed, swathed quality to it, I thought, well
befitting a collection of small villages of so bleak a position and so
ominous a reputation. Not far from the main village there stood a
vast eighth-century Coptic necropolis that admirably represented,
it seemed to me, the personality of Kharga. It was a genuine city
of the dead, akin to that vast conglomeration of fair-sized villas, for
all the world like some prosperous suburb, that houses the Muslim
dead of Cairo. There were neat streets of big mausoleums, domed
or pillared, with such an air of normality to the arrangements that
I almost expected to find a village store at the corner tomb or be
harassed by some insidious postcard seller; but all was dead, not a
mourner crept among those crumbled structures, and the sand was

seeping into the doorways. Some of the tombs were decorated with gay mosaics. I saw one enchanting representation of Paradise, a sort of baroque arcade in the Osbert Lancaster manner; and in another picture a resigned martyr was sitting quietly on a bench being bisected with saws. Generally, though, the atmosphere was one of melancholy and rather sinister dereliction. Half-way up the main street I peered through the grill of a little domed shrine to see inside it the headless, mummified body of an ancient Copt, his arms lying there beside his trunk, surrounded by scattered miscellaneous intestines.

On one side of this disquieting place stood the green fields of the oasis, and deep in the palm trees I could see the brilliant white façade, etched with bulls and goddesses, of the little Ptolemaic temple of Hebi, a fragile and entrancing dream. On the other side was the desert; and the sand, moving restlessly and irresistibly with the prevailing winds, was in fact marching upon Kharga inch by inch through the years. Some of the outlying settlements had already been swamped. Some had built great protective walls around themselves. In one small hamlet a single householder was left in possession, and he too was preparing to leave, for a brutal yellow sand dune was poised above his shack. "The sand has its needs," he said philosophically. "We must allow the sand its rights." Everywhere there were broken walls, shattered houses, and discredited barricades, all half-buried in the dunes.

The detention camp was several miles away in the desert, and nobody seemed very keen to take me there. The government maintained several such centers of internment, in which the residual opponents of the regime (Communists, members of the fanatical Muslim Brotherhood, or old-fashioned diehards) were locked up for security and re-education. From time to time rumors leaked out of cruelties in these camps, and certainly it was very easy for a man to disappear into one of them without warning or appeal; so that people usually preferred not to talk about them, and would be chary of guiding an inquisitive foreigner to see one. So I settled down in the main village of the oasis, hoping to find some friendly guard or prisoner at large, but content enough to sip my coffee in the rambling main square of the place. Its manner was deadened but soothing; its people (mostly Berbers) listless, stupid but friendly. Many of the narrow streets were roofed with wood and earth, to dissuade the wild Bedouin marauders of old from riding down them pell-mell. Along these shady paths the people moved with padded footsteps, carrying baskets decorated with odd little tufts of wool; and at night lanterns swung down side streets and over the open fronts of stores, with piles of beans, big glass pots of spices, and silent shopkeepers lounging against shutters. Hardly a woman was to be seen in this town of rigid tradition; only one cringing soul, embalmed in black, did I meet scurrying from the square in the shadow of a wall. The weather was excessively hot, and the hours of Kharga passed heavily.

On market day, though, the place was transformed, and then I found a trail to my prisoners. The main street was lined with butchers' stalls, piled high with white, fatty camel meat, which the butchers, after a few brusque strokes with the chopper, tore between their bloody hands with a noise of rending flesh and muscles. Piles of this horrible stuff, I noticed, were being loaded into a small truck guarded by a couple of policemen, and when I asked where it was going they said: "To the prisoners." Oho, said I, might I come too? Certainly not, I was told. They were political prisoners, and obviously no foreigner could talk to them—what would the governor say? However, somebody added with the suspicion of a wink that I might be interested instead to visit the hospital of Kharga, just over there, turn right at the square, and very interesting I would find it. So I went along that morning, and an agreeable young doctor showed me round the place. In one ward we found a number of grumpy and scrofulous patients sleeping on palliasses on the floor. "What's this?" I asked. "Not enough beds, then?" "Oh, we have enough normally," said the doctor casually, "but just at the moment we've got a ward full of political prisoners from the camp. Care to meet them?"

And there they were, those successors of Athanasius, propounders of very different faiths: some of them Communists, some Muslim Brothers. They looked a murderous lot, all the more sinister because of the bandages and plasters which, thanks to the kind ministrations of the doctor, covered their eyes or supported their limbs. We talked of this and that, of the past and the future, of the conditions of their detention and their hopes of release. Every

morning, I learned, they were given a lecture of indoctrination by
a representative of the regime, but something in their eyes told me
they were far from brain-washed. Two gray-haired police guards
watched us benevolently from the verandah as we talked; and now
and then a savage old reprobate lying on a bed in the corner inter-
vened with some caustic witticism, delivered in the most cultured
of English accents and with the bite of an educated and incisive
mind. Thus Nestorius might have spoken, I thought, during *his*
exile at Kharga; and thus, by the impact of Egyptian individualism
against the successive grinding stones of government, the traditions
of the oasis continue to be realized.

The heritage of Assiut seems less sure of survival, for this is the
capital of the Coptic community, and in a state like modern Egypt
there is little room for racial disparities and pockets. In its early
years the revolutionary government built up a reputation for
decency and tolerance in such matters—General Naguib's Christmas card used to depict a Christian church, a Jewish synagogue,
and a Muslim mosque, side by side in Cairo—but nationalism and
racial tolerance do not march easily together, and there are signs
of mounting official prejudice against the Copts and other minorities in Egypt. If you are a Christian in government service, you will
find promotion slower than ever. If you are a Coptic landowner,
all kinds of special pinpricks will burn your life. Christian missionaries in Egypt find their task ever more difficult, and there are
signs that the government is planning to take over all foreign
schools and merge them into the national system. The Jews, tarred
of course with the Zionist brush, do their best to ingratiate themselves with the regime, but are poised nevertheless upon a dangerous tightrope; and the Copts, the greatest minority of all, sometimes
feel themselves a people toppling on the edge of persecution.

Assiut is thus a memorial to the vanished heyday of the Copts.
It lies on a bend of the Nile about eight hundred miles from the
sea. High cliffs enclose it and beyond them the deserts stretch away
to Libya and the Red Sea. It first became important as the beginning of a caravan route to the Sudan, and parts of the town still
have a dark African feeling to them. The slave market, for instance,

still stands in the *suk*, a dim square courtyard with a balcony, and little shuttered alcoves in which the shackled Dinkas and Shilluks from up river used to be exhibited to buyers. A butcher inhabits it now, and if you ask him nicely, the mangy, stuffed body of a two-headed water buffalo, which his small son will drag around the courtyard on a string, powerfully contributes to the atmosphere of the place. Nearby there is a deep and cavernous bath, built by the Romans, into which I was politely ushered one stifling July afternoon. Through narrow corridors and down winding stair-cases we passed, my guide pausing now and then to assure me that the mosaic on the floor was eight thousand years old; until we came to the big, gloomy bathhouse in the center, heated by huge fur-naces, wet and steamy. Here, through the darkness, I could see the glistening forms of naked men; some hugely corpulent, lying on their backs asleep; some laughing at me and slapping themselves with soap; one, with his head bandaged, sitting on the floor being massaged by a small boy; one, who was near death or heavily under the influence of hashish, gaunt and unshaven, his eyes open but vacant, lying lonely and forlorn in a little dripping alcove. Many of these men were Negroes, and with the steam rising from the floor, and the black bodies gleaming, and the air heavy with heat and damp, I felt very close to Africa that afternoon.

But though Assiut retains some of the manners of the caravan-serai and the frontier, its character is dictated by the Copts. Four or five Coptic families have set the pace of the city for generations and are still indissolubly associated with its fortunes. They form a proud but pathetic oligarchy. Christians no longer control Egypt, even indirectly, and the Coptic minority no longer has powerful friends at court. The great families of Assiut are therefore deci-mated and relatively impoverished, and their crumbling mansions near the river are as evocative of a retreating era as are the peeling plantation houses of the American South.

When I went to Assiut to learn something of this moribund society I was met at the station by an elderly Copt whose astringent intelligence was characteristic of his breed. The educated Copt is immensely quick in the uptake, humorous and unsentimental, and often a trifle pleased with himself. So was my guide. We sat in the station café for a preliminary cup of coffee; he undid the buttons of his tight linen jacket, and wiped his balding head fastidiously with a silk handkerchief. "I come from a family of priests," he said by way of introduction. "There have been Christian priests in my family since A.D. 48, when St. Mark paid his visit to Assiut; and before that my family, through unnumbered centuries, provided priestly acolytes for the local god of Assiut, Leci."

This struck me as a promising start; and he went on to discuss, with the same endearing loftiness, the origins of the great Coptic families of Assiut. "Now the So-and-Sos, though I hate to say it, for some of them are my very good friends, can only be described as a family of intelligent upstarts. They dealt in ivory, you know, until recently—until the reconquest of the Sudan, I suppose. Ivory, yes, and a little gum arabic and ebony and that kind of thing. A few slaves, perhaps. You might call them," he added with a sniff, "general dealers. Now the This-and-Thats, on the other hand, dealt exclusively in slaves. A fine, upstanding lot they have always been, and some of them reached quite high positions in the priesthood of Leci."

It appeared that these families, though prosperous enough for several centuries, reached the apogee of their fortunes late in the nineteenth century. In those days the system of Capitulations was still in force in Egypt. All sorts of queer things happened under the aegis of this anachronism, which exempted foreign nationals from the jurisdiction of the Egyptian state, and one of the queerest of them was that in Assiut, the most important city of Middle Egypt, nearly all the Powers established consulates. Each consular office had, at the very least, a consul, an interpreter, and a dragoman; and they were responsible not only for the usual consular activities, but also for hearing legal cases in which foreigners were involved—cases which, on appeal, might suddenly be transferred across the continents to Washington, Stockholm, or Madrid. When the Powers wished to appoint such local representatives, more often than not they chose members of the prominent Coptic families, and by the nature of their appointments these people acquired foreign diplomatic privileges, if not foreign nationality. As early as 1875, long before general land ownership was authorized in Egypt, foreigners could acquire property, and many a commercial privilege was accorded them which was denied the unfortunate native.

Thus there arose in Assiut an indigenous community largely above the cramped and corrupt Egyptian law of the time, and consequently unusually well-equipped for self-advancement.

"Oh, they were very delicate about it," said my friend. "A little discreet persuasion could work wonders, even in an embassy. Nothing so blunt as money, you understand me, but a nice little work of Egyptian antiquity, some priceless little statuette, say, could easily procure a vice-consulate. Old What-d'you-call-him, now, he was—let me see—he was vice-consul of Russia and Austro-Hungary, I know for certain, and I think he was the French consulate interpreter, and he *may* have been the Portuguese dragoman too. No job was too menial for those great men, you see, if it brought them extra diplomatic advantages. There were forty consulates here altogether, so there were plenty of positions to be filled, and the old families shared most of them out among themselves, in a gentlemanly sort of way."

"And never looked back?"

"And never looked back, such were the advantages of the thing—and such, I might add, the position they had already achieved, through the industry of unnumbered centuries, in the life of our city. Ah!" said he, looking like an elderly actor preparing a curtain speech, "ah! we say they never looked back! But now the captains and the kings have departed, my dear friend, and I need not tell you, an educated man, about the lizards. Come, finish your coffee while I settle this infamous account, and we shall visit the halls where my fortunate coreligionists drank so deep."

They stood in the grander part of the town, well away from the two-headed water buffalo, and I have never seen houses so infused with piquant character, or so instantly redolent of notable yesterdays. One in particular I remember, for it stood in the middle of a perfectly ordinary street, lined with unpretentious houses, as a corpse might decompose on a family bathing beach; its brown, rotting grandeur loomed at me balefully, far down the pavement, as I walked warily towards it. It was a long building on two floors, very knobbly, like an enormous Christmas cake made of brown suet; and it was surrounded by a dilapidated wall and a garden neglected for so long that it was a chaos of briars, tangled trees, and drab, harsh grass. We walked up the broad steps and through

the front door and found ourselves in an entrance hall that reminded me at once of Grand Central Station in New York. It ran
from the bottom of the house to the top, and a large staircase with
busts upon it circled its flanks to the upper floor. Every inch of its
walls, from floor to ceiling, was covered with reproductions of
Pharaonic scenes—gods and monarchs and sacred birds, cross-
legged scribes and tortuous serpents, painted in colors of astonishing freshness and clarity.

One dowager lived in this vast house, which had been built for
her when she married in 1904 at the height of the prosperity of the
Assiut Copts. (The monogamous customs of the Copts, *vis-à-vis*
the polygamous Muslims, also helped them economically, for they
prevented the frequent division of estates. "Why, the barbarous
Mamelukes," my guide told me, "when they battened themselves
upon Assiut, used to have four wives as a regular thing—an Egyptian for child-bearing, a Mameluke for sentimental reasons, a Turk
for policy, and a Sudanese for fun! Uncouth creatures!") We
found the lady in her drawing room, wearing a black frock and a
headdress not unlike a nun's, surrounded by visiting relatives, all
either intelligent or attractive, and sometimes both. Most of the
family, she said, had gone away to Cairo and Alexandria, where
they were lawyers, doctors, and university professors; but they
were very faithful still, and often came down to visit her in her
mausoleum. A small, portable wireless played in the corner as we
talked, and now and then a very old-fashioned telephone on a
stand rang tinnily. The decor of the room was muted in color but
florid in form, and there were pictures on the wall of prosperous
forebears, visiting celebrities, and flouncy garden parties of long
ago. The house grew on me as I talked; the old lady was very
charming; the relatives discussed with vehemence the true meaning
of the Christian witness; and only a whispered reminder from my
companion ("The Egyptian dusk draws on apace!") dragged me
away from the gathering and down the staircase between the
divinities.

There are many such houses in Assiut, the remnants of its golden
age. Some are grander still, with decorations by imported Italian
craftsmen, and urns on pedestals beside the river, and memories of
royalty. Some are more derelict and crumbling, advertisements

stuck to their garden gates, and boards in their windows. One prominent Copt lives in a houseboat on the Nile, equipped with air-conditioning and an organ; other old gentlemen, with scholarly stoops and walking sticks, are sometimes to be seen emerging, still with dignity, from the cracked front doors of sadly tumble-down mansions.

"A melancholy spectacle," said my friend as we stepped from our garry at the station, "but few things are constant in this world, my dear friend, even in Egypt; and since, I am sorry to have to tell you, they do not include our splendid train service, may I suggest a final cup of coffee?"

Nothing could be more different than Alexandria; but it too lives on its memories and looks over its shoulder to a more munificent past. In the storm of activity that has recently swept Egypt, changing the face of Cairo, hurling roads and factories throughout the country, Alexandria has remained generally aloof and inviolate. Cairo nowadays is a Babel of steamhammers and electric drills, a forest of scaffolding; but few new buildings are going up in Alexandria, and there has settled upon the city a muffled, backwater feeling, such as you sometimes experience in railway stations that are at any moment to be abandoned, or in villages that are scornfully ignored by glittering new highways. It is true that Colonel Nasser's Communist arms are shipped in through Alexandria, and the dock area is sometimes sealed off for weeks, roads are blocked and bridges closed, airliner pilots are forbidden to fly overhead, and the whole port is shrouded in hushed secrecy. But in general the revolution has passed Alexandria by; and the reason perhaps is that this great Mediterranean city, with its splendid white waterfront, its coffee-shops, and its high memories, is not an Egyptian city at all, but a ghost, a shade, a shred of the days when Egypt was a spiritual province of Europe.

I have always found it a place of melancholy. You drive to it through the marshes of Lake Mariut, where the fishermen sail out into the wastes on craft so slim and fragile that in the distance they look like insects balancing themselves on sticks; and almost before you are out of the desert you can see its tall buildings gleaming in the sunshine, as the American skyscraper cities often beckon to you across the prairie. In a moment your head is full of Alexandria's magical past, Alexander himself drawing its ground-plan with a fork, the Pharos flashing on the mole, the pipes of Hercules as he abandoned Antony, the philosophers and mathematicians who once strolled those celebrated boulevards. But somehow when you enter the city, and pass through its faded shopping streets and sniff its air of despondent submission, this sense of history fades and evaporates, the bottom drops out of your preconceptions, and you are left with a place that has some of the baffling pallor of the albino. It is a faceless, blank, hollow kind of city; and nowadays a pall of provincial depression hangs shabbily over its squares and palaces.

Only a few years ago this was the most dazzling metropolis of the eastern Mediterranean. Every summer King Farouk came here with his government, to settle at Montaza or Ras el-Tin; and with him trailed the embassies and legations of the world, officials of every sort, and all that complex social caravan that attaches itself to the affairs of government. During those bright summer months the presence of His Majesty—with his sunglasses and gaudy swim suits—injected a stream of rather dubious lifeblood into the veins of Alexandria; for the entire "palace set," with all its eddying and sometimes unsavory relationships, moved scented and tarbooshed through the salons of the city. For three months in the year Alexandria was a royal capital, and its familiars were the mixed Turks, Albanians, Greeks, and Italians of the royal household, pampered valets and chauffeur-pimps, a companionship bound by the common interests of sex and sycophancy. In the same sunshine there basked, too, a large and prosperous foreign community, with many a banished but imperturbable nobleman, and many an astute wartime profiteer—so that to British officers, entertained during the war in some chromium-plated pleasure house, there sometimes came, between the *pâté* and the salmon, blurred visions of ramshackle army cinemas in the desert, or those millions of ill-printed erotica which circulated among the Allied armies. There was an exiled king or two, who might indeed have given Farouk some disturbing presentiments. There were comfortable English cotton magnates, with yachts riding in the harbor. There were Italian plutocrats and Greek millionaires. There was the fat Turkish aris-

tocracy of Egypt, with a hint of the seraglio in their ponderous
flirtations, and more than a suggestion of the Mamelukes in their
philosophies. What with the Albanian monarch, this motley court,
the old Turkish upper crust, and the cosmopolitan society of the
Alexandrian summer, the city was at once full-flavored, sophisticated, and ridden with satisfying intrigue.

Now all is gone. The King has found other resorts and other
confidants. The revolutionary government, resolutely bourgeois,
spends all the year in Cairo. The pashas are humbled, and, unless
they have managed to make special arrangements, exist on the
meager remains of their capital, listlessly playing tennis at the sporting clubs, or going to the pictures. The sparkling foreign community, discouraged by the constant succession of convulsions and
crises in Egypt, has drifted away with its pigskin suitcases, leaving
that big, colorless residue of miscellaneous aliens that lingers everywhere along the quaysides of the Levant. The big business houses,
surviving with discomfort in what Colonel Nasser likes to call "a
cooperative state," have lost much trade to the Lebanese, and now
seem musty and depressed. The shopkeepers are apathetic. There is
none of that sharp Levantine bite, pungent and stimulating, which
used to be so characteristic of the city. In the summer the crowds
that mill along the beaches are raucous and unkempt, and only now
and then does a delectable French hat give a flicker of elegance to
the tired corniche.

For the wheel of historical fortune has turned, and a city that
was built upon the cultures of Europe is a sad misfit in an Egypt
fervently dedicated to Afro-Asian nationalism. Only a century
after its foundation Alexandria was the greatest city on earth, with
a population of more than a million. The glories of classical Europe
poured themselves upon Alexandria. Its great libraries were the goal
of scholars from all over the civilized world. This was no cold
Pharaonic treasure house, but a glorious ornament of the age in
which the Mediterranean was truly a European lake, in which the
warmer splendors of European thought and architecture were
scattered all along its shores. Euclid, Aristarchus and Herophilus
taught and studied here. Alexander, Caesar, Antony and Cleopatra
marched magnificently through the city's chronicles. The Christian
scholars of the Patriarchate conducted their controversies in Alex-

andria; Napoleon said of the city that it "could not help becoming the capital of the world"; and here, within our lifetime, the gentle Greek poet Cafavy worked and died. All through the centuries Alexandria has flourished as an outpost of Europe in Africa; the Arabs who captured it in the eighth century did little to embellish its splendors; and it remains, poor peeling city, harshly out of sympathy with the Bandung era.

Sometimes, only occasionally, on a steamy summer evening, you may fancy you catch some glimpse of Alexandria's many-colored past: when the lights are beginning to appear along the corniche, and the fort on the mole stands square and squat in the dusk; when there is the clink of coffee cups from the open-fronted shops beside the sea, and a fragrant smell of scampi and curry from the swinging doors of the Union Bar; when a ship steals by outside the harbor, with a muffled thudding of its engines; when a garry labors past, clopping and squeaking, its tattered driver half-asleep on his seat; and when from the jumbled darkness of the Arab quarter there come the first faint sounds of illicit pleasure, a shrill laugh, the beat of a drum, the strains of a drunken song.

Then, for a moment, you may imagine scholars arguing in the coffee-shops; kings at their food in the Union Bar; triremes in the harbor; white ties and taffeta in the garries; and young men of high spirit, with black and perfumed hair, roistering through the arcades of indulgence.

A DITCH IN EGYPT

LONG BEFORE Alexandria was conceived, perhaps even before the rise of the priesthood of Leci at Assiut, the Pharaoh Necho began a canal to link the Mediterranean with the Red Sea; and several millennia before the advent of the British Empire, the Isthmus of Suez, through which that waterway fitfully ran, was of supreme strategic importance to the Egyptian Empire. We generally think of the isthmus as a link between the Mediterranean and the Indian Ocean, between Europe and India; but to the Egyptians it has always been a bridge between Africa and its neighbor Asia. When the British occupied the Canal Zone, they stood astride Colonel Nasser's principal foreign communications—his railway links with Palestine. When my Israeli colonel led his tanks to the shores of the Suez Canal he was hammering at the ramparts of Egypt itself.

It is all too easy nowadays for a foreigner to forget this, for the Isthmus of Suez is now so completely dominated by the presence of the canal. This is a strip of land more than one hundred miles long, with three cities on it, a big military base, airfields, parks, and holiday resorts; yet it lives almost entirely in the service of the Suez Canal. Only the visionary may conceive the isthmus as running east and west, linking Africa with Asia; to the ordinary eye its orientation is firmly north and south, connecting seas. If you fly over it, from the sparkling Mediterranean, you will suddenly grasp, with the shock of recognition, this immediate significance of the place. There below you in the yellow sand stretches a narrow ditch, for all the world like those little precarious rivulets that children dig with wooden spades on beaches; but as you leave the Mediterranean behind you and glimpse the Red Sea in front, it is abruptly and violently brought home to you that this particular channel links no sand castles, nor does it meander irritatingly between the legs of deck chairs, but instead is a highway between worlds. Behind is Europe, *edelweiss*, and Chartres; in front are the crags of Arabia and the bottomless blue seas to China.

It is, superficially anyway, because of the importance of the Suez Canal that the affairs of the Middle East have reached such a dizzy and rumbustious climax; but the isthmus is also a place of pleasure and constant fascination. I know of no procession more exciting to watch than the long line of a convoy navigating this marvellous waterway. If you approach it by car across the desert you may catch sight of a smudgy line of smoke moving all but imperceptibly north from Suez; and if you drive very fast you can settle on the sandy banks of the canal to watch the ships go by. It is nearly always hot in the isthmus, and nearly always sunny, and the air is nearly always oppressively still; so that before long you will hear the muffled beat of engines, and then over a bump in the bank you will see masts and funnels and upperworks creeping through the sand, and then miraculously the ships will appear. Their speed up the canal is very leisurely, giving them the air of matrons of honor walking up a nave; from a distance there is only the swell of the bow waves, the lazy wisps of smoke from the funnels, and the hum or the pounding of engines, to show that they are moving at all. Nevertheless, in a moment or two they are beside you: a white Norwegian tanker leading, as clean and shiny as a tube of toothpaste; and then some old British freighter, generally the dirtiest of them all, rust on her hull and peeling paint on her funnel, with a brawny Geordie singing a song from a galley porthole; and two or three huge, modernistic tankers, streamlined and bulbous, flying improbable flags of convenience, Liberian or Panamanian; and a yacht-like Italian; and a tumble-down shambles of a Greek; and, if you are lucky, one of the great British liners steaming home from Sydney, summer frocks and white ducks all along its rails, and stewards with trays, and the suggestion of an Australian accent seeping across the water. (Not so long ago there were civil servants from India lining such shipboard rails as these, missionaries from China, or French Legionaires from Saigon, who frequently seized the opportunity, as they passed through the canal, of leaping overboard and deserting, sometimes fifty or sixty at a time. This is the Bandung age, though, and even the passenger list reflects it.)

Not long before the nationalization of the canal I sailed through it on a Royal Navy frigate, partly because I wanted to experience that stately progression for myself, partly to see how the canal pilots did their work. In those days the Navy and the *Compagnie Universelle du Canal Maritime de Suez* enjoyed a friendly system of liaison, and there were always stout British pilots available to guide the White Ensign through the canal. The atmosphere on the bridge of the warship was therefore supremely calm and confident. The elderly pilot was in charge; the youngish captain stood beside him; and the helmsman, richly bearded, took the orders. Only now and then did the pilot issue a murmured command. Generally the bridge was silent, except for snatches of desultory conversation, and the sun streamed over the canvas shields most pleasantly. So quiet was our movement, so still the water, so smooth and uniform the banks of the canal, that we seemed to be in a butter boat cruising on a sea of cream. There was no sense of tension or potential danger; indeed the whole operation looked perfectly simple. It was the wind, said the pilot, that sometimes upset things, and the sudden currents set up in the canal by the bow waves of preceding ships. Sometimes you would find, all of a sudden, that you must reverse your helm to keep the vessel in midstream; sometimes an unexpected breeze or current would swing the ship around broadside on, and you would need a clear head and experienced judgment to straighten her again. I liked and respected the pilot, and believed him; and the Company used to say that on the average two or three ships got out of control every week. Just the same, I always suspected that there was some exaggerated mystique attached to the job of the Suez Canal pilots. They were extremely highly paid, and the Company, in justifying the employment of so many foreigners, always used to claim that only a most experienced master could safely pilot a ship through; but I remember with affection the letter of a Royal Navy officer who once wrote to *The Times* to say that he had often taken his own destroyer through the canal by dint of simply ordering his helmsman: "Steer down the middle!"

The Company has gone now, and the genial Frenchmen in their shorts no longer sip apéritifs on their terraces beside the water, and the omelettes are no longer delectable in the little French Club at Ismailia. But the towns of the Canal Zone will not soon lose their last trim traces of Frenchness. Ismailia in particular, the local headquarters of the Company, has a delightfully green, summery, pro-

vincial feeling to it. With its souvenir shops and its perpetual sunshine, it sometimes used to suggest to me some modest little French
ski resort with no mountains and precious little snow. The Company built itself unusually comfortable premises. Its offices were
long, low, unpretentious structures with verandahs and colonial
temperaments; but the homes of its senior staff were grand and
sometimes luxurious, with lawns round about them, tall palm trees
shading them, and excellent wines in their cellars. These houses,
along the principal boulevard of Ismailia, still set the tone of the
town (though the prints in the drawing rooms of *L'Audace*, sixty-
two guns, sinking H.M.S. *Formidable*, eighty-four guns, off Cape
Finisterre may have been replaced by something more assertive).
There are big public gardens, pleasant, tree-shaded squares, a golf
course and some handsome avenues. De Lesseps would feel at home
in Ismailia still; and indeed he could set up his brass-knobbed bed-
stead in his same old chalet, for it still stands there among the
gardens.

Port Said, up the road, also possesses, in normal times, a certain
bright French exhilaration. On the balcony of the great echoing
store of Simon Artz (camel saddles, dowdy fashions, and suitcases
with pictures of the pyramids on them) you may drink your coffee
overlooking the busy entrance of the canal. There goes your convoy, still creeping northwards, with the Australians in their floppy
hats waiting to come ashore; and there, lined up like hams, is a
row of tankers waiting to sail south to the oilfields. Along the mole
are rows of bright bobbing fishing boats, and there is a murmurous
rankling from the fish market on the quay. Below you, hastening
towards the dockside, are the dragomen in their long robes, the
bumboat men with their boxes of Turkish delight, the pompous
customs men, the gulli-gulli men with their chickens, the big-
mustached policeman, the man who squirts Flit, the doctor and the
Representative of the Regime—all in a hurry to board the big liner,
for coffee, formalities, or the prospect of profit. To the north there
is a tall, striped lighthouse, standing bashfully in a street. To the
south you can see, moving machine-like against the glittering water,
rows and rows of blackened coolies, dressed in a few meager rags,
bent double with sacks, chanting mournfully as they fill the coal
bunkers of a freighter.

At nighttime, though, Port Said is still one of the rumbliest, raw-
est places on earth. Its tall balconied buildings feel barred and foreboding, and there is a muffled sense of ill will abroad. Perhaps,
indeed, some ragged urchin will dig his dirty nails into your wrist
as you pass by, trying to steal your wristwatch, while a villainous
accomplice on a bicycle threatens you with a stone; but more
probably it will simply be the touts and the pimps, the relentless
salesmen, the shouting taxi drivers, who will make you feel obscurely ill at ease. Anything might happen in Port Said, you feel;
and a great deal does. Tucked away in the sleazy shambles of its
backstreets, in houses of tacked flotsam or in peeling, rambling
tenements, the purveyors of sin are at work. The brothel-keepers
beckon from their doorways; the leering garry-men clip-clop down
the alleys; and in the *salles des exhibitions* the lipsticked, naked
girls prepare their perversions. Sailors lounge through the streets,
trying to look experienced. Old men with sacks over their heads
cough heavily over their stalls of roasted nuts. The beam of the
lighthouse flashes gloomily across the city. Before long you may
wish you were back on the balcony of Simon Artz, among the
blue crêpe dresses, writing your picture postcards and watching the
ships go by.

For the Isthmus of Suez is a place of power and turmoil, and
Port Said, for all its daytime charm, is correspondingly tough. It
was a just coincidence that picked upon Port Said, that terrible
November, to symbolize for a day or two all the conflicts and
hatreds of the Middle East, to illustrate the rising rivalry between
East and West, and to remind the world that a taste for violence
is still one of the primary human emotions. At our chosen moment
in history there were no sequined dresses in the windows of Simon
Artz and no coffee cups upon its balconies. Soldiers in battle kit
patrolled those dim backstreets, and big gray warships had driven
the fishing boats from the mole. The canal was littered with sunken
ships; the houses along the sea front were pitted with shell holes;
only a few frightened touts offered their beastly souvenirs in the
streets.

For this was November, 1956, and the British army had invaded

Egypt. When I stood in the Sinai that day the Union Jack was flying defiantly over Port Said; but the brief triumph soured into a nightmare, and not all the coffee of Simon Artz, not all the good wines of the French Club, could wash the taste away next morning.

HIGH DAM

COLONEL NASSER's seizure of the canal was both successful and spectacular, and gave a powerful fillip to the self-esteem of the Egyptians. Much more crucial to the future of Egypt, though, is the nation's second great waterway, the Nile. If the canal might be said to symbolize Egypt's foreign adventurings, which have always played a lively part in the affairs of this queer state, the Nile might represent the second half of its rather schizophrenic character. For two years I rented an elderly houseboat moored on the Nile in Cairo. It was a paddle steamer with a slim white funnel, once a ferryboat, now securely fastened to the grassy bank, only to be released by our cheerful watchman (an old sailor himself) when the inexorable rise of the Nile demanded it. I therefore became accustomed to the dignity and rhythm of that noble river. The great white sailing boats would come drifting past our bedroom window in the small hours, tall and ghostly, silent but for the creaking of wood or the muffled singing of a helmsman. The rich mud would swirl by in floodtime, as if half Egypt were being washed away; and in the winter we would sink with the water, far below the level of our garden, as though before long we would be resting ignominiously on the bottom. There were antique ceremonies to be seen upon the river; and swimming races, in which the gigantic Egyptian long-distance champions pounded by like greased machines; and sometimes huge, mysterious fish would cavort beside our hull like porpoises. (In the Museum of Natural History one of them is stuffed and mounted behind glass, but is described, unhelpfully, simply as "Nilotic Fish.") The Nile at Cairo is often thick with filth; but its nature is genial and humorous, and when our Siamese cats fell in, as they did from time to time, it always treated them kindly.

Egypt is the gift of this old great-heart, as Herodotus observed, and depends upon the Nile for almost all her wealth. Compared with the bounty of the Nile, the royalties of the Suez Canal are chicken-feed. It was the intelligent use of the Nile flood that made

Egypt the granary of the world in ancient times; and throughout
the centuries the Egyptians have been adept at waterworks, at
irrigation, damming, and the astute exploitation of floods. Nowadays, indeed, for all the bluster of the regime, the throwing of
weight about, the shouting and the bullying, the survival of Egypt
as a Power depends upon the fuller use of the resources of the
river; for the economic situation of Egypt is nightmarish, and the
Nile is almost her only natural resource. The population of Egypt,
scarcely aware of the mysteries of birth control, increases at a rate
of half a million every year—in other words, it will double itself
by the end of this century. The standard of living is already desperately low. Bilharzia and tuberculosis are rampant, the incidence
of blindness is the highest on earth, the vast majority of Egyptians
are illiterate. With such a basic situation, the effects of a doubled
population are terrible to consider.

Until the rulers of the new Egypt began to fritter their energies
away in *realpolitik*, they seemed to be doing their best to solve this
appalling problem. The remedy they proposed was dual: to increase by irrigation the agricultural land of Egypt, and to indus-
trialize the country. More food would thus be produced, more jobs
would be provided, the standard of living would be raised, and at
the same time Egypt would be helped to stand upon her own economic feet. This program was launched with commendable energy.
German constructors built a big steel plant at Helwan, outside
Cairo. Work was begun on a great new fertilizer factory. With
Russian help, an atomic energy laboratory was founded. With
American help, areas of the western desert were reclaimed for
agriculture. The grandiose Liberation Province scheme was started.
All sorts of minor industries were fostered.

But the basis of any such Egyptian development plan must be
the Nile—the immense power of which is largely untapped, for a
large proportion of its water still flows unimpeded into the Mediterranean. So the foundation of Colonel Nasser's schemes was a
dramatic new exploitation of the resources of the Nile. Very early
in its career the revolutionary government adopted a scheme of
development proposed in the past, but shelved, which would trans-
form the relationship between the Egyptians and their river. In the
upper part of Egypt, where that country trails away in deserts and

cataracts towards the Sudan, the government proposed to build the greatest dam the world had ever seen, containing seventeen times as much masonry as the great pyramid of Cheops (though an American expert estimated that it would cost only about five man-hours per cubic yard, compared with four hundred man-hours per cubic yard for the pyramid). Not only would this great thing, it was thought, increase the productive land of Egypt by a third; it would also provide hydroelectric power for the new industries; it would revivify the stagnant provinces of Upper Egypt; and it would ensure (a hollow triumph, this) that in twenty years' time the standard of living of the Egyptians would be no worse than it was already, despite the increasing population. Moreover, the dam would stand as a symbol of the new Egypt, to remain in future centuries as a memorial to its vision and labor. "Our new pyramid," Colonel Nasser used to call it, handing his visitors an illustrated leaflet on the subject; and the High Dam, *Sudd el Ali*, became one of the staples of the regime, something it was always tactful to discuss, and in which the Egyptians began to take justifiable, if premature, pride.

The High Dam was to be built at Aswan, only a few miles to the south of the existing Aswan Dam—which, when it was erected by British engineers fifty years before, had a comparably revolutionary effect upon the agriculture of Egypt. The river steamers sailing southwards from Shellal pass the site, and one day I boarded one of them to see it. The Sudanese captain invited me to join him in the wheelhouse as we sailed past the spot, and I settled myself there on a high wooden stool and ate a banana. Although scores of engineers had contributed to the plans of the High Dam, they were still rather hazy and tentative; so that the pamphlet I spread on my knees seemed to me more imaginative than precise, and contained indeed two totally different pictorial impressions of the structure, both presented as equal certainties. Still, everybody seemed to agree about the size of it all. It would be, declared the pamphlet baldly, the biggest thing ever made (God and the weather permitting, as the paddle steamer timetables used to put it). "For thousands of years," Colonel Nasser was quoted as saying, "the great pyramids of Egypt were the foremost engineering marvels of the world. They ensured a life after death to the Pharaohs. To-morrow the gigantic High Dam, more magnificent and seventeen times greater than the pyramids, will provide a higher standard of living for all Egyptians." Indeed, the dam sounded a marvellous conception. Its height would be two hundred and fifty feet, and it would be in all three miles wide. Thirty-four thousand tons of iron and forty-two million cubic meters of other building material would be used in its construction. Sixteen electric turbines would generate nearly two million horsepower and every year ten thousand million kilowatt hours of electrical power would be produced. No water would pass through the face of the dam. Instead, seven vast tunnels would be bored through the east bank of the river to allow the passage of the river; and four on the other side would drive the turbines in a monumental underground powerhouse. All this, it was thought, would take fifteen years to build and would cost something like $750,000,000. It was, in truth, an idea of breathtaking splendor.

Early one blazing afternoon our big steamer approached the site of this marvel, and the passengers crowded forward to the bows. It was very hot and dazzlingly sunny, and the harsh brown rocks around us looked pitiless. Beyond them there was only the desert. There was no life along these banks, no villages or fishing boats, and only an occasional launch chugged by on its way to Aswan. Presently there was a blast on the ship's siren. The passengers craned their necks or prepared their cameras; the siren blew again majestically; and we passed through the site of the *Sudd el Ali*. One day, I thought, the dragomen might practice their talents here, and very revealing their statistics would be; but there was not much sign of life to be seen that day. Tucked away beside the east bank was a tumble-down old houseboat; high above it was a small white office building; moored in midstream were two big barges of convoluted appearance, from which engineers were testing the nature of the river bed. For the rest, all was quiet and placid in the sunshine.

But the captain tapped my shoulder. "Look at the banks," said he; and there I saw something far more suggestive. Painted on the rocks on each side of us were a series of vertical white lines, running down to the water's edge. They showed where the buttresses of that gigantic structure would stand, where the seven huge tunnels would pipe the Nile northwards, where the powerhouse would pulse through the years; and they showed (at least to the imaginative) exactly how the new pyramid would one day block the channel of the river as a cork stops a wine bottle. In so empty a landscape, unfriendly and ill-disciplined, there was something bold about those simple lines, and I found them exciting. So did my fellow passengers. The people on deck, gazing at that drab and ancient place, stood silently beside the rails; and the old helmsman at my side, who sailed past it twice a week, smiled at me, clicked his tongue, and shook his head like a man foreseeing wonders.

The creation of the High Dam would affect the whole of Egypt. Desert areas would be made fertile, irrigation water would always be plentiful, factories would be given birth. But in particular it would alter the face of Upper Egypt, a region of traditional tranquillity and tourism, where Aga Khans still spend their winters with Somerset Maughams, and where I once encountered a honeymoon couple from Indianapolis holding hands in a *felucca*. Luxor, one hundred miles downstream, would not be touched, but the character of Aswan itself, which stands on the first cataract, would be drastically altered. It is a pleasant place with many gardens, and a grand hotel overlooking the cataract, and a tree on a neighboring island which is inhabited by hundreds of egrets, their wailing cries echoing across the water like a multitude of cats. But it has long since passed its days of glory, and the tourists who go there now (rather intermittently, between international crises) are not as affluent as their predecessors. Now the regime sees it as the capital of a new industrial region. There are iron mines near Aswan, known to the Pharaohs and still exploited; and there is potential power in the Nile. When I was in Aswan, engineers were already adapting the old Aswan Dam to generate electricity, with French and Swedish contractors, British consulting engineers, and Swiss and Swedish turbines brought down the river by barge from Alexandria. This would, in particular, provide power for a fertilizer factory. Thus the town was already changing, and in my hotel room I sometimes used to feel that I was already in the backstreets of a great productive city, so constant was the noise outside as the laborers brawled beneath the street lights and the jeeps and lorries rumbled out to the dam.

These changes are as nothing, though, compared with the metamorphosis that would overcome the region if the High Dam were completed. Not only would there be new industries and irrigation works, transformer plants, powerhouses, the influx of workers and shopkeepers: the dam would also create, beginning only six miles south of Aswan, the largest man-made lake in the world. It would be two hundred and fifty miles long. The whole of the country historically known as Nubia would be flooded, and the ships that now bustled so easily up the river would have to navigate their passage through an inland sea. The shape of Egypt would be altered almost as dramatically as it was by the cutting of the Suez Canal; a fifth of riverain Egypt would be submerged.

My steamer, plowing southwards, took me through all this sentenced territory rather as a surgeon might conduct a visitor through his wards, for though sympathetic I could not help feeling comfortably detached from it all. But there was a poignancy to the journey, all the same. Nubia was a land of noble historical associations, which had provided splendid fighting men for the Pharaohs, and in which some of those unpredictable potentates had built magnificent shrines and temples. Almost within sight of Aswan, for example, the Ptolemies built the temple of Philae, a delicate masterpiece upon an island in the Nile. It is only visible for a few weeks in the year, for the building of the old Aswan Dam created its own substantial reservoir, and this promptly flooded the temple. As we passed southwards from Aswan I strained my eyes for a glimpse of this wonderful thing, fretting the years away beneath the reservoir; but all I could see were the thin black lines of its pylons, looking no more evocative than a pair of moldy black logs drifting downstream with the current. If the High Dam were ever built, though, Philae would emerge again in all its glory. The level of the present reservoir would be slightly lowered, and this would allow the engineers to build a protective dyke around Philae, and to drain it of its water; so that there would be a kind of sunken island in midstream, and visitors, carefully climbing over its dyke, would see before them, in a little green pocket, those sublime buildings, dry and unmuddied; with their surrounding fields fertile

again, and the goats wandering among their columns, as fabled
cities are often seen, serene and prosperous, beneath the waters of
legendary lakes.

Some such hostage to the gods would perhaps be advisable; for
elsewhere the lake of the High Dam would submerge scores of
other temples and memorials, and hundreds of the picturesque
Nubian villages which cling aridly to the banks of the river. At
almost any hour of the day, as we progressed upstream, now and
then interrupting our observations for a vast, white-napkined
lunch, one of these quaint settlements would be in sight, tumbled
about some slight inlet in the river bank, or waiting wide-eyed for
the little white boats that always seemed to be approaching from the
opposite bank. There are no other villages quite like them; neither
African nor Arab, nor even properly Egyptian, but of a style that
seems to have grown, willy-nilly, from the brown and formidable
landscape of Nubia. Their houses often look like forts, so squat,
square, and uncompromising are they. Sometimes they are decorated with hands, diagrams, or cabalistic symbols, to keep inimical
spirits away, or perhaps to prevent, by alliance with the occult,
the construction of the dam. One of the sailors, pointing out an
open hand painted on one such house, told me that each finger
represented a Muslim saint—Mohammed, Ali, Fatima, Hassan, and
Hussein; but I suspect the Nubians, who had their minds on the
evil eye, were impelled by only the haziest eschatological instincts.
Many of these places looked deserted already, except for the rows
of bright-painted fishing boats lined up beside the shores. Most of
the men went away to work in Cairo, the sailor told me, where
there was money to be earned. The rest grew a few dates, caught
a few fish, farmed a few *feddans*, and generally labored their lives
away in unrewarding toil. The desert came down to their back-
yards, and behind the escarpment which stood over them the lone
and level sands stretched far away.

Now and again we saw some lonely riverside temple, half engulfed in the sand or proudly reflected in the water: with two big
figures of a Pharaoh, perhaps, or a smooth and simple image of a
falcon, poised upon a pedestal; with a compound reaching to the
escarpment behind, and a little track through the sand along which
the superstitious Nubians still crept, at times of danger or anxiety,

to pay surreptitious tribute to the ancient gods. There were tombs and temples all along this blazing river bank, steles and cartouches in the rocks, and images of emperors. This was the way to Kush and Napata. In the confused pages of Pharaonic history many a glittering army may be discerned moving up or down this waterway, looking for slaves, quelling insurgents, or establishing new dominions. Resonant names of ancient places dignified the map of our route—Dabud and Qirtas, Dandur and Affedunia, El Dakka and Garf Hussein, which stands below the Jebel Umm Shaghir, southwest of the Sinn el Kaddab, opposite Kushtamna; and late one night, when the stars were reflected fuzzily in the Nile, we arrived out of the darkness at the most thrilling of all Egyptian monuments, the *tour de force* of Rameses II, the rock-temple of Abu Simbel.

Like the little Nubian villages and the palm-studded river banks themselves, it was threatened by the prospect of the High Dam; and through those days and nights archaeologists were at work inside it and on its great façade, recording every crack and carving before committing it sadly to the waters. So as we slid quietly towards the bank, a blue-robed sailor shouting instructions from the bows, we found the temple ablaze with light. The banks of the river stretched away as black as midnight, and the water rippled darkly beneath us, and the sky was an impregnable blue; but there gazed at us brilliantly, from the rocks in front, four colossal images of the Pharaoh, cold and white and imperturbable. They sat there with their hands upon their knees, vast and square and rather fleshy; and so endearing was their manner that I felt quite a pang of sympathy when I saw that one of those wistful heads had fallen from its body, and lay bang on its nose on the ground beneath. Inside the temple there were ladders and tarpaulins and draftsmen's tools. The shadowy columns were lit, the dim alcoves had planks in them, and the mosaics recording the Pharaoh's invariable victories were wonderfully vivid. No lovers maundered through this bright-lit cavern; no pimpled youths took combs out of their breast pockets to smooth their greasy hair; but it reminded me a little, all the same, of a subway station very late at night, just before the last train. It was odd to emerge from the rocks to the dark sandy bank outside, and to hear the captain, high in the wheelhouse of his vessel, calling throatily for his passengers to reembark; and odder still to reflect that this glorious monument, which had stood there beside the river for three thousand years, come flood, come low water, come Roman, come Arab, come galley, come steamboat, might soon be drowned and whittled away by the slow motion of the waters.

But the High Dam has never been started, and Abu Simbel is still dry. Long and protracted were the negotiations by which Colonel Nasser hoped to raise, from the West, the enormous sum of money he needed to construct it; subtle and misty the suggestions, from time to time, that Russia would provide the money without conditions; disconcerting the suddenness with which the United States, closely followed by Britain, announced that she would not, after all, help with the project. Within a month or two Colonel Nasser, seizing upon a pretext, nationalized the Suez Canal, declaring (without much conviction) that its fees would pay for the *Sudd el Ali;* and for the moment one waterway replaced the other as an expression of Egypt's triumphs and aspirations.

It may be that Colonel Nasser can feed his populace for a few more years on the intoxications of foreign policy, and that he can afford to let the economy of Egypt stagger on towards the dreariest kind of Nemesis; or it may be that the High Dam will crop up again not as a political sop or a project of prestige, but as an urgent economic necessity. Whatever its future, our setting is November 1956; and the dam is still only a dream, still no more than a noble design upon a very preliminary drawing board.

THE AMERICANS

THE SUDDEN AMERICAN DECISION to withdraw financial support for the dam came as a shock, but not as a surprise. It was a shock because it was so obviously a rebuff to a regime that had hitherto enjoyed the favors of Washington; but it was scarcely a surprise to those who had followed the fluctuations of American policy in the Middle East, and who knew how hazy, ambiguous, and contradictory were American intentions towards the region.

American associations with the Muslim Middle East were much older than most people supposed. Washington had enjoyed treaty relations with the Sultanate of Muscat, for example, since 1834; there was an American military mission in Egypt in the nineteenth century; Americans had played an important part in the economic life of Persia since the beginning of this century; for generations American missionaries had been honorably, if sometimes misguidedly, active among the Arabs. In November, 1956, the United States still took second place to Britain in the actual exertion of power, in physical presence, in direct influence and prestige; but this was misleading. It had been many a long year since American oil interests became predominant in the Arab world (in 1939 the American share was thirteen percent and the British sixty percent; by 1956 the American share was sixty-five percent and the British thirty percent). Moreover, since the British evacuated the Canal Zone in 1955, the principal Western military forces in the Middle East had been the astonishing American Sixth Fleet, ceaselessly roaming the Mediterranean, and the American bombers which used the United States air base at Dhahran, in Saudi Arabia. Even in 1956 most Egyptians and most Arabs, by force of habit, thought of Britain as the paramount Power in the Middle East. The mythical gunboats of the Westminster diehards were very real to the Egyptian mind; there is every evidence that Colonel Nasser, when he seized the canal, expected an instantaneous and terrible British retaliation. But the truth was that Britain no longer had the power to exert her will; despite superficial appearances, the Americans had

taken over ultimate responsibility long before the attack on Port
Said or the Sinai offensive.

The American stake in Middle Eastern affairs was already enormous. The activities of the Russians in the Middle East, especially
in Egypt, demanded counteraction from Washington before the
whole place crumbled into Communism. The American base at
Dhahran was an important link in the chain of strategic bombers
which, in this pre-missile period, surrounded Soviet Russia like an
iron ring. The Arabian-American Oil Company, which operated
in Saudi Arabia, was the greatest single American overseas investment. In several other oil states American capital was heavily invested, and healthy American dividends were being produced.
There were two states in the Middle East—Iraq and Persia—which
had frankly joined the American alliance, and might therefore be
regarded as American wards. American policy had been largely
responsible for the creation of Israel, and there was still an influential body of American opinion ready to exert pro-Zionist pressure on American policy. There was also Britain to think of; she
was, after all, America's principal ally, and she still had sizable
Middle Eastern investments and responsibilities, some of them
worthy of American encouragement. At the same time, it was a
prime principle of American policy that self-determination among
small countries should be cherished and supported. Finally, the
Middle East was a kind of power vacuum, and there was always
the horrible possibility that America might one day have to use
force to fill it.

As may easily be seen, these stakes and aspirations were very
often conflicting. You could not easily support Israel and ingratiate
yourselves with Saudi Arabia at the same time. You could not at
once bolster the position of Britain and concede all the demands
of Arab nationalism. If you provided arms for the Baghdad Pact
countries, you antagonized the Egyptians. If you gave tanks to the
Jews, Standard Oil might object; if you reequipped the Egyptian
army, you stood to lose the Jewish vote (for what that was worth
—the political experts seemed to disagree). If you tried to check
the advances of Communism, you were accused of intervention
in the affairs of small Powers. If you did your best to stay aloof from
the affairs of so quixotic and trying a region, you were accused

of isolationism. No wonder the policies of the Americans, throughout the difficult postwar years, were distorted and contradictory;
idealism, the saving grace of Americanism, strikes few chords of
sympathy in the Middle East.

In particular, American policy was characterized by sincere but
confused attempts to be all things to all men. The Americans supported the thesis of the Baghdad Pact, smiling upon its programs
and arming its members; but they would not take the decisive step
of joining it—the only step which would give it the necessary sense
of power and permanency. They paid lip service to Anglo-American cooperation (and indeed among Americans and Britons in the
Middle East there was the closest community); but they were
largely responsible for the withdrawal of the British from the
Canal Zone, and for the subsequent drastic reduction of British
influence throughout the region. They forced the creation of the
State of Israel, by insisting upon more Jewish immigration during
the British Mandate; but they did nothing to break the Arab blockade of that beleaguered state, or to restrain the Egyptians from
their reiterated threats to obliterate it. Even after Colonel Nasser's
purchase of Communist arms, they paid careful court to the revolutionary government in Egypt; yet their withdrawal of help for
the High Dam was blunt to the point of insult.

These ambiguities were one reason why the Americans were
regarded with distrust throughout the Arab countries—though not
with that peculiar respectful loathing reserved for the British. Another reason was the close connection between American Jewry
and the State of Israel, and the undeniable fact that Israel existed
upon American bounty, both official and unofficial. The character
of Israel, at least in its early years, was overwhelmingly American;
and few Arabs doubted the assertions of their propagandists that
American arms were being poured into Haifa and Tel Aviv. A
third cause of distrust, paradoxically, was the devoted work of
the Point Four officials, whose ill-informed enthusiasm was often
mistaken by the natives for some sort of colonialist zeal. In Arab
eyes Israel and Point Four were equally manifestations of dollar
imperialism—that ill-defined, mistily envisaged bugbear which so
harasses America's relations with the smaller Powers.

Thus America's first groping and half-hearted attempts to impose serenity upon the area, after the enforced withdrawal of the British policeman, were handicapped by an almost universal unpopularity. It was virtually impossible to convince the young Arab that the American ideal was precisely what he himself wanted, that the American Revolution was the prototype of his own struggle towards emancipation, and that the American Republic was the godmother of independence movements everywhere. The more money the Americans spent in good works, the more their motives were suspected; the more they fawned upon the Arabs, the less they were liked. For all their anti-colonial sentiments, they found themselves indiscriminately lumped together with the British as imperialists and Zionist stooges.

But gradually, during 1956, some degree of decision entered into American policies, as the nature of the Communist offensive in the Middle East became apparent. Those in Washington dedicated to the wooing of the Arabs were clearly gaining the ascendancy; and those who favored the encouragement of Israel and support for Britain were losing ground. There was a gradual but unmistakable shift in American sympathies. This was partly because the Russians were conducting so successful a flirtation with the Arabs that the American competitive instinct was aroused; and partly because it was dawning upon the planners in Washington that the Bandung group of nations would soon be more powerful (and were already more influential) than the democracies of western Europe. Israel was not crucial to the future of the United States. Britain was becoming less so. But every year the Arabs and their friends gained in stature; and every year Arabian oil was growing more important to the Americans, not only because they were importing large quantities from the Middle East, but also because their oil companies were constantly expanding their activities in the Arab countries. A new kind of understanding with the Arab world was essential for the welfare of America.

As the British position weakened, and as the hounds of nationalism hurled themselves upon the carcass, the British connection became ever more embarrassing to the Americans in the Middle East. The longer Britain retained her dwindling hegemony, the wilder Arab nationalism became, and the more danger there was of instability and insurrection in the oil-bearing countries. The British

habit of confusing politics and economics particularly upset many
Americans, for it was a cardinal point of policy of the Arabian-
American Oil Company that there should be no meddling in local
politics—an attitude that led the company to some sad excesses
of subservience to Saudi Arabian whims and prejudices. ("I know
of no country in the world," a high official of the company announced publicly about this time, "in which oil royalties are more
wisely spent." He was referring to the Saudi kingdom, where almost all the vast oil monies were devoted to the personal gratifica-
tions and salacities of the ruling house.) It could thus hardly be
expected that American policy, if it was at all affected either by
the oil lobbies or the call of idealism, would consistently support
the efforts of Britain, that gnarled old imperialist, to maintain her
grip upon the Arab world. Long before the Suez crisis, which cast
so shaming a spotlight upon Anglo-American differences, the policies of the two Powers often clashed disastrously.

But if America would not share in any Anglo-American suze-
rainty in the Middle East, which of the rival indigenous factions
should she support? Should she put her money on Colonel Nasser,
much the most influential of all the Arabs, the prophet of the
nationalists? Or should she make friends with those old-fashioned
conservatives who still controlled the oil resources of the Middle
East—the feudal princes of the Arabian Peninsula, the landlord-
governments of Iraq and Persia? The traditions of American liberalism were on Nasser's side, I suppose; the instincts of American
capitalism favored the princes. To be sure, it looked in 1956 as if
all the feudal autocrats of the Arab world were due for a tumble;
but for the moment, anyway, they controlled both the oil and the
money-bags—and by the nature of things they were anti-Com-
munist. Anyway, Nasser himself decided the issue by throwing
himself so rashly into the hands of Soviet Russia. America would
certainly continue to support Nasserism against imperialism; but
she would, apparently, do her best to prop up the rich princely
houses of the Middle East against Nasserism.

Thus, painfully, the shape of an American policy emerged from
the unhappy events of 1956. The United States must inevitably
fill the vacuum left by the general (and unlamented) expulsion of
the British; but she would do so chiefly by economic means, and

by the weight of diplomatic pressure at the United Nations. Britain would be dismissed as a major force in Arab affairs, except insofar as she still controlled the oil territories along the Persian Gulf. Israel would be maintained but not favored. King Saud of Saudi Arabia, rather than the recalcitrant Nasser, would be fostered as the leading figure of the Arab world, thus placing America's weight firmly behind the forces of the establishment in the Middle East. There would be an attempt to reconcile the conflicting dynasties of Saudi Arabia and Iraq; and a general stepping-up of economic aid all round. Colonel Nasser would be treated with courtesy (as befits a leading statesman of the Bandung Powers) but with reserve (as befits a fellow-travelling troublemaker with nothing to offer the West but the power of words).

This plan did not display any Socratic wisdom, but it was perhaps the best that could be achieved. The paramount Power in the Middle East, whichever she may be, must pick and choose her friends. She cannot run with the kings and ride with the revolutionaries. As it happens, it is the kings, not the rebels, who presently control the oil sources of the Middle East; and it is, naturally, the rebels who are most amenable to the blandishments of Communism. Britain found, during her period of supreme power, that there was no negotiating class in the Arab countries but the pashas, and in the long run her series of agreements with feudal autocrats led to her decline; now the Americans, faced with just the same problems, were adopting just the same tactics. The pashas and the landlords might not be ideal associates, and they seemed doomed to eventual dispossession; but for the moment no other class in the Middle East offered even so fragile a straw of stability and integrity.

So, with the flick of a pen, the High Dam subsidies were withdrawn; and so, when the assault went in across Sinai and the parachutists dropped upon Port Said, the British and the Israelis found themselves suddenly and totally abandoned by their ally and benefactor. America, that noble amateur of Middle East diplomacy, had turned professional, and followed the well-marked footprints through its market place.

NEIGHBORS

IT WAS NOT ONLY finance that postponed the construction of the High Dam. When our steamer left those poor, condemned divinities at Abu Simbel, she turned her hefty prow southward again, against the stream. Next morning the sun was paler and harsher than ever. The Nubian villages still lined the bank, the white-sailed boats still scudded across our wake, the same desolate escarpment brooded over the water. We were still in territory that would be flooded by the dam, and to the informed eye all looked fated and forlorn. Presently, though, we approached a large town upon the river bank, and there was a sharp toot from the siren. The ropes were readied, the gangplanks prepared, and the old Abyssinian priest on the lower deck, with the clothes of a hermit and the manners of a diffident saint, picked up his sack of possessions and prepared to disembark. We slid alongside with scarcely a bump; and behold! (as the Abyssinian priest might say) on the flagpole beside the deck there flew an unfamiliar flag, green and white, and very new. In our ceaseless progress through the hinterland of the High Dam we had crossed the frontier of Egypt and were in the young Republic of the Sudan.

It was the easiest, most natural, the least abrupt of transitions. In the days when the British were advocates of Nile unity, they used to encourage their officials to travel by these means to show them how naturally united was the Nile valley, how obviously Egypt and the Sudan formed a political entity. Slowly, imperceptibly, one country edged into the other, complexions growing gradually duskier, temperatures sliding upwards, the imperturbable old river narrowing a little, until Wadi Halfa stood beside you on the shore, and a different flag flew above you. Winston Churchill, discussing the reconquest of the Sudan under Kitchener, once wrote that the purpose of the campaign was "to unite territories that could not indefinitely have continued divided; to combine peoples whose future welfare is inseparably intermingled; to collect energies which, concentrated, may promote a common interest; to join together what could not improve apart."

At this particular moment in time, the Egyptians were more

ready to recognize this affinity than the Sudanese were; for the latter had just achieved their national independence (after flirting, indeed, with the idea of unity with Egypt) and they were in no mood to contemplate dilutions of their sovereignty. In particular, by an age-old paradox, it was the Nile, bridging the two countries so easily, which was the principal cause of their differences. There were old disagreements about sharing its water; there were newer ones about the best ways of exploiting it; and the Sudanese had strong criticisms of the High Dam project, which would, as we have seen, flood a substantial slice of Sudanese territory.

Certainly one had to admit, as one stepped off the boat, a distinct change in atmosphere. In Aswan the formalities had been prolonged but haphazard; here there was an English accent still; the bow-legged policemen at the quayside ushered one ashore with polite decision, and the customs officer asked, perhaps with a slight suspicion of social consciousness, whether one happened to know Sir Willoughby Carruthers, his old chief at Khartoum, and such a nice gentleman. There were very few Englishmen left in Wadi Halfa (indeed, there never were very many). The little Anglican church beside the river was closed, and a young German couple ran the Nile Hotel; but the District Commissioner's house still had its gardens of gorgeous bougainvillea, and its guns outside the gate; and the trains in the station, waiting to steam south to Khartoum, were still cream and clean. The place retained a sort of white-ducks-and-pith-helmet serenity very different from the tumble-down vigor of Egyptian provincial life.

So as I wandered about that frontier town I encountered often enough a contemptuous distrust of Egypt (the distrust possibly more genuine than the contempt); and this was expressed most coherently in opposition to the High Dam. Wadi Halfa itself would be extinguished by the lake, and so would many a little Sudanese village still higher up the river. There was strong resentment of a scheme which would flood so much of the Sudan without offering the Sudanese anything very obvious in return; there was also, I fancied, a sort of vague, instinctive, inherited feeling that people really ought not to mess about with the Nile. As I walked down the street one morning I overtook a dignified citizen in a blue silken robe, hastening under the palm trees, and we struck up a conversation. It was intolerable, said he, that the Egyptians could flood this entire district simply at a whim of theirs. The Sudanese would not stand for it. It was worse than imperialism. Why, it was a return to anarchy, and a flagrant flouting of the universal law that those living upon the upper half of a river must respect the rights of those living upon the lower half. No, no! the Egyptians would have to realize that the Sudan was independent now, and not to be disregarded—"Good *morning*, my friend, and the peace of God go with you!" In the ugly little bazaar a man who sold radios told me that his father, now a very old man, had already had to leave home once because of a reservoir—he was flooded out of his Nubian village by the building of the old Aswan Dam—and the family would not take easily to the idea of another such convulsion. "If the Egyptians want to move us, they'll have to move Wadi Halfa too, the whole town, and the railway, and put it all up again somewhere else. That's what the government says, and quite right too!" A third informant, of religious temperament, told me that God had willed that the river should be moved, and if God decreed that Wadi Halfa should be built elsewhere, then he would uproot himself and his belongings without complaint, God willing.

The District Commissioner, in his cool white headquarters beside the river, confirmed that on this subject feeling in Wadi Halfa was running high. (On his desk I noticed the obviously home-made casing of a fairly large bomb, and I asked him if this was an expression of such sentiments. No, he said, they'd had a flower show recently, and this was one of the more unconventional exhibits in the handicrafts section. "It didn't seem quite in keeping with the spirit of the occasion, so I took it in charge.") There had been noisy meetings in the town to protest against the dam, and every now and then he would find that his petitions box, on its pedestal outside the door, was stuffed with impassioned protests and appeals both to the Almighty and to the Ministry of Irrigation.

This was only one of the squabbles without number, personal and public, restrained and belligerent, that have invariably accompanied the harnessing of the Nile. Countless savage feuds have arisen in the villages of the valley because one family has appropri-

ated too much of the precious irrigation water, or one estate factor
has illegally opened his sluices, or somebody has installed a pump
without authority. Old friendships have been ruined by the Nile,
international relations embittered, sorcery summoned, and violence
fostered. In medieval Cairo the great Mameluke Sultan Qait Bey
was humiliated during a public audience by the Ambassador of
Ethiopia, who impertinently reminded the assembly that his Em-
peror could, at any moment, deprive Egypt of her livelihood, the
Nile water. Much more recently a British Minister of State dropped
a hint to Colonel Nasser that Britain had it within her power to
impede the headwaters of the White Nile. For decades there have
been differences between Cairo and Khartoum concerning the
division of water, methods of storage, flood control, and "established rights"; and the feelings of Wadi Halfa on the dam were
the reflections of deeper anxieties. Without the Nile the young
Sudan, so confident and hopeful, would stagnate among its plains.

For the Nile is a complicated thing, and in its upper regions it is
sometimes perverse and contradictory. On the map it looks straightforward enough. The White Nile rises in the region of Lake Victoria and Lake Albert; and the Blue Nile rises in Lake Tana; and
the two join at Khartoum and roll majestically down to the sea,
watering the valley as they go. But in fact this process is full of
difficulties. The White Nile does rise in the Great Lakes, fed by
the rains of the Ruwenzori; but once it has entered the Sudan
more than half its water is lost in the greedy marshland of the Sudd,
and it is only kept alive by the arrival of a tributary, the Sobat,
which flows in from Ethiopia. The Blue Nile does flow down from
Lake Tana, just as the map shows; but it contains two hundred
times more water in the autumn than it does in the spring. The
rivers indeed combine at Khartoum; but at some times of the year
the Blue Nile is so powerful that none of the water of the White
Nile can squeeze a way through. The Blue Nile is thick with silt;
the White Nile relatively clear. The White Nile is steady and
sensible; the Blue erratic and flamboyant in the extreme.

Yet upon this ill-matched brotherhood of streams depends the
entire agriculture of Egypt and, to a lesser extent, of the Sudan.
The control of the Nile presents the oldest, and one of the most
exacting, of all engineering problems—more difficult even than the

taming of the Mississippi, for that vast river must be mastered more to prevent floods than to irrigate fields. At Wadi Halfa, opposition to the dam was based partly upon emotion, partly upon instinct. On a higher lever, the disagreements between Egypt and the Sudan about the High Dam arose from a basic difference of approach to the technical problems of the river. A controversy was raging (through the closeted medium of pamphlets, conferences and scholarly papers) of great historical and geographical importance; upon its outcome would depend the future flow of the Nile, the shape of large areas of Africa, and the way of life of thousands of its people.

The Nile, governed by the equatorial rains, floods for half the year and is in low water for the rest. The peasants of antiquity therefore allowed the flood to irrigate their land and deposit its fertilizing silt, and then grew crops upon it during the low-water season. This was called basin irrigation. In parts of Egypt it is still done, and you may see the villages perched on high mounds among the plow-land, to escape the swirling flood waters. The system, though, produces only one crop in the year, and in the middle of the nineteenth century the Egyptians, with their foreign advisers, devised ways of providing water for the land throughout the year— in other words, of using the surplus of the flood water for irrigation in the low-water season. They built a number of barrages to raise the level of the water, and they cut large canals to distribute it where it was needed. The old Aswan Dam, with its big reservoir, enabled almost the whole of Egypt to be converted to this perennial irrigation, and vastly increased its fertility and production.

But the Nile is inconstant. If the flood is generous (or even dangerous) one year, it may be stingy the next. Throughout history the Egyptians have watched with anxiety the progress of the river's rise, and the chronicles are interspersed with disaster years when the flood water never came at all. (In a Hellenistic statue of the Nile in the Vatican, a small boy has clambered up the cornucopia and looks down from it with an expression of triumphant satisfaction: he is the genius of the sixteenth ell, the height on the Nilometer that the river must reach to ensure a good inundation.) At the same time, the populations of the riverain states are rising startlingly. There is an urgent need for more fertile land and for

more electric power. The problem of the Nile has therefore resolved itself to this: how to ensure plenty of water for all these
needs, both for the Sudanese and the Egyptians, at all times of year
and in every kind of year, whether the river is bountiful or mean.
The conception of annual storage, to provide water simply for
low-water months, is now supplemented by over-year storage, to
provide water at any time of any year, in a regular and adequate
flow. The British Nilologist H. E. Hurst, faced with the difficulty
of estimating an accurate average mean flow, set himself the task
of producing a mathematical formula which would represent the
reservoir capacity needed to maintain an average discharge over
one hundred years. There were no very long river or rainfall
records available, so he turned for information to the rings on the
giant redwoods in the United States, and the annual layers of mud
deposited on ancient lake beds; one gave him meteorological data
stretching back one thousand years, the other four thousand years.
By collating such natural evidence with the laws of probability, he
reached the following formidable formula (which, unfortunately,
I have not the space to interpret): $R = 0.6\sigma N^{0.72}$. Dr. Hurst called
his concept century storage; and it was around these esoteric calcu-
lations, culled from the redwoods, the bottoms of lakes, the rainfall of Ruwenzori, and the spasmodic affluence of the river, that
our controversies now revolved.

The Egyptians claimed that the High Dam at Aswan would
effectively provide century storage on the main Nile. It would,
they said, be both practical and economical; it would provide
power for Egypt and much new farmland, and it would also (they
sometimes added) bring certain technical benefits to the Sudan.
The Sudanese, on the other hand, not only demanded a much
higher share of the passing water if the High Dam were built; not
only insisted that the fifty thousand inhabitants of the Wadi Halfa
region should be resettled first, on specially irrigated land, with
new mosques, schools, and hospitals, all at Egyptian expense; not
only demanded the right to be consulted at every stage in the construction of the dam; but also said, fairly forcefully, that they did
not think it the best plan anyway.

This was partly because they thought the High Dam reservoir
would lose a great deal of water by evaporation, and would also

be rapidly silted up; but it was partly because, in common with many hydrologists in all parts of the world, they supported the principle that the Nile was a "hydrological unity," best developed as a whole. The Tennessee Valley Authority was an obvious model for such a method. It was no good, said the advocates of this approach, merely plumping a great dam here, a huge reservoir there, without coordinating all the work in all parts of the river, and without making use of the Nile as an entity in all five riverain states, from one end to the other. This conception entailed no single structure so gigantic as the High Dam; but it meant a series of works extending across twenty-eight degrees of longitude. The best-known plan for the unified control of the Nile envisaged eight big dams, a canal nearly two hundred miles long, and an intricate system of controls so regulating the waters of the river that in some regions the very seasons would be virtually reversed.

First, the Owen Falls Dam (already built in Uganda) would convert Lake Victoria into the greatest of all reservoirs, and another dam would control Lake Albert. Century storage would thus be provided at the top of the Nile, where there would be no wastage by evaporation or clogging by silt. A canal, the Jonglei Diversion, would carry the waters of the White Nile safely past the wasteful swamps of the Sudd, so altering the conditions there that the tribesmen who grazed their cattle and fished their fish in those humid marshlands would have to be taught an entirely new manner of living. There would be an annual storage reservoir on the White Nile at Gebel Aulia, below Khartoum (it already exists). Meanwhile the Blue Nile would also be dammed at its source, Lake Tana, providing another reservoir for century storage; and the existing Sennar Dam, south of Khartoum, would continue to provide annual storage. When the rivers had combined they would be blocked by a new dam at the fourth cataract, south of Wadi Halfa, and again by the existing dam at Aswan, both these reservoirs providing annual storage; and there would be extra storage in a reservoir at Wadi Rayan, south of the Fayoum in Egypt.

Every mile of the river would thus be controlled, its flow would always be constant, and the dams would provide hydroelectric power for Uganda, Ethiopia, Egypt, and the Sudan. There were, I need hardly say, supplementary problems innumerable, some of

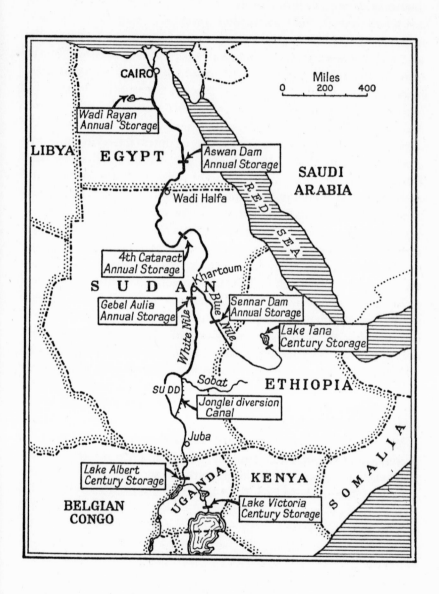

them crucial to the differences between Egypt and the Sudan—
questions of evaporation, of silt, of navigation, of weed on the
river bed, social and agricultural problems, matters of finance,
questions of control and priority; but this was, in essence, the
scheme of things preferred by the Sudan, and it was one of the
reasons why relations between Khartoum and Cairo were, perhaps,
rather less neighborly than Mr. Churchill foresaw in 1899.

No such high-sounding technical disputes intruded into my
conversations in Wadi Halfa. Nobody ventured to disagree with
Dr. Hurst's formula. Those pleasant citizens knew nothing of
evaporation or creeping flow, but argued from the heart; they recalled to me the Pharaonic ceremonies in which the people of the
valley, creeping obsequiously to the river's edge, offered it gifts
and propitiations to avert some nameless and ill-imagined catastrophe. Wadi Halfa existed to serve the Nile. It was a station upon
the river, through which had passed, over the millennia, successions
of kings and conquerors, and millions of travellers moving, by one
means and another, up and down the line of the stream. Here the
big steamboats ended their journeys from Egypt, for they could
not negotiate the cataracts below; here the train puffed off to
Khartoum; and here the charter aircraft flying north from Kenya
landed for petrol and refreshments, while their passengers spent
the evening buying wooden elephants and carpet slippers in the
lobby of the Nile Hotel.

No wonder, when their every activity is bound up with the
presence and the slow cycle of the Nile, and when the territory of
their virile neighbor stands almost within sight across the sands, the
people of Wadi Halfa take their birthrights seriously.

KHARTOUM

THOSE HOT DISTRICTS of the northern Sudan face down the river, rather than up, and are ornamented with the engravings and temples of northern rulers. Not only have Egyptians often ruled the region of Wadi Halfa, but for a century kings from Napata, near the fourth cataract, ruled Egypt. The superficial flavor is Sudanese enough, but so impregnated is the air and the soil with memories and reminders of Egypt that you do not feel too remote from Aswan, Assiut, or even the Delta; a Kharga butcher or a woman with a goose on her head would feel fairly at home in Wadi Halfa. In Khartoum, though, you are among other philosophies. The air of the lower Nile is spiced with mystery and ancient influences, echoes of old legends, pyramidical, catacombesque, sphinxian things. But Khartoum, the capital of the Sudan, seems at first sight a quiet little city of prosaic provincial tendencies. I first approached it by air, and looked out of my window to see the confluence of the Blue and White Niles, which occurs just above the capital. On one side of the river was Omdurman, the Mahdi's city, an enormous sprawling clutter of a town; on the other, Khartoum sat among trees, infinitely respectable. When Kitchener replanned it, he laid it out in the shape of a Union Jack, not simply to impress the lesser breeds, but because streets so arranged would provide fine fields of fire for machine guns. Khartoum has long spilled over the plan, and the railway sidings have upset it, so that I could make out only the extreme corners of St. Andrew's Cross, obstinately resisting; but the city still feels orderly and symmetrical—not indeed with the resplendent symmetry of a Paris or a Washington, but rather with the rectangular gentility of a suburban housing estate. There is a pleasant promenade along the river, shaded by big trees, with a zoo upon it, and the old palace of the Governors-General, and a few platforms where women do their washing or devout Muslims, preparing for their evening prayers, perform their ablutions; and there are many nice houses occupied by government officials, and a university, and a research laboratory, and mosques and schools, and various other edifices more worthy than inspiring. The city moves leisurely and rather fitfully. A strict speed limit restrains the old taxicabs, rattling earnestly along the promenade; and when the garbage is collected no brash German diesel trucks come roaring along the gutters, as they do in Cairo, with a hiss of hydraulics and a clang of automatic gates; instead two crotchety camels saunter from bin to bin, pulling a quavering cart.

It is only a year or two since the British left Khartoum, and the city is still feeling its way through the heady mists of independence. Here, as in Wadi Halfa, you sometimes feel that the English are only just around the corner, and that if you hurry down to Kitchener Avenue, past Barclay's Bank, you may glimpse a last departing flicker of their helmet plumes, or hear a fading drumbeat from the railway station. Outside the palace two old British guns still stand, gazing across the Nile; when they showed signs of tarnishing, two Britons from the local brewery bought a bottle of Brasso and polished them. There is a *Sudan Morning News*, and a plethora of official publications in English; many of the civil servants talk with excellent English accents, and very often speak of Sir Willoughby Carruthers. The big hotel on the waterfront (supplemented by a houseboat of supreme discomfort) is still very much a tea-and-biscuits hotel; the servants who sleep on blankets on its roof will rise smartly to their feet as you pass, in a manner sharply expressive of the imperial past. English cars are everywhere; *The Times* sells well (it has particular associations with the Sudan, for two of its correspondents were killed in nineteenth-century battles there); the admirable maps and stamps are English-printed; and the unsuspecting stranger may be surprised to find in his change a genuine British two-shilling piece, legal currency in the Sudan.

For the English, by methods exemplary but insidious, ingrained themselves very deeply into the life of the Sudanese. There were never more than a few thousand British officials in the country, but their quality was high, their opinions were contagious, and it will be many a long year before the echo of their manners dies away. Often and again, interviewing some Sudanese official in his office, I have suddenly detected, in a turn of phrase or tone of voice, a vicarious donnish memory of New College; and when the District Commissioner puts on his helmet with its gay tuft and leads you out into the desert, you may see reflected in his stride mornings in Shropshire long ago, or happy shooting parties on the moors. When I first went to the Sudan the Anglo-Egyptian Condominium was still in existence, and self-possessed British officials still sat trimly in their Khartoum offices. They were highly educated men, well-informed, courteous, and sometimes unconscionably smug. Hardly a word of self-criticism passed the lips of these remarkable bureaucrats, and never a doubt about their own supreme competence to take care of the Sudan, a country, they sometimes used to say with a modest smile, as big as the United Kingdom, France, Holland, Norway, Germany, Switzerland, and Denmark all put together. An air of hygienic certainty surrounded them; and when, in later years, they came to write their memoirs, very often the penultimate paragraph thanked the Sudanese "for a lifetime of happy memories," and the ultimate one told the Sudanese how grateful they should be for services rendered. Most visitors were dazzled by this unshakable confidence and integrity. A few found it, though admirable, a little trying. But for the Sudanese it provided an education in administration that could hardly have been bettered. The Condominium Government had the ease and flexibility of an organism characterized by unquestioned self-respect; and some of these qualities have been inherited by the Sudanese. Very often you will find some petty problem, a waster of days in Egypt, solved in a matter of moments by a big Sudanese smoking a pipe. Occasionally you will be astonished by some quite unexpected ability for compromise or initiative. Some of the gears of the government machine still move smoothly and at a sensible speed.

But others, you will very soon find, do not. Behind its façade of cool, Westernized competence, you will find that Khartoum is not placid and prosaic at all, but a city of concealed doubts and tensions. The Sudanese, though a few of them talk with an Oxford accent, and some of them make admirable administrators, and a few hundred are men of real culture and education, are not by any manner of means a Western people. A century ago this was, more or less, a country of savages. To this day about ninety percent of its inhabitants are illiterate. The veneer laid on so skillfully by the British administrators, though it still shines in patches, masks a structure of rough and sometimes cracking ebony. In the Sudan

Assembly you will find a speaker in a wig, and a master of arms
in an elaborate uniform, and parliamentarians referring to their
honorable friends from Northern Fung, and ministers saying they
would like notice of that question from the honorable member
from Nyala Baggara East; but as you watch those gleaming Negro
faces, and listen to the grave intonation of their voices, you may
sometimes feel that it is all some kind of sad game, and that this
assumption of alien traditions is only a sham or a screen. Passions
more violent than the disagreements of Westminster seethe below
the surface of Sudanese life, instincts more primitive, values much
nearer the Sudd than the Thames. I sometimes felt in Khartoum
that this young nation, born of the Nile but nurtured from Whitehall, was suffering from some kind of dichotomy, some traumatic
disturbance.

Certain expressions of the condition are merely amusing: for example, the appealing attempts of semi-educated government servants to keep up with the demands of official English. During one
of my visits, two Sudanese foresters were killed in local disturbances, and the government was forced to recall from England the
two British foresters who had done the job before independence.
Explaining this sad circumstance to its readers, a government organ
remarked that the two Britons had to be recalled "because they
were the only people who knew what their later successors were
up to." I also remember with pleasure a moral injunction offered
by a Sudanese Cabinet Minister at a press conference I once attended. The duty of the press, he said solemnly, was "to produce
thrilling, attractive, and good news, coinciding where possible with
the truth." The Sudanese government publishes an annual booklet
of information about the Sudan; it was touching and rather pathetic
to compare the issues for 1952 and for 1956 and to observe the
slow disintegration, both of grammar and of typography, which had
overcome that little book during the years of transition.

But these are surface cracks or aberrations, more piquant than
significant. There are deeper fissures too. You may first sense that
something is wrong in the bar of the Grand Hotel, that shuttered
palace of Gentleman's Relish beside the Nile. This is the haunt of
the British business community in Khartoum, and the barman has
acquired his skill in response to many years of brisk or blurred

British orders. There is no reason nowadays why Sudanese should not get drunk in the bar of the Grand Hotel just as the English do. The old laws governing the sale of alcohol to Sudanese have, of course, been abolished; the licensing hours apply to everybody; this is a country in which there is, mercy of mercies, no suspicion of a color bar. Cheerful living, too, is a Sudanese tradition; there was once a king in Sennar whose favorite dish was human liver washed down with beer. What comes as a shock is to find some young Negro, just down from the university, drunk not in the Sudanese but in the British manner; facetious with the sweaty banter of his British companions, not with any African drollery; with his tie loosened precisely as their's are loosened, and a cigarette sticking to his lower lip. When the government officials are clipped and assured, they are Oxonians by proxy. When this young man slurs into the maudlin it is the maudlin of distant smoky pubs in Birmingham, where the girls pick at their Smith's Crisps and the evening paper on the bar is folded greasily at the racing results. His grandfather charged across the plain at Omdurman, brandishing a spear and screaming; his father, in a white turban and a long robe, conscientiously added up figures in a downstairs office, while the fan turned wheezily and the Englishman upstairs quoted the classics on a spindly telephone; but the new Sudanese enjoys no certainties, absorbing his values like a *bouillabaisse,* all mixed up and fishy.

There are older cleavages too, older by far than the British administration in the Sudan. I once walked down to the junction of the Niles in the company of a Sudanese of culture and perception. In silence we watched the waters join, the clear stream of the one not mingling with the mud of the other, but flowing down side by side with it, as oil keeps itself aloof from water. "That reminds me of the Sudan," said my companion. "We are one country, but some of us are thick and some of us are thin, some come from one direction, some from another, and so far we have not learned to unite." I am not in general sympathetic to such sententious symbolisms, and indeed I shied away from him as he spoke; but when I thought about it, it did strike me as apt. The differences that still divide the Sudanese are deep and ancient; and when I was there they were not yet soothed into reconciliation by the delights of

independence. The country was still split, to begin with, by the
old feud between its two most prominent and durable figures, Ali
el-Mirghany and Abdel Rahman el-Mahdi (both of whom, by an
endearing paradox, are knights of British orders). Most Muslims
of the northern Sudan are followers of one or other of these two
old warhorses, and in Khartoum you can scarcely elude the rumbling rivalry between their respective sects, the Khatmia and the
Ansar. These deep-rooted antipathies are partly religious, but they
simmer side by side with political bickerings of diverse and complicated kinds. The party system is all-pervasive in Sudanese life.
All the catch-phrases and offices of parliamentary democracy have
been transplanted to this alien hothouse; and there have been
national elections in which those voters thought capable of making
any kind of pencil mark—a scribble, a dot, or a tremulous cross—
were officially defined as "sophisticated urban populations." There
are bitterly contested issues of foreign policy, some of them given
added interest by the occasional judicious greasing of relevant
palms. What should be the Sudan's relationship with Egypt, for
example? Was she right to join the Arab League? Should she accept
Russian arms? Upon such issues the politicians have clamped themselves, making use of them as unscrupulously as ever a crooked
chancellor manipulated the budget in some motheaten Balkan republic. Nobody bats an eyelid if a Sudanese politician changes his
views entirely on a crucial issue from one month to the next; for
in this context democracy is almost as uninhibited a struggle for
personal power as were the savageries between slave dealers, the
vendettas between chieftains, in the black days of the old Sudan.

   I once had occasion to call upon the first Prime Minister of the
Sudan, Ismail el-Azhary, at his home on a sweltering evening in
August. A policeman guarded his gate, and I was asked to wait in
the drawing room of his pleasant little house while the Prime Minister was called. Coffee was prepared; the policeman and the servant
were polite and attentive; Ismail el-Azhary, when he arrived in his
dressing gown, was cordial. I began to feel that any nagging doubts
I had about the state of the Sudan were unfair and ill-founded. But
as we talked I found my instincts slowly changing. The Prime Minister was a big, thick-set, clumsy-looking man, with spectacles upon
his broad nose and a flashing smile; and as he chatted, amiably

enough, I thought I detected in his conversation a rather more distinct streak of coarseness and insensitivity, perhaps (you might say) a stronger strain of self-interest, than the inamorato of Sudanese independence had led me to expect. He talked in the language of Western democracy, decorated with a certain indigenous floweriness of idiom; but I suspected the fibre of his thought was a good deal thicker and older than the conceptions of Burke or Jefferson.

So, with such stresses and instincts never far below the surface of life in Khartoum, before very long you may feel that the security of the city is a delusion, and that the Sudan is not quite so stable and sensible as it seemed when you first stepped off the steamer at Wadi Halfa. All the same, the Sudanese, by and large, is a friendly and attractive figure, and there is always something appealing about a brand-new nation struggling towards maturity. When I returned to the hotel from my interview with Ismail el-Azhary, I picked up that little annual booklet (1952 edition). The scrubbed and saintly British administrators of the Sudan had a wonderful knack of making you feel slightly ashamed of yourself; and whoever wrote the last paragraph of the booklet managed to do it again. "A new nation is being born," he had written, as a vicar might rebuke an errant choirboy, "and in the difficult world of today the new arrival needs all the sincere sympathy and disinterested help you can give it or get for it." I blushed; but it did not matter, for the electric light had failed.

THE SOUTH

SOME OF THE DISSENSIONS of the Sudan have been most skillfully exploited by the politicians. Others are too grave and too fundamental for exploitation, and lie at the very root of Khartoum's insidious anxieties. The Sudan is not only divided politically; it is a racial disunity too, and a country of tribes and country people in which power is almost exclusively in the hands of the townsmen. Ismail el-Azhary and nearly all his colleagues are Muslims and speakers of Arabic, drawing inspiration from the Arab world, from the ulemas, universities, and disputants of Egypt. Khartoum, with its mosques and prayer mats, and its memories of the Mahdi across the river, is recognizably an Islamic and Arabic city. But the name of the Sudan is Arabic for "country of the blacks." The whole of the south of the country is neither Arab nor Muslim, but pagan or Christian, and indisputably African. It is a country of rains and mountains, of tribal heritages, of Negroes in mud huts and grass hovels, with elephants and lions and zebras around them, and missionaries in their midst; as wildly different from el-Azhary's environment as a cheetah from a plump Labrador. The Muslims of the northern Sudan, self-governing at last, find themselves saddled with their own colonial empire, baffling and alien, sprawled across the distant country on the threshold of the Equator.

I was in Khartoum once when this vast territory broke into armed insurrection. There were rumbles and rumors of a mutiny among the forces in the south, of violence in the main centers, and of troops being flown south to deal with it; but the government spokesmen, with excruciating distortions of official syntax, did their best to persuade the world that it was merely some trifling disturbance within the Sudan Defense Force, not political at all, and easily to be put down. It was difficult to find out what was really happening, partly because the government clamped down on every source of information, partly because the government knew precious little itself. It was a thousand miles from Khartoum to Juba, the principal town of the south. The public air services had been suspended, and so had the telephone service. Moreover, it was the rainy season. No car could make the journey down the

Nile, and the steamers took several days. Gathering information in Khartoum about events in the distant south was rather like trying to find out, in nineteenth-century Boston, just what was happening in the Indian wars upon the frontier.

One afternoon, though, I happened to meet an English clergyman who had just returned from the south, and his conversation put an altogether different complexion upon the situation. This was not mere mutiny, it seemed, but popular insurrection: the southern tribesmen, incoherent and unorganized, were rising against their new northern masters. There were road blocks on every country road, angry tribesmen with spears roamed the countryside, there had been murders and pillaging in the villages, most of the locally recruited forces had deserted and taken to the hills. The worst fears of the Khartoum administrators (both British and Sudanese) had been fulfilled. If I wanted to see the basic dichotomy of the Sudan vividly illustrated, said my informant, I should visit the south now.

I begged a lift in a Royal Air Force aircraft flying to Juba. ("Lie low at the airport," said the captain conspiratorially, "and try to look official when you come on board.") Early in the morning we flew off down the line of the Nile: from the Muslim, Arabized north to the pagan African south. It was a lesson both in geography and in sociology. Far more abrupt than the transition between Egypt and the Sudan is the transition between the north and the south. At the beginning I was looking through the pilot's window at endless brown desert-like country, hot and sparse, with figures in Arab dress riding donkeys or carrying petrol tins to water wells. For a moment or two I glimpsed the great agricultural scheme of the Gezira, stretching away from the river, glistening and rectangular. Then all of a sudden, or so it seemed, we were in equatorial Africa. The grass was rich and thick; the Nile small and twisty; there was a green, wet, squashy, sticky feeling to the landscape. Twice we flew low over herds of elephants, waving their trunks boisterously. Once we saw a family of lions crouching in the long grass. (In the Sudan elephants, tigers, hornbills, rhinoceri, cheetahs, and snails are all protected, but the poor lion is classed as vermin.) There were small villages of mud huts, huddled rather cozily beside the river, and sometimes a lean black figure, half-naked, would stand solemnly on the bank, leaning on a spear. Narrow,

tortuous tracks meandered through the grasses. There were herds
of white long-horned cattle. This was the country of the Dinka
(who regarded their mothers-in-law as socially taboo); of the Shil-
luk (who had their own king, a reincarnation of divinity); and the
Nuer (who liked to drink the blood of their cows by tapping their
neck arteries with hollow reeds). Such tribesmen lived in a sort of
spiritual communion with their cattle, and the cow was the center
of their being—at once their friend, their idol, and their source of
income.

Soon there squelched below us the vast, oozing swamp of the
Sudd, so impenetrable that for centuries it blocked the way of
explorers to the source of the Nile. Here Nero's African expedition turned back in A.D. 65, hastily reporting, after taking a look
at the place, that the country was too poor to make it worth while
going any further; and here the Nile itself, swallowed into the maw
of those grasses, all but dries up and disappears. There was not a
sign of life in the marshes as we passed over them, except for the
hastening shadow of our aircraft; but a solitary paddle steamer was
chugging through, its stern wheel churning up the mud and agitating the rushes. Presently we passed over Jonglei, a tiny hamlet
on the edge of the swamp, not unlike some remote bayou village
in Louisiana. From here it was proposed to cut a canal northwards
to avoid the wastage of the Sudd; and here the river steamer would,
in a few hours, emerge from the morass, shaking itself free of the
clinging weeds and pounding more comfortably towards the
Equator. Even in the air there was a sense of relief as we left that
disconcerting landscape behind us, swung cheerfully along the line
of the emancipated river, and found ourselves over Juba.

This was the heart of the Sudanese south. It was an agreeable
little place, clean and rustic; but such were the stresses of the time
that I found it almost in a state of siege. Just as my clergyman had
said, the whole of Equatoria province, six hundred miles from end
to end, had, with a growl, shaken itself free of its new northern
administrators. Throughout this huge area, which marched with
the Belgian Congo, French Equatorial Africa, Uganda, Kenya, and
Ethiopia, there was now no government. Only Juba remained
under the authority of Khartoum. The Equatoria Corps of the
Sudan Defense Force had deserted almost to a man, and was now

entrenched and defiant on the east side of the river. All the northern administrators and businessmen had either been murdered, or had fled across the frontier to friendlier foreign territories, or had withdrawn within the perimeter of Juba. Northern troops had been flown into the place to maintain order there and, if possible, reassert the sovereignty of Khartoum in these remote and dissident regions.

No wonder, I thought, Khartoum sometimes seemed a city of suppressed anxieties. Few countries in the world had so desperate a problem as this: a situation in which one half of the population loathed the other half with a desperate and senseless intensity. At every step I found evidence of the baffling fissure between north and south. The smart northern officers, with their British trucks and Bren guns, talked of their southern fellow citizens as "the enemy." A grizzled shopkeeper told me his grandfather had been taken away to slavery by Muslims from the north. "They're the same now. They haven't changed. How can we trust them?" The local commander of the Sudan Defense Force, organizing operations, told me he had never been in the south before in his life, and sounded as though he didn't much want to come again. An Englishman, returned from the out-country, said the tribesmen at their road barriers had shouted to him: "We don't want to kill the English. We want to kill the northern people, for they are slave traders and treat us like dogs!" A kindly missionary told me that though many of the northern administrators were devoted and able, others —how could he put it?—veered a little in the direction of self-satisfaction. The average northerner, Arab and Muslim, thought the southerner a savage; the average southerner, pagan or Christian, thought the northerner inhuman, arrogant, and likely to put you up for auction in a slave market. The air was heavy with suspicion and foreboding, and Juba felt like an anxious island among barbarisms.

The town was half empty, for many of its inhabitants had fled to the countryside, fearing northern reprisals against them. There was no petrol for sale, so the only cars about were military ones. In the native quarter, towards the river, the neat rows of huts looked at once so trim and so deserted that they reminded me of the grass-and-plaster African villages one sometimes used to see at

Earl's Court exhibitions. Many of the people, agile but skinny, were totally nude, but would walk into the Greek grocer's store for a yard of calico with all the assurance of a dowager sweeping into Fortnum and Mason's. Others wore a pair of shorts, a casual skirt, a trilby hat or a necklace, and yet managed to look, owing to some innate dignity and self-possession, neither coarse nor ludicrous. They were a polite and kindly lot, not at all like revolutionaries.

Poor southerners! They were the victims of rivalries, political and spiritual. Egyptians, Britons, and northern Sudanese had all fought to gain the loyalty of the south. Many a wily Khartoum politician had cast his bread upon these shifting waters, and in Cairo you would often see, vociferously shouting Nasserite slogans at public gatherings, a few bribed and bearded stalwarts from Equatoria. The British, masters of the Sudan for eighty years, had insulated these southern regions against all outside influence. Entry to them, even for Sudanese, was prohibited without license. It was an ordinance of humane intentions, meant to protect the simple southerner (generally content with his cow, his hut and his ox-horn pipe) against alien exploitation—that is to say, exploitation by Egyptians and northerners; but half a century of such protection had left the southerners defenseless against the sudden onslaught of modernity. The British had left, and the poor tribesman was in the condition a mountaineer might be in if his oxygen were to fail high on Kanchenjunga. He was not acclimatized.

Nor were they proof against the influx of Islam, or amenable to the sudden emergence of a Muslim government for the Sudan. Throughout the era of the "closed districts," Catholic and Protestant missionaries had been active in the south with British blessing. They had built their schools and hospitals all over this wild place. They had mastered the countless indigenous dialects, and had often reduced them to phonetic alphabets. They had taught thousands of tribesmen to read and write, and to speak English. They had cured thousands of sick, nurtured thousands of babies, helped countless poor people. And they had caused many of those trusting pagans to abandon their idols and become Christians. "Of course they dislike us," the northerners would tell you. "They have been taught to loathe all Muslims. The British always intended to keep the south for themselves—perhaps to unite it with Uganda—so they naturally encouraged the missionaries." There may have been a half-truth in the charge. I thought I detected among some of the Juba missionaries traces of antipathy to the northern government, an undercurrent of sympathy for the southern insurgents, perhaps a suggestion that they were proud of their rebellious protégés. The leader of the mutineers was a Catholic. "A fine boy," said one priest of him, "honest and intelligent, and a gentleman—like all these people." (It proved to be true: this rebel leader, defying the opinions of his colleagues, crossed the river one dark night and gave himself up, hoping to arrange a surrender.)

It was strange to think that this equatorial town, with its manner of tropical colonialism, had been thrust into the turmoil of Middle East politics; but so it had. This was the southernmost outpost of the Muslim Middle East. These nude bucolics in their mud huts were represented in the Arab League, whose turgid discussions affected the course of events from the Turkish border in the north to the Gulf of Oman in the southeast. The angry disputations swirling around us at Juba (destined to last for many a long month, with bloodshed and reprisals) were the sparks that arose when an Arab government was applied to an African hinterland, and were thus the distant echoes of those virile energies radiating outwards from Cairo. When the Israelis swept down through Sinai, and the Anglo-French parachutists descended upon Port Said, these benevolent, ignorant Africans were represented in the impassioned protests of the Arab world.

I walked down to the river one evening, avoiding, but only for an hour or two, the watchful northern military posts, and looked across it to the wide grasslands beyond. The river was dark and brooding, a stream of crocodiles and hippopotami. The southern rebels were massed somewhere on the other bank, among the high grasses, and mutineers were in anxious conference in the mountains whose lovely blue ridges I could see dimly in the distance. The sunset was golden, the trees around me rich and shady, and the only sound was the timorous rustling of some minor creature in the bank behind me. I was in the heart of Africa.

But in a moment or two a sentry surprised me. The officer he took me to talked in Arabic; the soldiers of his headquarters had unrolled their prayer mats towards Mecca; and in a day or two an aircraft flew me down the Nile again, back to the tanks and the dragomen.

PART TWO

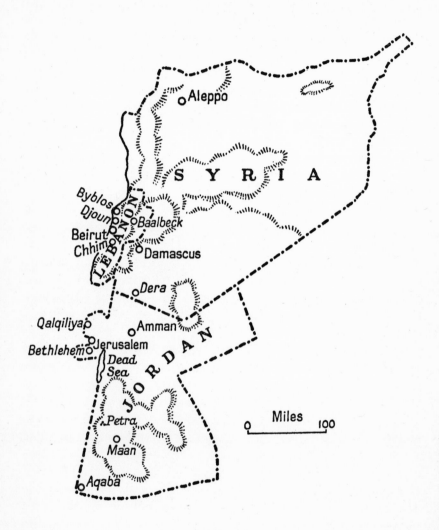

Aleppo

S Y R I A

Byblos
Djoun
Beirut
Chhim
LEBANON
Baalbeck
Damascus

Dera

Qalqiliya
Amman
Bethlehem
Jerusalem
Dead
Sea

JORDAN

Petra
Maan

Aqaba

Miles
0   100

PHOENICIA

UNDER THE SPELL of Nasserism and nationalism, the African Middle East is not an easygoing place. At this moment of history the atmosphere of Egypt is scarcely soothing, and even in the Sudan, charm and serenity are not easy to find. There is a sense of brooding in the air, of squalor and foreboding, a mingling of immense age and brassy promise. The tide of affairs eddying outwards from Cairo is a muddled and tumultuous current, and there is malice in the air.

To the northeast, though, there lies the little Republic of Lebanon, which is a community of very different temperament, an oasis of gifted commercialism set in a desert of power politics. Lebanon lies delectably on the eastern shore of the Mediterranean, with mountains running down to the sea, and citizens skiing and bathing on the same day. It is the gateway to the Fertile Crescent, that slab of productive country encircling the Syrian Desert; and through many centuries it has been the channel by which the ideas and philosophies of the West have passed to the peoples of the Orient. Innumerable civilizations have thrown themselves, thick and fast, upon this little country. Most of them have receded into the halls of scholarship, but they have left many a piquant trace to remind you of the varied history of the place—a stele here, a castle there, an abandoned pillbox on a beach. Egyptians, Aramaeans, Phoenicians, Assyrians, Hittites, Persians, Greeks, Romans, Arabs, Crusaders, Turks, French, British—the armies or administrators of them all have found their way to Lebanon; and the result is not, as in Egypt, a fetid mongrelization, but a synthesis of grace and pungency. Half Lebanon is Christian, and has links with the Western churches; half is Muslim, and prays to the south, towards Mecca. Many of its citizens have made their modest fortunes in the United States, faithfully sending remittances home over the years before returning themselves to Lebanon in the fullness, or more pertinently the richness, of time. These wide associations and liberal tastes make Lebanon a hybrid country, half West, half East, one foot in the intrigues of the Middle East, one firmly on the floor of the Stock Exchange.

As an introduction to this strangely layered and divided society, it is a good idea to visit a small fishing port called Jebail, which stands on an inlet north of Beirut—schooners in the bay, and a white sail or two scudding away towards Cyprus. It is a minute place nowadays, demurely perched beside the sea, but outside it a notice in French—"To the Diggings!"—tells you that this is the ancient city of Byblos, which gave its name to the Bible and was one of the most famous seaports of antiquity. You enter it through a narrow Arab market place, lined with open-fronted shops, like busy little caverns, selling panama hats, fruit, picture postcards and fly swatters. At the end of this *suk*, though, you pass through a handsome stone gateway and find yourself in a Crusader city. The castle stands high above the sea. The city wall frowns formidably. From the great cathedral-church of Mar Yvhanna (St. John) you may hear devotions being conducted in the all-but-forgotten Syrian language. Below the hill there is a little fortified harbor, like a toy port. A few delicate fishing boats now ride reflectively upon its waters; but once it held the galleys of the House of Embriaci, most tenacious of the Crusaders, until their last crews sailed away to Europe leaving Islam triumphant.

This is one historical stratum of the Lebanese scene, but Byblos illustrates several more. The Pharaohs, for example, shipped their cedar trees through Byblos, and the remains of their temples still stand on a little plateau above the harbor. The Phoenicians had a port here; just above the waterline there is a tank cut in the rock, to which (so it is said) the ladies of the Phoenician royal palaces used to slip in secrecy to bathe discreetly within sound of the surf. Wherever you look there are stumps of masonry or crumbling antique walls. There are Greek columns and Roman sarcophagi; and there is a peculiar sort of garden of obelisks, rough and truncated, erected by successive kings over many centuries as a dwelling place for divinities. There are mosques built by the Arab conquerors. There are cannon balls lodged in the walls of the city by the Royal Navy, in pursuance of some forgotten nineteenth-century end. There are French archaeological guide books. There are Turkish houses. Even America contributes to the *mélange:* in a dusty yellow street outside the Crusader walls there stands a rusting gambling machine, into which from time to time some rash

urchin inserts a piastre, or cheats the management with an antique
coin, Roman or Phoenician, picked up on the sands.

The whole of Lebanon is like this: criss-crossed with cultures,
like one of those cheeses whose texture displays, beneath the smooth
surface of its rind, innumerable vein-like streaks of blue. In Europe,
of course, you can find countries of immensely complicated historical structure; but they have long evolved a composite culture
of their own, giving them cohesion and stability. In Lebanon the
cultures are still fermenting: the melting pot is still at work. It is a
moot point, even in 1956, whether Lebanon will go East or West;
whether she feels herself nearer Bandung or Paris. Confronted by
many different climates of thought, affected by many separate
streams of influences, poised between opposing compulsions, the
Lebanese have a national character that is complex and unique
(and more akin to the Israelis than to the Egyptians).

Above all they have sharpened and perfected that tangy Phoenician commercialism that has been driven from Alexandria by the
earnest affronts of politics. Lebanon is a land of money makers. It
lives by its itchy palm. Its burghers are rich, shrewd and greedy,
and in its banks you can acquire any currency under the sun. I
once bought a book of American travellers' checks by converting
East African rupees, Maria Theresa dollars and a British gold
sovereign (though some Muslim bankers, it is said, fight shy of
Victorian sovereigns because they portray an unveiled woman;
in the eyes of orthodox Islam even Queen Victoria was an invita-
tion to sin). They say that, just as the bumblebee is aerodynamically
incapable of flying, so the Lebanon is an economic impossibility;
but it lives on lavishly, a place of ski-lifts and nightclubs, black-
heeled nylons, air-conditioned hotels and American cars. It does so
by being frank about its morals. Beirut is a port where nearly anything goes, and in Lebanon the stranger feels that if he has his
check book handy (any old check book will do) he will never be
in trouble for long. The landowners only prevaricate for a moment
or two before telling you about the hashish growing in their fields.
The businessmen build their splendid villas and drive their magnificent cars with a manner of frank opulence not at all unattractive

to see. If you admire the gusto and earthiness of private enterprise, you will respect the mercantile flavor of Lebanon.

For the Lebanese are merchants of brilliance, and they have made their country the clearing house of the Arab world. Oil pipelines from Iraq and Saudi Arabia have their terminals in Lebanon, and contribute handsomely to the national revenues. The international airport at Beirut is the best in the Middle East, and a staging post for many of the airlines serving the Far East. The Lebanese have no natural resources except their talents; they live by providing what the economists austerely call "services." When I first went to Beirut I disliked this deep-rooted sense of the mercenary. The setting of the city is delightful: white modern buildings and a few tall, antique Turkish houses, encouched in trees between the mountains and the sea. But I used to find something missing from the fabric of the place. It felt obscurely purposeless, frivolous, and insincere, like some extraordinarily corrupt and sophisticated girls' school. The heart-rending anxieties of the Middle East seemed to pass it by, and there was a half-hearted and dilettantish flavor to its politics. But I have changed my views. Nowadays, when I arrive in Beirut from Cairo or Iraq, from Cyprus or the Persian Gulf, I breathe more happily when I step off the aircraft; for I know that the passions animating this little state threaten no lives, insult no ancient dignities, tamper with no ideologies, but are concerned only with homely and mundane matters of personal profit. In the United States, a land of pervasive idealism, the profit motive sometimes comes as a rude shock to the traveller; in the Middle East, embroiled in a ceaseless quest for power and revenge, it strikes the senses as a soothing balm. Such is the unsuspected philanthropy of the Lebanese.

There are, though, determined cultural overtones to Lebanon. The two universities of Beirut—one American, the other French—are the principal intellectual centers of the Middle East; and there is an active Franco-Levantine society which deals resolutely in modern art, sculpture, advanced architecture, and Tennessee Williams. The resilient President of the Republic, Camille Chamoun, rather sets the tone of all this with his manner of smooth and knowing cosmopolitanism, strikingly at variance with the plumes and striped trousers of the picture-book soldiers who stand guard outside his house. The rich business society of Beirut likes to dabble in culture; some of the press has higher yearnings; and in the coffee-shops you will encounter a plethora of intellectuals, actively subscribing to whatever philosophy was fashionable in Paris or Greenwich Village a year or two ago.

This is as it should be. Lebanon is a conduit of ideas. From these hills Flecker watched his old ships sail, like swans asleep, for Famagusta and the hidden sun; and from the breakwaters of Beirut the graceful steamers still steam to Greece and Italy. The rehashed audacities of Beirut conversation are couriers from other civilizations. All the same, it is sometimes rather overpowering to experience the efforts of the Lebanese intelligentsia to impose a pattern of European culture upon a society still fundamentally oriental. I once found myself in Beirut at the beginning of an international music festival to be held among the prodigious ruins of Baalbek, in the Bekaa Valley, and I asked a taxi driver to take me the sixty-odd miles there to a concert. Certainly, said he, and if I didn't mind he'd bring his family along too, just for the ride: they liked a nice festival. So we set off into the evening—the taxi driver, his plump wife in black, a little boy in jeans, a very small baby girl with enormous brown eyes. Like so many Lebanese, the taxi driver had spent some years in America, and his English was sprinkled with rather dated Americanisms. "Say!" he would remark from time to time, as we swept up the hillside from Beirut, "there's a swell ice-cream parlor round the corner. What you say we stop for a sundae, hey?" Or: "How d'ya feel like a Coke, hey, baby?" Sometimes he would burst into a few snatches of raucous rhythm. Sometimes he would withdraw from an innermost pocket a picture of his brother, or his house in Detroit, or demonstrating to me that he had landed in New York on January 14, 1945—a fact about which he appeared to think, Heaven knows why, that I might have some doubts. Thus we progressed through the balmy Lebanese night towards the festival.

It was also a religious feast day of some kind, and we frequently stopped in villages for some quick refreshment among the festivities. Candles were burning in many windows, and there was a constant cracking of fireworks and whizzing of rockets. The church towers were decorated with huge illuminated crosses. Gangs of young men strolled about the hilly streets, singing and shouting. Innumerable friends or relatives of the taxi driver emerged from houses to impede our progress, and we had so many bottles of pop that the baby girl was visited by a long, staccato series of burps. "What feast day is this?" I asked the taxi driver. "Christmas, friend," he replied without a smile (it was the middle of July).

But at last we found ourselves near Baalbek. It might have been a disconcerting approach for the music lover accustomed to the suavities of Edinburgh or Salzburg; for the valley of the Bekaa was pitchy black, and only an occasional string of camels swayed past us, or a pair of armed policemen peered out of the glare of our headlights. "See, they're looking out for the hoodlums," said the driver. "They're plenty of bums around this place, yessir." Baalbek was calm enough, though, and the glorious pillars of the temple, the tallest on earth, were grandly floodlit against the black of the valley. I abandoned the taxi and walked to the threshold of the Temple of Jupiter, richly embellished with carvings and monumental lions. The concert had begun; a German orchestra was playing the overture; and an earnest young man, thrusting a very large and expensive program into my hand, ushered me to a nearby lion and invited me to sit upon its paw.

It was a wonderful spectacle. The *Jeunesse de Musique*, which had organized the festival, had done so with vigor and imagination. The columns and battlements of the temple were softly floodlit, leaving their crannies and doorways shadowy and suggestive, and a myriad of gargoyles and sculptured animals stared down at us queerly. Armed soldiers paraded about the place, and their huge shadows, cluttered with rifles and accoutrements, were projected most romantically upon the masonry of the Temple of Bacchus. Big country insects sometimes flitted muzzily into the light; on the high ramparts of the temple a man in some kind of white robe was crouching among the stonework. The sound of the orchestra was rather lost in the immensity of these surroundings, but the players looked both graceful and capable, up there on the temple steps, and the conductor seemed oblivious of the peculiarity of the setting.

For peculiarities there undoubtedly were, as I soon began to sense. Some incongruities were apparent in that place of culture. For one thing, a group of young men launched a ferocious argument about the price of hamburgers near the exquisite Corinthian gateway which gave entrance to the arena. For another, a woman swathed in nebulous draperies was giving suck to her baby on the next lion to mine. Sometimes some men in very obvious fancy dress (local peasants in costume) shuffled self-consciously past on their way to the refreshment stalls. Beside the orchestra, I suddenly noticed, two ravishingly beautiful girls in very short skirts sat cross-legged on chairs, gazing with fixed smiles at the assembly. They were too slim to be members of some neighboring harem, and too refined to be Miss Baalbek and her runner-up, so I assumed them to be members of the *Jeunesse de Musique,* but I had never seen their like at Edinburgh. Between the movements of the symphony the audience clapped vociferously, to the annoyance of a few enthusiasts who sat in intellectual attitudes near the temple steps; and one or two music lovers opened big picnic baskets in the middle of the Beethoven, with exuberant crackling of paper, popping of corks, and dropping of tinny forks. At the end of the interval the President of the Republic suddenly emerged from nowhere and bestowed the Order of the Cedars upon the conductor; he also appeared to bestow it, by what seemed rather arbitrary judgment, upon one of the back-desk violinists, who slouched sheepishly out of the darkness to receive it, to the half-hearted applause of those members of the audience who had managed to drag themselves away from the man dressed up as a Bedouin who was serving coffee at the buffet.

But I must not be unkind. I enjoyed the Baalbek Festival. Its setting was superb and its spirit, to one of catholic tastes, infinitely beguiling. The taxi driver was waiting for me at the gate (his family was fast asleep, in attitudes of ungainly abandon, in the back seat of the car) and we drove away down the Bekaa, leaving the columns of the temple shining behind us. The driver and I smiled at each other, for neither of us was very much at home in the ambiance of the *Jeunesse de Musique;* and in a moment or two the darkness of the valley enfolded us.

The driver, despite his vocabulary, was unashamedly a man of the East; America, he said, had been too swift and obvious for him, and he had come home gladly to the bitter subtleties of Lebanon. He wanted neither Menuhin nor Sinatra, but wallowed in the bosomy quartertones of the Cairo serenaders. He liked the hugger-mugger family relationships of the Arab world, and he enjoyed his haggling and petty Phoenician deceits. Though Lebanon is a country of immemorial Western affinities, a place of mingled faiths and tastes, most of its citizens are Easterners still, and only the thinnest of occidental veneers camouflages its character. When the music lover cracked his hard-boiled egg during a tender silence in the symphony, he was striking an instinctive blow for his right to be oriental.

It is not only in Lebanon that such protests are being registered, for the conflict between European and oriental ways is evident everywhere in the Middle East. We have seen its effects already in Egypt, where for several generations men have been trying to evolve some compromise between cultures. It is even apparent in Israel, for most of the recent immigrants have been oriental Jews from Yemen and North Africa, and their traditions are already pressing hard upon the customs of the earlier settlers. The affinities between Arab and European civilization are easy enough to see. Greek and Roman thought tempered the ideas of Egypt during their respective periods of domination; in the Middle Ages there were constant cultural exchanges between Arabs and Europeans, by way of Spain and the Danube Basin; in recent years many thousands of Arabs have chosen Western ways of education, and translations of the Western classics flood the Arab market.

But on the whole the rifts have been more significant than the forces of union. Throughout the eighteenth and nineteenth centuries, when Europe forged ahead into new fields of thought, the Arab world remained stagnant and sterile. More important, the twentieth century has seen the revival of Asia as a Power, the birth of a new concept of continentalism, the new philosophies of Bandung—all of which have stimulated that part of the Arab dichotomy which faces east rather than west. Nobody could now call

the Levant a province of Europe, or even the Mediterranean a
European lake. Fifty years ago the struggle was between rampant
Westernism and fading Orientalism. Nowadays the tables are
turned.

In Lebanon especially this division of loyalties, amounting almost
to schizophrenia, affects the conduct of daily life. This country is
the prime example of the conflict. Because it has apparently been
Westernized so thoroughly (Cadillacs, Simone de Beauvoir, and
Baalbek festivals) the underlying archaisms of thought and custom
come as the greater shock. Because it prides itself on its worldliness,
its business sense, its sophistication, its culture, the clash is the
more profound between its Western externals and those pertinacious Eastern values (so charming, so insidious, so suspect to Arab
progressives) that linger everywhere behind the scenes.

In 1956, despite the *Jeunesse de Musique*, the East seemed to be
holding its own in Lebanon. The Muslims were outnumbering the
Christians. The mainstream of Arab thought, momentarily attracted eastward, was sending its strong subsidiary channels to
Beirut. If you drove up the mountain on a summer evening, you
would find the countless coffee-shops and pleasure houses of its
resorts crammed to suffocation with Arabs from Kuwait and the
rich oil kingdoms; with their flowing headdresses and their white
robes, their languid hubble-bubble poses and their flamboyant
disputes, they were a reminder, at once gorgeous and squalid, that
of all the streams of influence passing through the Lebanon—from
Pharaohs through Greeks to Frenchmen—the Arab strain remains
the most potent. And that piquant grasping Phoenician check-book
flavor, the essence of the Levantine, is oriental too, as anyone will
agree who has naughtily circumvented his sterling allowance in
some fusty, gas-lit coffee-shop beside the docks of Beirut.

In the Lebanese countryside, of course, the orientalism of the
place lives on most cogently. The Lebanon is a country of ancient
myths, of classical traditions passed down, through varying faiths
and centuries, to form part of the pattern of folklore. At the mouth
of the Adonis River you can see the blood-red waters of the stream
(colored by iron particles) mingling with the blue Mediterranean

just as they did in the dreams of the ancient world. In Beirut there is the very well from which the dragon emerged to give battle to St. George. At Tripoli, to the north, there is a pool full of tame fish, fed by the local inhabitants on chickpeas and watermelon: they are the descendants of creatures worshipped in a forgotten Phoenician cult three thousand years ago. Not far away the surviving members of an order of whirling dervishes still whirl once a year in their mystic dance. On the slopes of Mount Hermon, inland from Beirut, is the reputed tomb of Darazi, the founder of the peculiar religion of the Druzes, which still has many thousands of adherents in the Lebanon. There are monuments and memories everywhere, many of them transmuted into legend; in Beirut you can wallow in the pleasures of the West, but in the mountains of Lebanon you are never far from earthier and perhaps more resilient intangibles.

I was once in Beirut when there was an earthquake. The city is historically prone to such things, and has been destroyed by them more than once; so it was scarcely surprising that something approaching panic seized the place. The Westernized Levantine temperament is volatile and excitable. The Beiruti is not made to withstand sudden blows of fortune. After the first few tremors half the population made a dash for the countryside, and camped out that night among the olive groves that sprawl seductively down to the sea. Some families had only a few blankets and a mattress or two; some had grand camp cookers and motor cars. Whatever their circumstances, they preferred to take no risks, and for many a long week afterwards the shopkeepers of Beirut would describe to you with gesticulations the horrors and dangers of that night.

Among the country people, though, the effect of this phenomenon was very different. More than one hundred people were killed in the earthquake and many thousands were made homeless. The epicenter of this disaster was among the hills to the southeast of Beirut, a country of Muslim highlanders. The little village of Chhim had been most gravely damaged, and the road that ran up to it had collapsed, so that when I went there the next morning I had to leave the car and walk. Below the village, like a warning talisman, there stood a mosque. The earthquake had lopped the top off its minaret, as neatly as a knife slices cucumber, and it stood

there looking forlorn and obscurely foolish. Nearby there was a
sadder sight. A small stone house had been completely shattered.
Only a pile of stone remained, and beside it a solitary woman in a
bright flowered dress was standing silently. She was as still as a
statue, and as dry-eyed, and she described the night's events to me
with a creepy air of detachment—the great roll of thunderous noise,
the terrifying tremor, the disintegration of the house around her,
the death of her husband and their two children—as though she
were complaining of the vagaries of her grocer, or telling me the
plot of a novelette.

In the center of the village this weird fatalism dominated the
scene. Most of the houses had been destroyed, and everywhere
there were those sad souvenirs made familiar to us by war—the
house split down the center, so that gay country hats were left
swinging on hooks, and knives and forks were still on the kitchen
tables; the pathetic little objects left behind, a baby's pillow or an
old wooden pipe; the stunned families huddled in the backyard or
the orchard; the egg unbroken in its basket; the man who wanted
to tell you his personal earthquake story. The village square was
crowded with families, crouching among their goats and baggage,
and here and there a householder scrabbled among the debris of his
home. Somber groups of men stood in the streets among shattered
shops. A small crowd of women, their donkeys and cattle and
children wandering among them, sat speechlessly around the tomb
of a Muslim divine, to the headstone of which someone had attached a bunch of withered flowers.

It was tragedy as you may experience it all over the world; but
the peculiarity of this scene was its padded, muffled character. The
crowd was almost silent. There was scarcely a tear to be seen,
scarcely a child's whisper to be heard. The people sat there quietly,
talking in low voices, as if their sense of inevitability had developed
into apathy. In one corner, indeed, a very old lady of ferocious
aspect, surrounded by a group of onlookers, was delivering a shrill,
impassioned harangue with many a violent gesture and swishing of
draperies; and sometimes a woman would suddenly, on no immediate provocation, break into a high, tearless lamentation that was
terrible to hear. But such sounds of grief fell upon a silent arena,
and scarcely stirred the dull passivity of the villagers.

Some of these people told me they had supposed the earthquake to be the first gunfire of another war with Israel; but to me an overwhelming sense of natural and ageless catastrophe hung over those hills. Lebanon no longer seemed a smart, nyloned, night-clubbing sophisticate, but *au fond* only another harassed Arab, consistent enough through the centuries beneath the shifting veneers of history. There was something hauntingly remote and timeless about the scene, as though poor Chhim was no more than a sad ruined site of antiquity, like Baalbek up the road, or Babylon.

THE SYRIANS

SUCH QUIRKS of background or temperament mean that Lebanon can sometimes be a testy country; in particular, it has constant differences with its bigger neighbor to the east, the unpredictable Republic of Syria. Geographically the two countries are one, and when the French held mandates for both they were bound by the closest administrative and fiscal links. Since they achieved independence, though, their relations have been strained by innumerable petty squabbles and jealousies, economic and political, and one is always reading of Syrian demands upon Lebanon, or Lebanese protests to Syria, or exchanges of political prisoners.

Nor are these simply neighborly bickerings. Syria is a very different country from Lebanon. It is overwhelmingly Muslim, and it is much more remote from the sobering influences of Western thought. When you drive from Beirut to Damascus, you are driving from the Mediterranean seaboard (not so far from Athens) to the border of the Syrian desert (not so far from Baghdad). The road starts in the gay, bustling environs of Beirut and ends in the wide, dry, brooding plain that surrounds the oasis city of Damascus. When my great-uncle Alec travelled this way in the 1870s, he went by the little narrow-gauge railway that still puffs precariously over the mountains. The old post road, he remarked complacently, was practically deserted now, because of the advent of this mechanical marvel. He was wrong. The road is busier than ever, and is infested with the police posts and customhouses, the inspectors and gendarmes and health officials, whose function it is to give substance to an artificial frontier.

Dark are the expressions with which the Syrians, on their side of the line, will probably receive you; and careful the examination they will give your passport; and smudged and heavy the signs they will stamp upon its pages. Syria is a country of constant political intrigue, and it is nearly always in the middle of a crisis. The students are out on strike, or a government is about to fall, or some political party or other has been banned, or a delegation is arriving from Moscow, or there are rumors of an assassination, a kidnapping, a *coup d'état*, a border skirmish. No Arab country has toyed more carelessly with Communism; outside South America, no state in the world is so vulnerable to militarist ambition. It is a country bubbling with plots and controversies. Sometimes the current fad is Marxism; sometimes a kind of Syrian Fascism; sometimes Nasserism. For the moment Syria is firmly committed to alliance with Egypt, and is re-arming (with the encouragement of Colonel Nasser) with weapons bought from Czechoslovakia. She maintains an intermittent feud with the West, characterized, for example, by a successful campaign of blackmail to raise transit dues on oil piped across Syrian territories. But she is at best a dubious ally, and her future is unforeseeable. She has no oil, and very few other resources; her economy is precarious; her frontiers wide open. It is true that Syria has refused to accept Point Four aid, on the grounds that it would compromise her sovereignty; but Syrian loyalties are adaptable emotions, and nobody regards her present political alignment as necessarily very permanent.

There is, nevertheless, an unchanging strain of xenophobia in Syrian life, and the foreigner is often likely to feel a trifle insecure. He must, for instance, be especially careful when he is taking photographs. The simplest and most prosaic object—an old lamp standard, a carpet factory—turns out to be, when the gendarmes arrive with surly imprecations upon the scene, something of vital military importance. The charming peasant woman, in her colorful costume, is banned because she does not represent modernity. The fine museum is banned because the French built it. The President must not be photographed without written permission. The station square must not be photographed because it is of vital military importance. In short, you must not take photographs. Why not? Because you are a foreigner, and therefore almost certainly either a spy or a Zionist. It is not easy for the Westerner to feel at home in Syria, and he will often find himself eyed with suspicion and distaste in the innumerable smoky coffee-shops that are the breeding ground of Syrian conspiracy.

In Damascus I have generally found all these seething plots and antipathies difficult to take very seriously. The capital of Syria is a desert city, facing the east and the Bedouin country, and its

atmosphere is rather bird-like and inconsequential, like the minds
of those who spend their lives in desert places. The students, you
may be sure, will be demonstrating for some quite different end
tomorrow. The kidnapping has probably never taken place at all,
or if it has, the victim is happily sipping sherbet in some secluded,
silky country house. The gendarme, if you treat him nicely, will
probably pose for his picture himself.

The city feels shaky rather than menacing. If nothing feels very
serious, certainly nothing feels very predictable: anything can
happen. Not so long ago political events in Damascus had the
profoundest effect upon affairs in the surrounding Arab regions.
Damascus was the obvious capital for the Arab Kingdom projected
after the success of the Arab Revolt; and it was the headquarters
of Turkish power in the Middle East. Nowadays, though, it has
rather the stringy flavor of a backwater, and its opinions are unlikely to have any decisive bearing on those of Amman, Baghdad,
or even Beirut. This is because there is little original political
thought in modern Syria. Beirut is, as we have seen, closely in touch
with Western ideas. Cairo is the showplace of Afro-Asianism.
Baghdad has the weight of oil behind it. But Damascus, the loveliest
of the Arab capitals, is a light-weight, fluctuating eccentrically
from year to year, whisked here and there by the breezes of opportunity.

It has, of course, elements of historical continuity. For example,
it was for a thousand years (and to a minor degree still is) the
starting place for the greatest of the *Haj* pilgrimage convoys to
Mecca. Damascus itself is a holy city to the Muslims, and its links
with the sacred centers of Arabia are living and intimate. It was in
the plain to the south of the city that Doughty joined his pilgrim's
caravan; there was, he said characteristically, "a new stirring of
this goodly Oriental city in the days before the *Haj.*" Later the
Medina railway was built, and a pompous station was erected in the
center of Damascus, and at the season of the pilgrimage thousands
upon thousands of pilgrims thronged its narrow platforms and
pressed into the stuffy confines of its carriages. The trains still run
from Damascus, though since the Suez war the railway has never
been restored to Medina—funny little trains they are, with prim,
cluttered engines, and they move ponderously with grinding and

snorting noises. Nowadays few pilgrims travel directly from Damascus to the Holy Place, except by air, but a good many set off in buses and cars to join a pilgrim ship at the head of the Gulf of Aqaba. They travel by the old routes still, down the traditional highway of the *Haj*, and at the season of the pilgrimage Damascus is still especially busy and bustling, though the craftsmen at work are the garage men, the welders, and the menders of tires.

It is a moving thing to drive down the broad, beaten track of a pilgrimage route in those places where it does not coincide with a tarmac road. The immemorial ruts and hoof-tracks are scattered widely over the landscape, so that it is easy to imagine that vast old cavalcade of horses and camel men, the grand canopies and pompous officials, the circling outriders of the protecting soldiery, and the whole immense mixture of profit and piety. The Turks built protective forts along the route of the *Haj*, and some of them are still standing, occupied by languid Arab soldiers. When Haroun el-Rashid and his wife Zobeyda performed the pilgrimage on foot, so the Arab historians say, new castles were built for them at each caravan station, with apartments splendidly furnished, and the whole road was covered daily with carpets, upon which that splendid couple walked in devout majesty. (The peoples of the Middle East love building palaces for distinguished visitors. When the Empress Eugenie went to Egypt to open the Suez Canal, the Egyptian government built her an enormous and very luxurious palace in Cairo, in which her personal apartments were exact replicas of those at home in the Tuileries.)

So, linked by these passages of terrain and of history, Damascus is never far in spirit from the Holy Places of the Hejaz. Of the more advanced Arab capitals, it is much the most fanatical in its religion, and it boasts all kinds of spiritual merits. (There is a hill above the city for which the following distinctions are claimed: Abraham was born there; Abel was killed there; Moses, Jesus, Lot, and Job prayed there; Mohammed lived there with his mother; and seventy thousand prophets and martyrs are buried there.) To be sure, there are plenty of young men drinking alcohol in its bars and restaurants, and many a worthy whose Islamic observances are more ostentatious than sincere; but the touchy, effervescent, almost whimsical political temper of Damascus is still closely linked with the prejudices of Islam. For one thing, Islamic fervor is a useful adjunct to nationalism; for another, one of the chief propaganda points of the Communists is the respect allegedly shown by the Russians to the Muslim communities within their frontiers. A third factor is that misty concept of Pan-Islam which contributes to Colonel Nasser's philosophies, and which from time to time crops up among the aspirations of the Damascus political parties. One such party foresees as the territories of the new Islamic Empire not only all those countries now professing the Muslim faith, but also all those which were Islamic domains in the past; on these grounds Sicily, Spain, and presumably part of France are thrown in—and Cyprus too, a fact that seems to have escaped attention in Athens. All the same, one of the pleasant things about Damascus is the agreeable strain of astringency or cynicism that tempers even the wildest of polemics. It was in a Damascus bar that a young Syrian told me the irreverent story of a pilgrim who had gone to Mecca to drink of the holy water of Zem-Zem. He drank so much of it, in his piety, that it began to do him serious harm; but the only cure he could think of for his overindulgence was to drink of the holy water of Zem-Zem. "In the infinite mercy of Allah," said my informant, "he burst on a Friday."

Damascus has none of the sense of power of Cairo, nor the raciness of Beirut; but it has a charm and beauty of its own, at once fizzy and mellow. It lies rather grandly among its sparse hills, projecting its roads into the deserts, surrounded by the lush green gardens of its oasis; and since you can never be altogether sure of what may be going to happen on any given day, nor who will be in power tomorrow, nor what particular ideology is fermenting in the bazaars that morning, a sense of uncertainty stimulates the activities of the city. The suburbs, stretching away up the hillsides, look trim but shuttered. The center of the city, speared with minarets and towers and criss-crossed with alleyways, is a place of lingering romance. And the shiftless nature of Damascus is the best conserver of its character; for nothing ever seems to last long enough to alter the place very profoundly, and in many ways it is still much the same as it was in the eighteenth century.

The *suks*, for example, are still very beguiling. Little that is remarkable is made in Damascus nowadays (the decline in artistic craftsmanship began when Tamerlane took away the best workers to his new capital of Samarkand, in the twelfth century); but the shops are gay enough still, and full of daggers and silks and carpets and perfumes, so that if you stroll about peering at the windows through half-closed eyes you may fancy yourself back in the scented heyday of the caliphs. The streets are jumbled and narrow and winding, and picturesque old men obligingly wander out of archways, and there are donkeys silhouetted in alleyways and veiled women, and fat businessmen in *tarbooshes*. Sometimes the dark-roofed bustle of a bazaar, crowded and clamorous, suddenly blossoms into a Roman arcade, decorated with splendid columns and sculptured blocks; sometimes you wander down a narrow Biblical backstreet to find yourself abruptly out of the shadows and on the threshold of a golden mosque, its courtyard inviting you through the gates like a fresh field seen through the crooked doorway of a barn.

Most wonderfully of all, you may find yourself stumbling in this way through the gateway of the Great Mosque of the Omayyads, the noblest thing in Syria and, to my mind, one of the two or three most fascinating buildings in the world. Of all the sensations I have ever experienced from proximity to architecture, the most compelling of all is the feeling I have when I emerge from the shade of the Damascus cloth bazaar to find myself at the doorway of this marvellous structure. It is a mixture of styles and periods, an amalgam of varying tastes, but it has the manner of some calm, unshakable organism, or perhaps a clipper ship, or a great mountain. In Damascus, of all cities, its rock-like serenity is wonderful to encounter.

Like nearly all mosques, it consists of space surrounded by structures. Its predominant elements are air, light, breathing-space, and a combination of wisdom and freshness. The Great Mosque also has a tinge of the eccentric, as befits a Damascene monument. Its principal minaret, for instance, is a peculiar affair with a covered verandah and a big round bobble on its summit. Poles and yard-arms and loudspeakers protrude splendidly from its walls, and it stands there with the clouds scudding behind it for all the world like the superstructure of a warship in that glorious period of naval architecture that spanned the transition from sail to steam.

On the other side of the great courtyard is the Basilica, based on a Christian structure. It crowns a monumental prayer hall, dim-lit and murmurous, with a shrine supposed to contain the head of John the Baptist, and a graceful forest of pillars. There is always a hum of life and worship in this cavernous building. Sometimes you may see a whole country family at prayer in the shadows, the woman demure and respectful, the children awed, the bearded father rocking slightly on his heels as he chants the prayers in a languorous, sweet tone from a holy book held very close to his eyes. I like to sit on the floor of this hall and watch the worshippers passing by. There is great sanctity to the place (no spider ever weaves its web there, so the faithful say, and the prophet Jesus will come to the mosque on the Day of Judgment); but there is also, as nowhere else in Damascus, a sense of tolerance. Outside in the bazaars you may meet suspicion and unfriendliness; here in the Great Mosque nobody will question the presence of a Christian, and if you like you may open your airmail *Times* and see who is engaged without incurring the displeasure of these passers-by.

And the courtyard itself: it is pale and flagged and exceedingly old. There are two strange little structures in the middle of it—one a treasure house, one a library—but its predominant character is one of venerable space. Pigeons fly about it, and Muslims wander here or there, praying or talking or simply thinking. High-vaulted arcades give it shade, if you prefer to withdraw from the bright yellow dazzle of the Damascus sun, and at the eastern end there is a series of bright mosaics, towns and trees and rivers and moun-tains, of infinitely surprising skill and humor. I have only to see a glimpse of yellowish sunlight, or remember for a moment the slow serenity of those worshippers, to be transported instantly to the Great Mosque at Damascus, and spend half an hour lapped vicariously in its charm.

Alas, it is not typical of the Syrian scene. Ask any ill-informed Londoner for his impressions of the Arab world and he will at once enumerate for you, with a pitying smile, all the national characteristics of modern Syria: flightiness, shiftiness, prevarication, a predilection for violence, political naivety, stubbornness, boastful incompetence. In Syria it all comes true. Mingle these sorry ingredients thoroughly, add a flash of humor and a basin-full of charm, flavor with brave memories and a trace of ineffectual nobility, soothe with a glimpse of magnificent architecture, and you have the essence of the Syrian Republic.

FRENCHMEN AND GERMANS

D A M A S C U S is not a sophisticated city. Those Westerners who
do not subscribe to the brittle charm of its Arab quarters are likely
to find it something of a hick town. The hotel windows do not
open properly, and there are grimy thumb-prints on the menus.
There still lingers, though, a thin film of worldly allure that is a
relic of the French mandate over Syria and Lebanon. French mandatory rule was in some ways admirable, in others dismal; but in
retrospect, at least to the baffled foreigner fighting for an exit visa
or a photography permit, it seems to have been admirably suave.

France abandoned her political position in the Levant partly because of pressure from the British government. Syria and Lebanon,
cocking a derisive snook at Paris, became officially independent in
1945. This was a blow to French pride. Ever since the Crusades the
French had cherished a special responsibility for the Christian communities of Syria and Lebanon, and they had done a great deal to
bring the benefits of European civilization to this part of the world.
What is more, though they had not hastened the advance of self-
government in their mandated territories, they had put a good deal
of money and effort into making them as trim and capably governed as possible. To understand French Middle Eastern policy
during the 1950s it is necessary to grasp the sense of national pique
induced by the expulsion of France from the Levant; and to remember that interlocked and coincidental with these disappoint-
ments was the protracted French campaign against the Arab rebels
of North Africa, who were always encouraged, and sometimes
armed, by Arab nationalists in the Middle East.

All over the Arab world the French genius has left its mark, and
it may well be that the French contribution to Middle Eastern
progress will outlive the British. The educative influence of France
in the Middle East began with Napoleon's astonishing adventure in
Egypt: for the corps of savants he took with him not only made
their survey of Egypt, but also introduced to the literati of Cairo
and Alexandria some of the delights of contemporary French culture. Since then the Western-style education of the Arabs has been
dominated by French institutions—the French University at Beirut,

for example, countless French private schools, the splendid government-backed *lycées* and French Institutes, and the great universities in France to which many a rich Levantine, in the heyday of European supremacy, used to send his fortunate sons. To this day French is the language of polite society in Beirut and Cairo—if any *politesse* is left in that ill-shaven capital. Many of the Arab scholarly reviews are printed in French. The philosophical fads of the Left Bank find ready adherents among the vestigial intelligentsia of the Middle East. Here, as everywhere, the inspired couturiers of Paris exert an influence of incalculable potency. Few people in the Middle East will admit to loving France, but a great many succumb to its old magic.

In more prosaic matters, too, the example or interest of France still has some importance. Many Middle Eastern legal systems are based upon the French code. French administrative methods are still extant here and there. In 1956 French investments in the Middle East, especially in Egypt, were still substantial. France had a share in Middle East oil, thanks chiefly to French part-ownership of the Iraq Petroleum Company and its subsidiaries; and she was a signatory of the Tripartite Declaration of 1950, which purported to guarantee the frontiers of Israel and her Arab neighbors against aggression from either side. French embassies in the Middle East were large and active.

But the sad truth is that long before the Suez debacle France's political stature in the Middle East had dwindled to insignificance. However grandly she might talk about her special connection with the Levant, she had no more sway over the affairs of Syria and Lebanon than she had over China or Ecuador. She governed no territories in the Middle East, maintained no troops there, and played no material part in the intermittent Anglo-American attempts to pacify the region. Hers was the politics of dog-in-the-manger. She refused to accept facts. When, from time to time, French spokesmen announced that no Middle Eastern settlement could be successful without the participation of France, it was splendid grist for the mill of those razor-keen Egyptian humorists whose particular pleasure it is to deflate misplaced pomposity.

This petty disgruntlement over lost glories was one motive behind France's misguided opposition to the Baghdad Pact, the agreement which drew both Iraq and Persia into formal alliance with the West. From the first conception of this association, France opposed it wholeheartedly. For one thing she supposed, in a hazy sort of way, that the pact would perpetuate British ascendancy in the Middle East at her own expense. For another, she was afraid it was a step towards the establishment of a Greater Syria, a union of the countries surrounding the Syrian Desert. Such a union, the French rightly thought, would lead to an Iraqi hegemony in the northern part of the Arab world; and this, because of her supposed special position in Syria, France would not happily contemplate. All this was, of course, utter nonsense. The Baghdad Pact made not an iota of difference to the condition of French authority in the Middle East, which was (culture and education apart) pure myth anyway; and the French were flattering themselves if they supposed their opinion had much effect on the course of the alliance one way or the other. For a couple of years I spent a depressingly large proportion of my time discussing the Baghdad Pact, and only three or four times did I hear the fair name of France mentioned at all.

The rebellion in North Africa was a more compelling, and slightly more understandable, reason for the French attitude. That protracted insurrection, which led in the course of 1956 to the emancipation of Morocco and Tunisia, was openly fostered in Cairo. Many an exiled rebel could be found, any day of the week, flattered by cronies as he smoked his hubble-bubble in the Cairo coffee-shops; and from time to time, indeed, one of the more prominent and coherent revolutionaries gave a press conference at the Semiramis Hotel. It was no secret that arms were going from Cairo to the French territories of the Moghreb, together with instructors and even fighting volunteers. Cairo radio constantly incited the Algerians, Tunisians, and Moroccans to rebel against French overlordship; Colonel Nasser, even in his public pronouncements, made no bones about his active sympathy for the insurgents.

Confronted by this brazen interference, the French dithered for a time. Sometimes they presented strong protests to Colonel Nasser, and huffed and puffed with all the spurious force of a second-class Power; sometimes they greased the unresponsive Egyptians with bland words. In such a sickly mood was engendered the French attitude to the Baghdad Pact, one of Colonel Nasser's several current anathemas. The marvellous logic of French literary thought is not always apparent in French foreign policy, and there seems to have passed through the collective mind of the Quai d'Orsay the improbable hope of a return of favors. If we oppose the Baghdad Pact, Paris appeared to be suggesting, why not call off, *mon cher Président*, your brave troublemakers in North Africa?

In this device, I need hardly say, the French were rudely disappointed. Far from relaxing their activities in North Africa, the Egyptians intensified them, and the fervor of Cairo's campaign of subversion became almost hysterical. There were strikes in support of the Algerian nationalists, wild Francophobe editorials in the newspapers, a constant stream of abuse and denigration. With Britain withdrawing from so many of her old strongholds, France became the principal target of Arab nationalism, and the old cry of the Arab imperialists—"The Persian Gulf to the Atlantic!"—became a slogan of liberation for the Arab communities of the Moghreb.

It was against this unhappy background, during 1956, that France turned to Israel. Thwarted and goaded beyond belief, subjected to insults and contempt, touchier than ever because of their fading position in the world, the French abandoned their hopeless attempts to conciliate the Arabs of the Middle East. Alone among the Powers, they openly gave their support to the Jews. An arms deal with Egypt was cancelled. Instead, new French tanks and aircraft went to Tel Aviv. Commercial links with Israel were established and cherished; cultural relations were fostered; friendly French influence became easily apparent in Israeli society. If American money still sustained Israel, it was France that was maintaining that country's affinities with Europe and the West.

So it came about, when I stood that day in Sinai, that French jet fighters were flying overhead and French tank-destroyers parked negligently beside the road. I find it impossible to believe that France did not collude with Israel to arrange the assault on Egypt that autumn—her primary purpose being to be rid of Nasser and his meddling once and for all. By then France was openly and unashamedly allied with the enemies of the Arabs. Alone in all the world, she stood by Israel at the bar of the United Nations. Of all the many states which sympathized with Israel during those bitter and depressing days, only France was not afraid to say so. After a long and disillusioning courtship, the French and the Arabs were frankly estranged; and this was a natural rupture, for there can hardly be two peoples in the world so alien to each other's spirit, or so born to disagree.

While France went out like a petulant lamb, West Germany came in like a lion. If France was irritated and cynical, Germany was buoyant, confident, and aggressive. Anywhere in the Muslim Middle East, throughout 1956, you would find German merchants and contractors hard at work, successfully carving themselves a place in the sun. The design for the High Dam was German in origin. German cars and diesel trucks swarmed through all the Arab capitals. German contractors labored on the new dams and bridges of Iraq, and German consumer goods, from cameras to nail scissors, found a place of honor in all the bazaars of Araby. The Americans and the Russians were the Olympians; but the decline of Britain, the virtual extinction of France, and the still amorphous gropings of the Bandung Powers left West Germany the nearest thing to a Third Force in the Middle East.

One cause was simple competence. German consumer goods *were* the best on the market. Their prices were low, their quality was excellent, and their servicing arrangements both courteous and elaborate. (I once remarked to a German in Cairo upon the difficulties of servicing my excellent British car—a local agent of obscure origins, a hodge-podge of rough Levantine mechanics, no spare parts, not much interest. Things were exactly the same with his Mercedes-Benz, he assured me. Did I realize that in the whole of his local Mercedes agency there were only three Germans, Mercedes-trained master mechanics especially brought out from the Mercedes works at Düsseldorf? A disgrace, he called it.) Strangely enough, the integrity of German design also seemed to appeal to the Arabs and Persians. Their products were not sham-American or mock-oriental, but plain, honest-to-goodness German; they combined originality with assurance.

But there were other, subtler reasons for the growing ascendancy of the Germans. They had never been unpopular in the Middle

East, for the good reason that nobody really knew them. The Kaiser's oriental ambitions had long been forgotten, and Rommel never reached Alexandria. The Germans had never administered territories in the Middle East, never been at odds with Arab nationalism, were never associated, even indirectly, with the hated mandatory system. In the 1930s many a frustrated progressive saw Hitler and Mussolini as the saviors of the Arabs, and during the war there were thousands in the Middle East who hoped for an Axis victory. Nasser himself, and some of his revolutionary colleagues, were in touch with Rommel during the fighting in the western desert; they hoped to integrate an Egyptian anti-British rising with a German victory in battle. Rashid Ali's pro-German rising in Iraq found many sympathizers. More than one demonstrating crowd in Cairo shouted, "Rommel! Rommel!" as the watchword of its desires. Arabs saw in the success of Nazi Germany the hope of an alternative to their several bondages.

Even the total defeat of the Germans did little to reduce their prestige, for after the war they were fortunately aloof from those international developments which the Arabs saw as affronts to their sovereignty. In particular, the Germans had nothing whatever to do with the establishment of Israel. They were the root cause of Jewish emigration from Europe; but this was perhaps more to their credit than their disgrace in a region which, though normally tolerant of race and religion, was developing some degree of anti-Semitism. It is true that German reparations to Israel were a useful economic prop to the new state, and that for a time they aroused the Arabs to anger; but this little matter, *purely* a political affair, not in *any* way an expression of German hostility to Arab aspirations, for which indeed she had a *great* deal of sympathy, was soon settled by the unobtrusive skill of German post-war diplomacy. Nobody could ever accuse the Germans of Zionist sympathies, and since Germany had no arms industry nobody could suspect her of arming the Jews for aggression. Of all the Great Powers (for even the Russians had helped the Jews in the early days) only West Germany escaped the stigma of Israel.

Then, too, she somehow escaped rigid classification into one of the two great power blocs. Even in 1956, when West Germany had committed an army to NATO, there surrounded her activities, at least in Arab eyes, an obscure aura of neutralism. More to the point, perhaps, she seemed to the Arabs to be prospering by the exploitation of Western fears and differences. They themselves, especially the Egyptians, were trying to go one further and play off Communism against capitalism; but they knew skillful opportunism when they saw it, and the Germans seemed to them to be excellent at the game. Germany was never lumped among the old unwanted familiars. She was recognizably different in temperament and intention from the great Western democracies. Even her language was strange; and nobody could imagine a nice West German manipulating a government (like the British) or rigging the cotton market (like the Zionists of Wall Street).

To such a people the Egyptians, in particular, willingly turned for help. Many an ex-Nazi espoused the cause of Nasserism, and contributed to its propagation. I was once at a ceremony at Alexandria at which some new Czech weapons were to be handed over to the Egyptian forces. As we waited for Nasser to arrive I noticed a crowd of Egyptian officers milling around a tall figure in a black beret on the corner of the grandstand. I elbowed my way across, eased myself through the mob, apologized once or twice, and pushed a few sluggards out of the way (for in such crowds I develop reactionary instincts) and found myself face to face with as obvious and disagreeable a Prussian officer as ever I saw. His face was congealed with hauteur; his movements were stiff and mechanical, like a robot's; and icy cold were the eyes with which, flicking his cane against his long legs, he turned to look at me. Those jostling Egyptian officers, with their seedy black mustaches and their high-pitched laughs, stood round about him, laughed at his jokes, applauded his opinions, copied his gestures with a greasy subservience that was pitiful to see. In the state tourism offices of Egypt you may find a brochure about the site of the battle of Alamein so dedicated to the glory of the German soldier that for a moment or two you may find yourself genuinely confused about the outcome of the battle; and indeed, much the most victorious of the several war memorials at Alamein is the great fortress-like structure being built by the Germans on the highest ridge, commanding the placid Commonwealth cemetery as completely as that displeasing brigadier dominated the gullible soldiery around him.

So at our moment of time the West Germans were the golden
boys of the Middle East. They stayed wisely aloof from the passions aroused by the nationalization of the Suez Canal. With France
brazenly committed to the Israeli cause, and Britain still the reluc-
tant imperialist, and the United States unavoidably suspect, Bonn
was admirably qualified as an agent of the West in the Middle East.
The Germans saw all kinds of opportunities arising, in which they
could exert great influence in these underdeveloped countries
without incurring political hostilities. If the Americans wanted to
pour their dollars into the Middle East, what better broker's man
than Germany? And what happier contractors to reap the profits
of development than the disinterested, unpolitical, down-to-earth,
untainted innocents of the Federal Republic?

Beside such gleaming competitors, the French looked frayed
indeed (but not all the froward earnestness of Bandung, not a
blocked canal nor a rampant dictator, not an Eisenhower Plan or
a Wehrmacht or a Cominform or a United Nations sanction could
keep the Paris fashion magazines from the gilded salons of Syria).

ALEPPO

I T   I S   O N L Y   when you observe this interchange of influence in
the Middle East that you realize how crippling is the backlog of
grievances borne by the old imperialist Powers. Whatever the subject of your conversation in the Arab world, the British and the
French can nearly always be blamed for something or other; and,
if you believe the Arab nationalists, there is scarcely an injustice
or a vexation in the Muslim East for which those two old sinners
are not ultimately responsible. In Syria, for instance, one of the
many grudges cherished against the French is their addiction to the
system of separatism. They deliberately separated Lebanon from
Syria in order to preserve its Christian character; and they did their
best, so the Damascus experts say, to weaken Syria by encouraging
regional differences and dislikes. The authority of Damascus in
some other parts of the republic is certainly rickety; and at the end
of 1956 there were severe disturbances in northern Syria which did
seem to confirm a lack of national cohesion or common loyalty.

The French may be partly to blame for this; but this is a patchwork region anyway, and many of its internal conflicts are ethical
or religious rather than political. To some degree this is true of the
whole Middle East. It is often conceived as a vast expanse of barren
uniformity, a big, sandy, indeterminate blotch upon the map. It is
true that one language is common to all its capitals, that cultures
are honored more or less in common, that the hero of one Arab
people is the hero of most of the others, that the Arab of any state
will feel reasonably at home across the frontiers of its neighbors—
as much at home, say, as the Englishman will feel in Massachusetts,
or perhaps Texas. But it is a region, nevertheless, of great variety,
of innumerable minorities and persuasions.

Lebanon is the outstanding example of religious multiplicity, but
Syria is a country of great contrasts too. It varies in terrain from
the huge, arid expanse of the eastern desert, speckled with the gay
hunting lodges of the Omayyad Caliphs and crowned with the incomparable ruin of Palmyra, to the high mountains of the Jebel
Alawi, near the Mediterranean, in which the mysterious Alawis live
and from time to time erupt into turmoil, secular or spiritual. In

the north Syria edges away greenly into Turkey. In the east its barrenness is interrupted by the Euphrates, and there are vast steppes of undeveloped cultivable land. In the south, in springtime, you can drive into the Jordan valley along a highway lined with a paradise of wild flowers. There are Kurdish, Armenian, Turkoman, Circassian, and Assyrian minorities in Syria. The religious sects include Sunni Muslims, Shia Muslims, Alawites, Druzes, Maronites, Greek Orthodox, Armenian Orthodox, Syrian Orthodox, Latin Catholics, Greek Catholics, Syrian Catholics, Armenian Catholics, Chaldean Catholics, Protestants, Nestorians, and Jews. Between the various Catholic sects the differences of dogma are sometimes so obscure as to be indistinguishable; but they do not prevent expressions of disagreement so forcible that they sometimes break into physical violence. To add to this militant confusion, the Druze will not tell anyone precisely what their religion is, and the Alawis seem to be inextricably enmeshed in a tangle of Muslim and Christian doctrines.

The most energetic center of regional activity is the city of Aleppo, in the north; and, as it happens, my own memories of the place are colored by one of Syria's politico-doctrinal imbroglios. This part of the country is studded with shrines and religious memories, and seems to have a peculiar facility for fostering controversies. There are the ruins of innumerable old Christian towns in the hills above Aleppo, and saints and martyrs beyond number have roamed the surrounding countryside. One of them was St. Simeon Stylites, who sat on top of his sixty-foot pillar for thirty years, achieving by these unorthodox means such an influence on world affairs that emperors and popes used to send their emissaries to him for advice, and their gorgeously sealed and beribboned missives were passed to the saint on the end of a long pole. It is an unhinged sort of countryside, exemplified by the villages of conical beehive houses, looking rather like inverted cake-molds, that are unique to these uplands; and it has never surprised me to know that after the success of St. Simeon, equivalent perhaps to that of some unusually seductive Italian film star, scores of other stylites laboriously erected their pillars in these hills; they ranged in age from infancy to dot-

age, and they sat there through the years meditating and performing sporadic miracles; so that in those days, apparently, it was not
at all untoward to come across such a holy man brooding on his
column in a gulley, or to see one silhouetted, a much holier Nelson,
telling his beads upon some distant ridge.

To this day Aleppo has a large Christian population, and the
schism most apparent when I was there was agitating the Armenian
community. I cannot pretend to have mastered this dispute. It was
partly religious, partly political, and to some extent it revolved
about the desire of Armenians all over the world to maintain their
national entity. The Russians had exploited this deep-rooted aspiration. The Armenian homeland lies within the borders of the Soviet
Union, and the Communists made much of the alleged autonomy
of the place, the vitality of its Armenian traditions, the flourishing
condition of the Armenian language. In the Middle East, as elsewhere, the Armenians (skillful mechanics, good businessmen, artists
and craftsmen of many kinds) suffer from a certain rumbling and
widespread prejudice, not so blatant as anti-Semitism can be, but
nearly as insidious; and throughout the Muslim world, not least in
Syria, such Christian communities are often unhappy and dissatisfied. So a number of Armenians had left Aleppo and had gone to
Russia, their journey sponsored by the Kremlin. Some of them
arranged systems of codes, so that when they reached Armenia they
could tell their friends in Syria what conditions were like; most
of them simply disappeared into the blue, into another world, and
their departure had left the community disturbed and divided.

More confusing still, the division of the Armenian world had
spilled over into matters spiritual, and there was a violent controversy raging over whether the Russian Armenian church authorities were the genuine ones, or those in the Middle East. I never
quite grasped the subtleties of this breach, but you could hardly
escape its implications in Aleppo. Misty, bearded figures moved
constantly through our conversations, prelates with resounding
titles, sees, archbishoprics and patriarchates. There was a dignitary in Jerusalem whom some seemed to regard as paramount;
and there was somebody from Russia who had recently been tour-
ing the Arab world proclaiming his supremacy; and there were
many obscure variances of faith and formality which I ignomini-

ously failed to digest. I have always liked Armenians, and if it were not for the undertones of tragedy to these asperities, they would have been very amusing.

As it was, they enlivened and embittered my stay in Aleppo, and emphasized the gulf that lies between the Syrian capital and its provinces. Anything connected with the Armenians of Aleppo has tautness and stimulation, very different from the heady Damascene spirit. I stayed in a hotel owned by Armenians. It was celebrated, old-fashioned, and full of character, and it was called Baron's. Why was that, I asked? Oh, "baron" was the Armenian equivalent of "sir," and since the original proprietor always had been regarded with respect, the people of Aleppo called it "Sir's Hotel." Everybody seems to have stayed at Baron's, from T. E. Lawrence to the Queen of Sheba, and it has some of the subdued self-assurance of one of the really great hotels. It has its individualities, though. I was once lying stark naked on my bed in the heat of a July afternoon when the chambermaid walked in, said good afternoon to me without batting an eyelid, and conscientiously placed some clean towels beside my basin. There is also a humble employee of the hotel, a porter or handyman, who suffers from the genuine and endearing illusion that he is in fact the proprietor, and greets the arriving guest as M. Ritz might have received a duchess; an aberration that mystifies some of the ill-informed, but pleases the dry and kindly humor of the actual owner.

The Armenians occupy a lovely, twisty, shuttered, high-walled, stone-built section of the city, with narrow streets and women stirring bowls of soup in open doorways. Life appears to be serene and simple, for all the squabbles of the patriarchs. The dustman does his rounds in the company of a donkey. He wears black baggy trousers and a checked scarf over his head, and he bangs vigorously on the wooden doors and shouts boisterously, so that the noise of his cheerful coming echoes down the alleys and around the little squares, and the housewives clatter through their courtyards to catch him. He loads the garbage into panniers; the donkey trots off down the street; and these sunny back alleys subside into a calm and mellow quiet. In the evening the Armenians sit on stools beside their doorways, while their womenfolk peel the vegetables in the courtyards. It is a far cry from the hysterical hubbub of the Damascus coffee-shops.

The Armenians are the leavening of Aleppo, for this ancient merchant city is deficient in fizz or abandon, and is in the main a heavy and uninquisitive place. By the high standards of the Arab world its people are humorless; they are also earnest and industrious. Ephemeral political theories are not often born among the Muslims of Aleppo. It is not a desert station, instinct with the flighty sentiments of Arabia, but a foursquare, rock-bottom, no-nonsense mercantile town. Its bazaars, among the finest and biggest in Syria, sell some objects of romance—sheepskin cloaks and saddle-holsters, tentage and thigh-boots—but their atmosphere strikes me as lumpish and heavy, and the grass that grows unexpectedly on their roofs (supporting a few depressed and tethered sheep) reminds me of stubble growing on the chin of some rather boring and self-satisfied old man. If you wander among the shadowy vaults of these bazaars, among the comfortable merchants and pre-occupied country people, nobody will view you with any particular interest or pester you with his wares; and though this can be a restful surprise, it can also be disappointingly flat, as though the bubbles have left the bottle.

But in any Arab city there are moments of piquancy, corners of delight. I remember one such moment, in a secluded corner of the Aleppo *suk*, when I happened to look through an open doorway down a flight of stairs. It was a public bathhouse; and there at the bottom in the gloom two portly and prosperous burghers were rubbing themselves vigorously with towels; they looked up suddenly as I stood there and I saw their two round and complacent faces peering at me goggle-eyed, pink from their exertions, with the heat glistening on their brows. Another old bathhouse, having something in common with that black catacomb at Assiut, has been turned into a felt factory. In its spacious entrance hall two elderly plutocrats lie luxuriously among carpets, sipping coffee and smoking hubble-bubble pipes; but inside the bathhouse things are very different. It is a windowless vaulted place, and at first you can see nothing at all; out of the darkness, though, there comes a series of guttural grunts, rhythmic and purposeful, in many different keys, the kind of noise I have always imagined sheep to make as they are plunged into the sheep-dip. As you peer into the shadows and the gloom dissipates, there slowly emerge the darker figures of the felt-makers. They are ceaselessly pushing rolls of felt around the floor with their feet. Some manage a roll alone. Some share the task with others. One is a boy of ten or twelve. Several others seem to be at least seventy. All of them, as they roll the felt round and round, round and round, like camels at a water wheel, emit that strange, throaty grunt, sharp and eerie. "It is traditional," said one of the plutocrats decisively when I asked him the purpose of this eerie ritual.

I also remember Aleppo as a city of milk and of cats. I used to eat daily in a little café near the center of the city frequented by country families doing their shopping in the *suks*. They were handsome people, gaily dressed, and with exceedingly genteel table manners (a soothing contrast to the voluptuous guzzling and dribbling of the Egyptian family at food); and what they chiefly ate was milk. To be sure, they had some bread, and perhaps some kind of kebab or minced meat; but the center of their meal was an enormous jug of *liban*, or soured milk. This liquid is common, and refreshing, in Jordan and Lebanon too; but it is chiefly characteristic of northern Syria, and Aleppo remains in my mind indissolubly linked with it. Some scholars indeed maintain that the very name Aleppo comes from *liban*, and others maintain (not with any very profound air of conviction) that Abraham himself milked his cattle on the central hillock of the city. For myself, I found that after a few days there almost everything had a milky taste to it; the peculiar dry flavor of *liban* seemed to pervade every dish, and even a bottle of pop I bought in desperation one morning tasted strongly of the stuff.

Perhaps the milk attracted the cats. Whatever the cause, I have never seen so many cats in a city as I saw in Aleppo, and most of them looked extremely contented. This is rare in the Middle East, a region that is not over-fond of its animals, and in which the cat is generally a scrawny and little-respected creature. It is many a long century since the cat was sacred to the Egyptians; and the beautiful Siamese I once lost in Cairo was speedily converted, I am quite sure, into a pair of exotic if ill-fitting gloves. In Aleppo, though, there is unexpected consideration for the welfare of cats. There is a mosque in the *suks* of Aleppo endowed by some antique benefactor for the purpose of feeding them each morning. When I walked through its carved doorway one morning an old, old man in a turban had just placed upon the stone-flagged ground a tin tray full of offal, and a vivacious assembly of cats, leaping from the medieval crannies of the building, was jostling for position around it. Elsewhere, among the cluttered foodstores of the *suk*, piled high with blood-red meat and gaudy vegetables, I encountered many another plump animal, and exchanged expressions of admiration with its owner.

Some of them may have English ancestry, for ever since the sixteenth century European merchants have been active in Aleppo, and an English trading company was established there in 1704. (The British Consulate in Aleppo is said to be the oldest-established in the world.) In the old days of Syrian adventure these merchants led a strangely segregated life. Except in the way of business they could not mingle with the local people, and they therefore lived lives of collegiate seclusion. Each company had its own *khan*, in which its members both lived and worked, only going out to the countryside *en masse* for a picnic or a game of cricket. So precarious were the conditions of the time, and so vicious the xenophobia of Aleppo, that the different companies (English, French, German, Venetian) used to connect their separate *khans* by overhead platforms, so that they could go visiting without running the gauntlet of the *suks*. Several of the *khans* still stand. In one of them I once ate a picnic lunch, and very restful and evocative it was. It stood behind a dark, dust-laden bazaar, and an old iron chain guarded its entrance. Inside there was a little quadrangle, shaded with trees, decorated with scholarly carvings; and the walls were colored gently with black and yellow stripes. The sun shone kindly in this little oasis; there was a murmur of bargaining from the *suk* outside; and as I munched my sandwiches and drank my *liban* I was torn in fancy between these brave old merchants of the English company, with their tabbies and their cricket bats, and Oxford on a long summer afternoon, when you can hear the distant shouting of rowing coaches muffled through the trees.

That *khan* was a faint Arabized echo of seventeenth-century Europe; in Syria it is much easier, if you enjoy such experiences, to be enthralled by the spirit of medieval chivalry. Sometimes the Crusaders are at your side, as you stand upon a castle battlement, or observe the crest of some knight-at-arms above the doorway of a church. At other times you are in a Saracen world. In Damascus there is the tomb of Saladin, a mausoleum among flower gardens; in Aleppo there is the citadel, one of the supreme examples of Muslim military architecture. It is the first thing you see as you approach the city, and the last to linger upon the hazy horizon when you leave; for it stands upon a great hill in the very center of the city, and looks around it, over the *suks* and minarets, like some magnificent old monarch in a state portrait. This citadel was heavily besieged by the Crusaders, but never fell; and it is easy to see why. The whole of its supporting hill is faced with stone. Its battlements are stupendously strong. Its entrance is guarded by towers and gateways ingeniously and powerfully built. A series of right-angle bends complicates the approach to the interior of the fortress, and lions and dragons of mystical defensive potency glare terribly from the walls.

When I first visited the citadel, in the dry heat of a blazing Aleppo afternoon—no river softens the aridity of this city—I found to my dismay that the outer gateway was firmly closed, and a notice in red chalk said emphatically: *"Fermé."* Blank was the huge wooden doorway that faced me, and stern the crenellated structure behind me. Everywhere there were arrow-slits and holes for the pouring of boiling oil, and the great glacis looked so steep and so slippery and so invulnerable to fire, oil, and mystic beasts as to be unclimbable. Above the great Saracen gateway a gorgeous inscription stood: "Our master, the great Sultan, Al Malik Al Ashraf, the learned, the just, the warrior, the champion of the holy war, he who fights for the faith, he who defends the frontiers, he whom God assists, the conqueror, the victorious reconstructor of the world and of religion, the incomparable king, the defender of Islam and the Muslims, the upholder of the dynasty, the keystone of the faith, the protector of the nation, the auxiliary of the Caliphate, the help of the Imamate, the lord of Kings and Sultans and those who proclaim the Oneness of God, the defender of the right by witnessing, he who gives life to justice in the universe, he who annihilates schismatics and apostates, he who exterminates infidels and heretics, the conqueror of rebels and revolutionaries, he who has vanquished the adorers of the Cross, the Alexander of his time, the conqueror of capitals, he who has put to flight the armies of the Franks, the Armenians and the Mongols, he who devastated St. John of Acre and the seacoast districts, he who put life into the noble Abbasid dynasty, the defender of the Muslim faith, Khalil, son of the Sultan Al Malik Al Mansur Khalaun, may God glorify his victories, has ordered that this construction, in poor condition, be restored in the 691st year after the Hegira on the initiative of His Highness, our master, the great Prince Shams-el-Din Kara-sankhar, Jukandar of the King Al Mansur, deputy of the King Al Ashraf, lieutenant-general of the province of Aleppo, may God glorify his victories!"

No wonder, I thought, that the infidel armies had never captured this noble fortress; and, like them, I prepared to slink away defeated. Before I left, though, on the principle that a cat may at least shake its whiskers at a king, I pressed that huge iron-studded door tentatively with my hand; and slowly, with creakings and echoing gratings, it opened at my touch, despite the dragons, despite the oil-holes and the exterminator of heretics, and I found myself inside.

OVER JORDAN

SOUTH OF SYRIA, down the be-flowered highway beneath Mount Hermon, lies the Kingdom of Jordan, presided over in an obscure sort of way by the young King Hussein, scion of the Hashemite dynasty. The road from Damascus passes through the small railway town of Deraa, on the Hejaz railway, where T. E. Lawrence was so appallingly misused in 1917; and Jordan itself is crowded with memories of the Arab Revolt. Its first king, Abdullah, was a prominent figure in the campaign under the leadership of his brother Feisal, and the country was established by Britain as a direct result of Arab participation in the 1914-18 war. As Lebanon was deliberately created by the French, so Jordan was, when the projected Arab Kingdom collapsed, carved out of nowhere in particular by the British government and presented on a diplomatic platter to the faithful Abdullah. Since then its size has been doubled by the adhesion of part of mandatory Palestine.

The borders of this kingdom are artificial. Its economy appears to be unviable. Its successful defense is almost impossible. Its character has been perverted by the presence within its borders of half a million Arab refugees from Israel, many of them living in camps in conditions of abject and embittering misery. Its future seems held in fee by the political propagandists of Egypt and Colonel Nasser's financiers in Saudi Arabia. In short, Jordan is a mess; and it is a moot point, at the end of 1956, whether it can long continue to exist as a Power, or whether it will be swallowed into the territories of its acquisitive neighbors.

When I first went to this country, soon after the Second World War (when it was still the mandated territory of Transjordan) its flavor was very different. Its little capital of Amman, tucked away in the mountains above the River Jordan, was infinitely serene. Its narrow, hilly streets were rural and uncrowded, with a milk-churn, crabapple, fly-whisk feeling to them. The benevolent hand of Glubb Pasha, the British commander of the Arab Legion, cast a gentle security over its people, and the aristocratic standards of the Bedouin tents injected into its thought and conduct a strain of ornate grandiloquence. In a modest palace on the hillside sat Abdullah himself, a splendid desert king, afraid of nobody, no not he, living in patriarchal state with high memories and an affectionate harem, the personification of the fighting Arab noble. There was a country calm to Amman in those days, quiet and confident, and backed by sterling.

Now all has changed. Abdullah has been gathered to his desert fathers (though his favorite Negro wife still lives on the hill) and his grandson drives through the streets in a succession of Mercedes and Cadillacs, a young man of courage but dubious stability, whose throne seems to be uncomfortably rickety upon its gilded legs. Glubb Pasha and most of his British colleagues have been rudely ejected (though Hussein, a Harrovian, did honor a school custom by sending the general a signed portrait of himself as he waited to board the aircraft of his expulsion). British subsidies are now politically tainted. The Arab Legion, an Anglo-Arab concept, has become the Jordan Arab Army, and is doing its best to discard the picturesque trappings (pink-checked headdresses, pipe bands, Sandhurst drill) that still link it with the mandatory past. Many young men of indefinable ambitions circle around each other in the arena of state, egged on by money bags and radio voices, some of them puppets of Cairo, some of them Communists, some merely shifty opportunists. The desert manners are dying. Amman is now a noisy, crowded, dissatisfied, jerry-built sort of town, a capital *faute de mieux*, and its government offices and royal palaces stand nervously and unconvincingly among its seven hills. The place simmers with the suspicion that something catastrophic may happen any day; and from time to time it does.

These changes are, of course, not all political. Jordan, like its Arab neighbors, is undergoing a slow but irresistible social transformation too. The feudal structure of its society, invested by education and political progress, is slowly disintegrating. The traditions of Muslim orthodoxy are, on the whole, fading. The Arabs may be looking East rather than West in 1956, but the impact of Western thought upon their manner of life is still immensely potent; and the Jordanians are still in a kind of schizophrenic suspension between the old shuttered Turkish ways and the brassy new ones. A good illustration of this condition was provided by King Hussein's wedding to Queen Dina, which took place, happily, in one of the lulls between internal convulsions. The palace authorities seemed torn between the demands of publicity and of decorum; but the wedding was remarkable because of the public part played in it by women of the royal household—astonishing to consider, when you recall that only one full generation before, Abdullah's womenfolk had been veiled, ignorant, second-class citizens of the Arabian desert.

Dina, though, was an educated person. She was widely read and intellectually inclined, had an Oxford degree, and had taught English literature at Cairo University. Vivid pictures were painted of the King, some years her junior and addicted to things like jet fighters and racing cars, enduring daily sessions of cultural improvement. Certainly nothing could be further from the old concepts of Arab womanly behavior than her advanced and businesslike approach to the ceremony. She went to Beirut to buy her trousseau. From Paris she summoned an Elizabeth Arden beauty specialist. From Cairo there came a number of her former pupils ("Her favorite poets were the Romantics," one girl told me mistily). It is a tradition in Islam that on the wedding day bride and bridegroom shall not meet until after the ceremony; but Dina swept this heritage aside cheerfully and appeared on a balcony that morning with her fiancé, wearing a gay mauve dress and a chiffon scarf over her head. She even granted interviews to a few women journalists, one of whom, foreseeing a ceremony conducted upon more traditional lines, had vaguely planned to make an entry disguised as some obscure princess of Scandinavian royalty.

The marriage contract itself was, it is true, signed in the presence only of men—the Queen was in another palace at the time—and a quaint ceremony it was. The guests assembled in a long reception room, holding glasses of heavily sugared raspberry juice. Glubb Pasha was there, standing by himself, in a corner, diffident but friendly, a legend in his lifetime. He had driven to the palace in a flurry of jeeps and Bren guns, one of the generic sights of Amman; but he was a modest and a kindly man, and if (as his critics had it) he was also an outdated autocrat, at least his despotism was a benevolent and beneficial one. Nearby was the singer Fair el-Atrash, the Bing Crosby of the Middle East. His family, Druzes from Syria, had once been granted political asylum in Jordan, and he was here to repay the debt by singing at the celebrations. A Pakistani brigadier carried his cine-camera unblushingly. An ecclesiast of undefined loyalties peered around him from the recesses of his black hood, fingering an enormous golden cross. Presently there emerged from an inner room the distinguished witnesses of the contract, which had been signed upstairs in private. The bride's father was a tall, cadaverous Egyptian, wearing hornrimmed glasses and a pale gray suit. The Emir Mohammed of Saudi Arabia was resplendent in Arab dress, a spotless white headdress, and a brown *aba* corded with gold. The Crown Prince Abdullah of Iraq looked suave and anglophile.

And the King himself stood at the end of the room, beneath a portrait of his father, the unbalanced King Talal. Beside him stood a royal cousin, King Feisal II of Iraq, grandson of Feisal of the Arab Revolt. How small and helpless and nice they looked, those two little kings, both of them youths, both absurdly small and stocky, in their somehow ill-fitting dark suits and their hands not quite at ease—Hussein, not long from Sandhurst, standing roughly to attention, Feisal, a little more experienced, with his legs apart and his hands clasped in front of him. Royal kings they were, but kings in a troubled and republican world. They received the wedding guests with shy smiles; and the celebrants, led by Glubb Pasha and the hooded ecclesiast, left the room clutching small be-ribboned boxes of chocolates, sent by Groppi's of Cairo.

But the really significant moment of that lavishly ceremonial day (for the capital was alive with parades and demonstrations from dawn to fireworks time) was the assembly, later that evening, at which the King officially met his Queen. In the past this would have been held behind the curtained doors of the harem, and the innumerable ladies of the household would not for a moment have been exposed unveiled to the gaze of the world at large. This time, though the affair was still predominantly female, some men were allowed to attend it; and the ladies, far from being veiled, appeared bewitchingly, or at least compellingly, uninhibited. I stood in a corner of the room while the assembly prepared itself for the arrival of the royal couple. Circassians in long black cloaks,

astrakhan hats, high boots, and cluttered accoutrements guarded
the entrance to the hall, as the eunuchs would have stood sentry in
an earlier age. At the head of the stairs were two bold lancers in
scarlet tunics and white breeches. But the body of the room was
a mass of women. They were dressed magnificently, a glitter of
satins and brocades and furs, a mosaic of lipsticks and mascara, a
tinkling kaleidoscope of earrings, a flurry of sequined handbags.
Chanel and Dior thickened the air. When the Queen Mother of
Jordan arrived, a sibilant Arabic whisper rippled through the hall;
for the first time she was appearing in public with no veil above
her sumptuous silk gown. All the same, I could not help feeling
that we were close in spirit, if not in textile, to the huddled jealousies and schoolgirl pleasures of the harem. How often and how brazenly did the women of the court eye one another's couture and
coiffure! How heavily accentuated were the outlines of their eyes,
like eyes seen through diaphanous curtains in forbidden corridors
of the Seraglio! How scratchy and talon-like were the fingernails,
how pinkly fleshy the figures, and how passive and doll-like those
emancipated ladies looked, in serried and perfumed phalanx, as if
some lascivious sultan were about to pass through their ranks, picking a beauty here and a beauty there, with a lordly gesture of his
forefinger!

But it was only little King Hussein who entered the room, with
his calm, intelligent, literary wife. The illusion vanished in a trice,
and as the court ladies smoothed their skirts and pressed the wrin-
kles from the wrists of their gloves, we were back in the world of
the film première, and a cameraman in a crumpled jacket suddenly
pressed his way past the Circassian guards and said, "Just one more,
ladies, please, give us a nice smile now."

At least Amman is still a country capital. In the spring the hills
that surround it are a heavenly mass of wild flowers, and its air
is still fresh highland air. Though its streets are jammed with cars,
and the jet fighters of the Jordanian air force have a disconcerting
propensity for flying very low over its rooftops, it is still graced by
country people selling their wares or doing their shopping. Some
are settled peasants, lean but hearty of face, their wives wearing

clean white headdresses or tumbled turbans. Some are refugees from Palestine, in snowy mantles and gorgeous blue gowns, embroidered face veils and bright, decorated sandals. Others are Bedouin, towards the northern end of that immemorial circuit which has brought them, through the centuries, slowly out of the Arabian desert towards the Fertile Crescent. They wear their hair in ringlets, and stride about with a beguiling but spurious haughtiness, like indigent eagles. Down by the main square a man sells fish from the Red Sea, presenting—with the flies crawling thickly over the great ice slabs—an appearance more exotic than appetizing. By the post office a butcher in a long brown robe hangs his beef on a spit above the pavement, to carve it with precision and presence among a crowd of rustics.

For though nobody could call Amman a picturesque city—its architecture is almost uniformly dreary—there is still enough of the Bedouin and the bucolic there to make it, on occasion, a gay place. The royal wedding, for example, set off the most rollicking sort of celebration, with innumerable bands, enthusiastic boy scouts, caparisoned horsemen, pistol shots in the air, fireworks, crocodiles of schoolgirls singing patriotic songs, sword dancers and fire-eaters in the streets. And when Amman was seething after the expulsion of Glubb Pasha (one of the chief links in the chain of events that led me to the Sinai) the most memorable sight of all was that of the Arab Legion pipe band going home by truck from some nationalist festivity or other: there they sat in their bright pink-checked headdresses, and one piper was playing his pipe on top of the driver's cab, and another had seized the bandmaster's staff and was twirling it wildly in the air, and the rest were dancing, laughing, singing with the music, beating their feet on the floor, conducting and swaying with the rhythm; and so they swept away up Jebel Amman, a fading skirl of melody, to the tune of an old Scottish air. Even those innumerable political demonstrations, which disrupt the life of Amman with their demands and complaints and threats of catastrophe, are often blessed by a certain gaiety of manner, leavening the bitterness and disillusion, so that the passing Englishman may find himself greeted more with quips than with bludgeon blows. (A British diplomatist in Amman returned to his home one day reporting that agitators in the town had molested him. When he bent over to change his shoes, so it was reported, there was seen imprinted on his trousers a number of tiny foot-prints, each bearing a trade name: "Kiddicumf.")

But it is only in patches, of time as of space, that Amman rejoices in these things. The gaudy costumes are here and there, the Bed-ouins are splendid, the soldiers are lean and soldierly; but generally the Ammanese look a drab lot, half Arab in dress, half European, with untidy *khuffiyahs* over dingy double-breasted suits. There is a frightened cardboard emptiness to the spirit of Amman. When the pipes or the *feux-de-joie* ring out it is rather an exhilarating place; but on any ordinary day of any ordinary week an air of threadbare futility seems to haunt it. When the British were still there, organizing the Legion, running the police, sticking together potsherds in the minute museum on the hill above Amman, there was at least some sense of purposeful competence. Not all the Legion officers were as efficient or as far above reproach as their legend would have them to be, and I remember with blushes the comment of a British army officer who had recently taken part in maneuvers with that well-publicized force; but there were oases in Jordan then where you could find integrity allied with profes-sional ability. Now there seems to be scarcely a department of state or a segment of society that is not riddled with tiresome rivalries and vendettas. The young men who run the army, suddenly rocketing from majorities to generalcies after Glubb's removal, were often brash and conceited. The politicians, with a few splendid exceptions, are soaked in the dreary polemics and ambi-tions of their kind. Governments are transitory and often powerless anyway. The monarchy is precarious. The civil servants in their offices seem to perform their grubby labors—all carbon paper and rubber stamps—with an air of bankrupt hopelessness.

The very character of the state is oppressive, for there is no very logical reason why it should exist at all. It is landlocked except for one small segment of coastline, four or five miles in width, at the head of the Gulf of Aqaba, the eastern fork of the Red Sea. The country has no means of earning its own living, and depends almost entirely upon outside contributions. Since 1948 it has been immured in a slough of half-war with Israel—an uneasy condition which intrudes into almost every conversation, colors the views of every citizen, squanders the dubious energies of politicians, and wastes the abilities of the army. The lavish schemes mooted since the war to irrigate large parts of Jordan and exploit its untapped resources (whatever they may be) never seem to come to anything; and the most promising venture of all, a development scheme in the Jordan Valley launched by the remarkable Palestinian Musa el-Alami, appeals so little to the Jordanian sense of pride that during one of the perennial periods of rioting demonstrators smashed much of its equipment in the frenzy of their fervor.

If this sounds a nation in a condition of paranoia, it is chiefly because of the presence in Jordan of the refugees—half a million unfortunate old men of the sea who hang lumpishly and frowardly on the shoulders of the state. They have been given Jordanian nationality, and seem to have little chance of ever getting back to an Arab Palestine; but most of them make no contribution at all to the economy or welfare of the country. On the contrary, they are a constant menace to its security. If you drive southwards from Amman you are bound to see one of their camps, blazing and fly-ridden if it is summer, bleak and chilly beyond description if it is the sharp highland winter. They are brown, huddled, miserable slums. Some of the people live in gloomy brown tents, some in piles of stones, some in caves or holes burrowed in the ground. They are fed by the United Nations and have their schools and clinics, and in some places they have been given huts; but since 1948 they have been immured in these places in idle hopelessness, and they move about their wretched enclosures with hangdog depression. In particular, they have nothing whatever to do. They brood the months and years away in bitterness, without a home of their own, a *raison d'être*, or even a humble job to perform. No wonder they are ridden with the politics of discontent—Communism, anti-Westernism, Nasserism, anarchism. Many of them are intelligent, not a few highly educated, and they have become a power in the land of immeasurable potency and danger. In them are crystallized all the rumbling miseries of the Middle East, with its poverty, its pervading sense of injustice, its disorientation, its hunger for positive leadership. Moreover, since they owe no real loyalty to Jordan itself, but are simply dispossessed Arabs, they are ideal material for those who seek to impose some sort of Arab unity upon the unconvincing frontiers of the Middle East—and for those who want to bolster their own power by exploiting the issue of Israel. The refugees are Arabs in the raw: the quintessence of mid-century Arabism. With a multitude of such unfortunates implanted upon it, the little country state of Jordan feels like a rectory infested with gangsters.

Disorder, ambition, even revolution is always in the air. Nobody knows what the mob will do next. "Picture postcards!" the street vendor shouts, and holds out a portrait of Colonel Nasser, smiling sweet-and-strong beneath his military cap, half Atatürk, half Peron —the refugees' Saladin, the pride of the Arabs. Any day, on one pretext or another, the mob may advance down the hilly streets of Amman, flags a-flying, shouting slogans and abuse—down with the imperialists, or the Zionists, or the colonizers, or the exploiters, or the Baghdad Pact!—and as they sweep through the city past the powerless or apathetic policemen, with the clash of their cymbals and the beat of their tambourines and the fevered hubbub of their voices, with a youth on his fellows' shoulders bawling a litany of subversion, and an inflamed soldier or two with uniform awry, the agitators in front, the excited young men in the middle, and the poor simple country crowds, out for the fun of it all, laughing along behind, as they tumble noisily past the palace hill with gun-shots and discordant songs, many a sensible, old-fashioned Jordanian peers from his upstairs window and sighs for the patriarchal days of the old Jordan, with Glubb Pasha cross-legged among his adoring Bedouin, and King Abdullah, the desert Arab, up there on the hillside in the loving company of his Negro wife.

THE FRONTIER

THE WHOLE of Jordan's western frontier marches with Israel. Except for Gaza, all that part of Palestine which did not fall into the hands of the Jews in 1948 has been incorporated into the Kingdom of Jordan, and a Jordanian is now a "west banker" or an "east banker" according to whether he lives on the west or the east side of the Jordan River—the former ex-Palestine, the latter Jordan proper. The Arab idealists maintain that one day Palestine will be restored to existence as an independent Arab state, but it is difficult to see the west bank, which includes the magnificent Old City of Jerusalem, ever being prised away from Jordan. King Abdullah saw to it that it was firmly attached to his kingdom as soon as the British Mandate in Palestine ended; and that shrewd old potentate thus became the only Arab ruler to gain any sizable chunk of territory from the Palestine debacle. It has been a mixed blessing, for with the west bank have come thousands of refugees, but it makes Jordan look much more imposing on the map.

In Jordan, as in Israel, you are never far from this frontier. From many places in the Jordan hills you can see the Mediterranean coast of Israel, with Tel Aviv sprawling beside it like a little Los Angeles, and the myriad ugly crescents and columns of housing estates creeping out across the plain of Sharon. From the Israeli side of the line this spectacle is redeemed by its sense of pathos and fortitude; seen from some tumble-down Arab village with a cracked and crooked minaret, it looks like a visitation from another world. The Israelis are understandably apprehensive that one day the Arabs may hurl themselves howling upon Tel Aviv; but the Jordanians are always afraid that the teeming, pulsing, ruthless little machine-state across the frontier will eventually spill over its confines in search of living room. The Israelis occasionally encourage these fears by vicious raids across the line, in which, by brilliant planning and exemplary discipline, they demonstrate both their military ability and their flair for *realpolitik*. The Arabs inflame the issue by sending hit-and-run commandos into Israel, and by more harmless forays in search of grazing ground or loot. Sometimes, it is said, Egyptian volunteers cross to Jordan from Sinai and operate from this frontier, attacking Israeli settlements and doing some minor sabotage. The frontier is always tense, and in Amman there are constant controversies about how best to defend it. (The Israelis have no such uncertainties.) Glubb Pasha used to think that much of the west bank would have to be abandoned if the Jews attacked. King Hussein and his young advisers disagree, and base their strategy on one of those heroic not-one-inch-of-the-homeland conceptions. The main body of the Jordan army, all the same, is kept behind the Jordan, and it is only at moments of great emergency that its tanks and guns and trucks stream across the hills of Moab in the night, guided by a series of gigantic white pyramidal markers striding towards Jerusalem.

When the Palestine war ended, the Israelis were in possession of most of the plain, and the Arabs were entrenched upon the escarpment which bounds it on its eastern side. Thus the armistice line was demarcated. Its authors were nothing if not literal. They marked the line on a map in Rhodes, and their decision was implemented with devotion. Sometimes villages are bisected. Once the line actually goes through a house. Often people are cut off from their water supplies, cattle from their grazing grounds, children from their schools, doctors from their patients. There is a place just outside Jerusalem called Beit Jala where the barbed wire of the demarcation line runs down the middle of the village street, and where you can stand among Arabs in Jordan and wave to Arabs in Israel. One old man told me that he sometimes talked over the wire with his married daughter, whose house was in Israel; but he was thereby guilty (thanks to the men with the map in Rhodes) of "communicating with the enemy."

A classic example of this traumatic situation is provided by the village of Qalqiliya, near Nablus. This is a smallish stone village which stands on the very edge of the escarpment, overlooking the plain. There is a shabby mosque, and a Muslim burial ground, and among the houses a group of Bedouin refugees has settled miserably. Some still have their black goat-hair tents, woefully patched and threadbare; others live in crude mud huts with thatched roofs. The people of Qalqiliya extract a meager income from the scratchy hill-fields behind the village, scraping among the rocks with their wooden plows. The women of the place still wear their bright traditional costumes—the old Palestine was a country of vivid blue and yellow dyes—but Qalqiliya on a bitter winter day is a picture of despondency.

Just below the village, though, there stand the casual white posts of the demarcation line; and beyond them, in Israel, are the old village estates of Qalqiliya. There are fertile groves of citrus fruit, stretching away to the skyline; wide fields of wheat; rich red soil. The poor Arab, shifting stones from an inhospitable hillside with his raw, bare hands, can look down the hill to see the skillful Israeli farmers working away there with their tractors and their trim, scurrying trucks, looking—at least through binoculars from Jordan—more like Middle Westerners than citizens of the Middle East. No Jordanian can legally visit Israel, for in Arab eyes a state of war still exists, and all this dispossessed peasantry may do is gaze in fury across the line towards its ancestral lands. I have travelled to this salient from both sides of the frontier, and I know that most of those Israeli farmers, though an unusually determined folk, are chiefly concerned with leading their lives securely and prosperously after generations of persecution. From Qalqiliya, though, through the eyes of a man who was born and brought up among those fields, who knows every inch of them as an English farmer knows his family acres, whose entire life and pride and ambition are bound up with that land—through the eyes of such a man, those Israeli farmers do look extraordinarily like thieves.

In Nazareth, an Arab city within the frontiers of Israel, a young man once told me blandly that he had just returned from a clandestine visit to Jordan; and nobody can be surprised that in these circumstances villagers from Qalqiliya sometimes sneak into Israel. They go to do a little pilfering from their old estates, or to visit relatives on the other side. They do a little smuggling. They continue, perhaps, that immemorial trade in hashish that has always colored the frontier activities of the Middle East. Sometimes, in the frenzy of their bitterness, they go specifically for revenge. Sometimes they go at the bidding of political extremists, or of opportunists who believe, in a woolly sort of way, that the more tension there is on the frontier the better it will be for them. Whatever their motives, they very often take a Sten gun with them, and the frontier at Qalqiliya is always nervous and often menacing.

Jordanian soldiers are thick on the ground, and usually seem to do their best (in the interests of peace, not from lack of sympathy) to prevent Arab marauders from crossing the line. From time to time, though, incidents increase, the death toll rises, the sense of emergency tautens, until suddenly something cracks in Tel Aviv or Jerusalem and the Israelis react with violence. One day in August, 1956, only two months before the battle in the Sinai, such a moment occurred at Qalqiliya. At the dead of night a powerful Israeli force burst across the frontier, headlights blazing, and raced through the village. Its momentum was overpowering. The police station, the Jordanian defense headquarters, was totally demolished with high explosive. Forty-five Arabs were killed, and many others wounded. By morning the Jews had withdrawn across the line again, and the surviving villagers were left, stunned and demoralized, destitute beside the ruins.

Of all the tragedies of this demarcation line, the most immediately moving is that of the city of Jerusalem. The frontier, established by bitter street fighting in 1948, runs clean through the place, with a tangle of barbed wire and a dingy strip of No Man's Land. From David's Citadel, headquarters of the Jordanian army command, you can look across to the Israeli position a few yards away; and from the King David Hotel in Israel you can gaze with thwarted longing upon the glorious walls of the Old City, as sacred to Jewry and to Islam as it is to Christianity. By a rare stroke of natural justice, all the old quarters of Jerusalem are in the hands of the Arabs, and nearly all the modern parts are in Israel. Refugees from New Jerusalem can sit with their coffee on the Arab side of the line and look across to their old shops and houses. On the Israeli skyline there is a big new building in modernistic style. It is a cultural center, in which the Israelis can indulge their passion for improving entertainment; but to the ordinary Arab it is a mystery, and an elderly merchant once asked me to let him know what it was, if I ever crossed to the other side, because it was just around the corner from his old grocery store, and he was curious about it.

For to the Arabs New Jerusalem is as firmly barred, as mysteri-

ous and totally inaccessible, as Bhutan or Inner Mongolia. Only
one narrow roadway crosses from one side to the other, infested
with barricades and watchposts. It is called the Mandelbaum Gate,
after an otherwise unknown merchant who once had a house
nearby, and who thus joins St. Stephen, Herod, the cities of Damascus and Jaffa, and the shining metaphysic of Zion in bestowing a
name upon a gate of Jerusalem. Traffic along this roadway is not
heavy. Officials of the United Nations pass through it, and con-
suls, parties of favored tourists, journalists, and the bodies of those
who are killed in frontier forays, who pass through this drab and
heartless portal to be buried in their own countries. For a few yards
people who pass through the Mandelbaum Gate are in a political
vacuum, the No Man's Land that divides Old Jerusalem from New.
When an American friend of mine once passed that way with his
family, his small daughter dropped a doll out of the window half-
way between the respective dragon's teeth. It lay there forlornly
in the road, spread-eagled, but nobody could get it back. They
could not stop the car. If an Arab soldier went out to pick it up
he would be fired upon by the Jews. If a Jew went out he would
be slaughtered by the Arabs. So the American doll lay abandoned
in the sunshine until, by the processes of diplomatic nicety, a consular official, flourishing his credentials, was able to walk into No
Man's Land to retrieve it.

Such are the sad antipathies of Jerusalem. Though they seem
horribly anomalous from a distance, somehow in the city itself
they do not appear altogether out of place. This has always been a
scene of bloodshed and bitterness, and it does not come as any
surprise, if you are wandering through the shuttered streets of
Old Jerusalem, to be reminded that a watchful enemy is only a
few yards away outside the walls. Despite it all, it remains golden.
It is still the holiest of holy places, still a magnificent Islamic city,
still a place of pilgrimage. If you climb to the Mount of Olives in
the evening you will find that its buildings, though scarred and
battered by the fighting, still look beautifully mellow and serene;
and through the shadowy, tortuous streets of the *suk* there still
move the pilgrims and priests, Bedouin, bootblacks, coffee sellers,
and gowned merchants of its tradition. There are Armenian priests,
ominously hooded, and Greeks in tall conical hats. The Muslim

women are thickly veiled, the Bedouin tribesmen are leathery, the Palestinian ladies dazzling. Parties of American pilgrims kneel at the Stations of the Cross in their cotton frocks; and there are adorable muddy-faced children, hurrying monks, and bent porters grunting their hoarse warnings to the passers-by. Wars may come and go, but Jerusalem remains miraculously the same, and the innumerable pious orders and institutions which function within its walls do so now as they have done, through all the wild vicissitudes of Palestinian history, since the beginnings of Christianity and Islam.

They have long been hardened to the danger and hatred that overhang Jerusalem. I climbed one night with a Polish nun to the roof of Dom Polski's, a little hostel for pilgrims in the very heart of the Old City. The city lay below us, softly illuminated, cobbles and high windows and a bright moon. From the bazaars arose the hum of the butchers and shoemakers and sellers of souvenirs; above the topsy-turvy jumble of rooftops the dome of the Church of the Holy Sepulcher stood solemnly. To the east the moonlight glistened on the Mosque of Omar, rivalled only by the Great Mosque at Damascus in its delicate solemnity. "Look!" said the nun, "the soldiers are practicing on the walls!" As she spoke, the white of her habit gleaming in the moonlight, I heard the familiar clink of a rifle butt, the clatter of ammunition boxes, and a muffled order from the battlements above the great Damascus Gate. "You see," she said, "they have cleared everybody away." Sure enough, the little square in front of the gate, hung with awnings like the deck of a tourist liner, was all deserted; and above it, on the dark face of the city wall, I caught a glint of metal and the flash of a torch. The Arabs, with an enemy literally at the gates of the city, were manning the walls of Jerusalem. This was an invested fortress, and the slightest incident—an accidental rifle shot, a stone tossed across the line in fun or bravado—could bring a storm of machine-gun fire and mortar shells over those high battlements. The nun sighed, but not, apparently, from fear or sadness. "Poor soldiers," she said, "they look so very young and they *do* seem to keep them working late."

To this protracted emergency, as to countless others, the Old City of Jerusalem has readily adapted itself. As somebody once remarked to me over lunch in the shadow of the walls, things were much worse in A.D. 70, when Titus was at the gates. The spirit of Jerusalem has withdrawn from the grand new suburbs, now in Israel, into the walled city. The streets are clean and seem reasonably prosperous. Big American cars are driven precariously up ramps and along ancient stepped alleyways. The Armenian postcard seller outside the citadel wears a new pair of shoes. An advertisement for a hotel announces spryly: "The Day, the Night, or as Long as you like. Your Room is Spacious and Airy, The Cosy Bar a Delight." The merchants seem to be fairly comfortable. To some extent this blithe spirit is whistling in the dark, for the whole of Jordan is suspended over economic doom, and Jerusalem depends to a dangerous degree upon the demands of tourism and piety. It is also, though, a reflection of the abnormally tough fiber of Jerusalem, where deaths and battles, hardships and privations, are perennial normalities.

Of course this sprightly commercialism pervades the holy things of Jerusalem, too, and repels some of the pilgrims who come to the city in their innocence, expecting all things bright and beautiful. The postcard man will certainly accost you outside the Garden of Gethsemane, and someone may well offer you a fragment of the True Cross, or a corner of St. Veronica's veil; but for myself, I do not feel that these activities tarnish the sanctity or delight of the city. The Church of the Holy Sepulcher has been infested for centuries by sectarian squabbles and commercial appetites; the various churches protect their respective rights of property and possession with a devotion that often seems to verge upon the vicious; and the building itself, constantly altered and extended, and propped up, since the 1927 earthquake, with a scaffolding of hideous iron girders, possesses something less than ethereal beauty.

And yet even for the skeptic or the unbeliever, there remains an incomparable magic to the church. In its great porch is the soft-carpeted divan on which the Muslim guardians of the church (hereditary officials) recline away the days; inside, the priests and pilgrims of a dozen different persuasions conduct their devotions. Here, down a dimly lit aisle, comes a procession of Franciscans: cultured voices and Gregorian chants, and a reverent visiting English priest, and a stream of pilgrims carrying lighted tapers, with two small boys at the back shuffling their feet. Hard on their heels come the Greeks. Harsh, grating and discordant is their music and their cassocks are rough and hairy. There are five or six young acolytes, their voices halfway between childhood and maturity, and hemmed in closely among them is an aged bishop, so enshrouded in his vestments that only his spectacles and a few white hairs can be glimpsed beneath his hood in the gloom; and he looks for a frightening moment as if he has no face at all, but is made of crumpled surplices. In every corner, in every secluded chapel, there are serious monks and whispering tourists, and guides whose rasping urgent murmurings echo among the gilded candlesticks. A family of Italians kneels to kiss the Stone of Unction (over the centuries such fervent kisses have worn away three stones already); and it is agreeable to observe the faces of visitors, cluttered with their cameras and guide books and lighted tapers, when they climb to a little upper chapel and realize suddenly, with awe or ecstasy, that they are standing upon the site of Calvary.

Spurious relics and grasping guides cannot spoil this place of sanctity. Indeed, I think they throw into relief the extraordinary magnetism of the place, which draws so perpetual a stream of pilgrims through every kind of danger and disturbance. I always remember the Church of the Holy Sepulcher as a place of pleasure. I once saw an old woman, horribly crippled, struggling down the last steps of the chapel of St. Helena, a dimly illuminated crypt. Her progress was agonizingly slow, but she was determined to reach the altar by herself. Slowly and painfully she shuffled down the stone steps. Her two sticks tapped and squeaked, and prayers were mingled with her heavy breathing. Each step was a torment. When at last she reached the bottom, though, and I peered into the dimness to watch her, she abruptly leaned down and placed her two sticks beside her on the ground. Then straightening herself as far as her old crooked frame would allow her, she raised her arms above her head in triumph and exuberance, more like some whip-corded young athlete at the moment of victory than a poor old woman, distorted and arthritic, who would soon have to face the steps again.

One other moment I remember with rapture from the Church of the Holy Sepulcher, a place of constantly shifting aspects and a building of unbelievable architectural complexity. The site of the sepulcher itself is maintained by the Greeks, and directly behind it there is a little chapel shrouded in black curtains. One morning, during a lull in the ceaseless round of the church's life, I found myself all alone beside the shrine; and as I stood there in the silence I thought I heard a faint ticking noise from inside. For a moment I stood hesitantly, thinking it might be the clicking of a perpetual censer, worked by some system of silver weights, or perhaps the swinging of an ornate lantern on its chain. But it was so regular and so insistent that I pulled the heavy curtains aside and looked in. There on the altar, all among the ikons and candlesticks, a red, moon-faced kitchen clock ticked away robustly, for all the world as if it were timing the eggs.

I laughed with pleasure at this unexpected discovery, and there was an answering chuckle behind me. Standing among the tall pillars of the rotunda, all but hidden in the shadows, there stood a gigantic Abyssinian priest in an attitude of serene meditation. When I turned to look at him, a white gleam in the darkness testified to the smile upon his black, bearded face.

Strong and resilient though the city may be, there is sadness enough in Jerusalem. You may not be wrung to tears by the lamentations of the refugee merchants, who will tell you all too often of the enormous stores, the vast estates, the bulging bank balances they invariably seem to have lost in the holocaust. But there is a genuinely tragic feeling to the spectacle of No Man's Land, which runs like a littered, disused highway, a blighted turnpike, between the two parts of Jerusalem. It is cluttered with derelict buildings, coils of wire, piles of miscellaneous rubbish. Into a few tumble-down buildings near the Arab line some humble house hunters have surreptitiously seeped. In the middle an Israeli housewife, in defiance of those map-makers in Rhodes, has hung out her washing. Away in the eastern corner of the Old City, near the Dung Gate, the old Jewish quarter lies depressed and destitute, inhabited only by scabrous Arab refugees, begging baksheesh clamorously as they scramble from their holes and ruins. The Wailing Wall is deserted, with never a pious paper inserted between Herod's gigantic stones.

Down at Beit Jala, only a mile or two away, that old man shouts a greeting to his daughter across the rusty barbed wire that separates them. Jerusalem retains as always its corners of sadness, its reminders of cruelty, and sometimes a veiled or hinted prophecy.

AQABA

If you board an aircraft and fly southward from Jerusalem, over the waste plateau of Qumran and the abyss of the Dead Sea, you will presently see below you the impossibly blue waters of the Gulf of Aqaba, with brown desert mountains rising on either side of them, and the fleck of coral reefs inshore. At the head of this gulf, tucked away among palm trees on the water's edge, stands the Jordanian port of Aqaba, an odd little place by any standards, and particularly individual in the inflamed and confused condition of the modern Middle East. When I first went to Aqaba, just after the war, there was nobody there but a few indigenous fishermen, a handful of merchants, an Englishman running a fishery, some soldiers of the Arab Legion, and the proprietor of a tumble-down hostelry called Claridge's, or perhaps the Savoy, who kept a small gazelle on the roof outside my window. Now Aqaba is important as well as genuinely exotic. The emergence of the State of Israel has blocked many of the Arab trade routes to the Mediterranean, and Aqaba is Jordan's only outlet to the sea. It is also immediately adjacent to the Israeli port of Elath, which lies resolutely on the other side of the bay, separated from Tel Aviv by the waste of the Negeb. The British still have troops in Jordan in 1956, and there is a small British base at Aqaba, chiefly to prevent any Israeli expansion across the top of the gulf. Its trim white huts and tank parks impose a patch of symmetry upon a wild setting, and its cheerful clubs and canteens brighten the beaches. (When King Hussein once visited the camp, he was greeted by a regimental sergeant-major with the magnificent formula: "Good morning, Mr. King of Jordan, *Sir!*")

Things military, though, sometimes seem falsely and crudely grafted upon the fabric of Aqaba. It is at once a shady and a distinctly romantic place. If you stand upon its sands and survey the surrounding scene you can see the territories of four countries—Jordan, Israel, Egypt, and Saudi Arabia—for here at the eastern corner of Sinai, Egypt shakes hands with her Arab brothers, around the barrier of Israel. Nobody can drive from Egypt to Jordan or Saudi Arabia, because the tiny strip of Elath, only a mile or two

wide, blocks the way; but the Egyptians fondly hope to build a
road across Sinai and run a ferry to the Saudi Arabian shore, thus
giving themselves a road link to the east for the first time since
1948. Aqaba is surrounded by enmities and subterfuges. Arab
dhows from the Peninsula anchor shiftily in its harbor. Bedouin
camel riders set out secretly from its hinterland to cross the unfriendly deserts of Israel to Egypt. In the small Crusader castle that
commands its main street, coveys of refugees brood revengefully
in nooks and crumbled crannies, cooking things over open fires in
old baked-bean cans. Often at night the distant chug of a motor
boat's engines whispers of hashish; and even when the day dawns
and the blazing sun lashes the sea, and the fishing boats ride merrily
out into the gulf, there lingers over the village the echo of last
night's illegalities, and the pungent promise of more to come.

Aquaba is set in country pregnant with history and fascination.
The old route of the Haj passed this way, *en route* from Damascus
to Mecca. A little way up the rough road, at Ma'an, is the present
terminus of the Hejaz Railway, with a little hotel outside the station hung thickly with faded mementos of the Arab Revolt, high-
collared English generals and hopeful Arab princes, and a curved
scimitar that smacks gorgeously of Lawrence at the apogee of his
heroics—and indeed at this very place Lawrence took part in some
stiff little skirmishes, and eventually pinched the station bell as a
memento of them. The rose-red city of Petra is not far away, where
the Arabs like to shoot at a stone urn on the façade of one of the
rock tombs in the ignorant belief that it contains treasure. "If it
doesn't contain treasure," remarked one hopeful to me as we stood
together looking at this ornate construction, "why put it there at
all?" And to this (for I am no admirer of the florid architecture
of Petra) I could find no very convincing retort. Farther north
stands the magnificent Crusader castle of Kerak; from it the bucca-
neering knights, swooping down from the mountains, used to harry
the shipping that plied uncomfortably up and down the Dead Sea.

It is a proud, high-vaulted hinterland. Only one road runs
through it; the terrain is desolate and unfriendly; and it is dominated by the presence of the Bedouin tribes that wander in it,

governed still by their own immemorial desert traditions. Under
the benevolent influence of Glubb Pasha, and within the molding
framework of the Arab Legion, the Bedouin of Jordan have been
moving with dignity away from their old lawless ways towards
some compromise with modernity. The Jordanian desert is now
one of the safest places on earth. Glubb's Desert Patrol will guide
you and protect you, and the tribesmen will welcome you with
their ancient hospitality untarnished. Too often the Bedouin of
the Arabian Peninsula, to the south, have been perverted by the
presence of oil. To the north, on the fringes of the sown land,
they are beginning to catch urban manners. Here in southern
Jordan they remain at their best. They have their schools and their
law courts and their government services; but they still inhabit
the land with pride, and their low, black, carpeted tents sprawl
there indolently with an air of spacious and well-bred poverty.

The Bedouin vary in habits from the genuinely nomadic, ranging
far across the Saudi frontier to the south and into Iraq to the east,
to the semi-settled tribes who till land and conduct their affairs on
the edge of the agricultural regions. The genuinely nomadic Arab
has advanced further along the road to Arab unity than anyone
else, for political demarcation lines, national boundaries, even the
identities of states have no meaning for him, and he measures
territories only as grazing grounds or tribal areas. In the old days
of incessant tribal wars, Bedouin raiding parties would travel to
the far corners of the Arab world to sell their booty in safety;
camels stolen in western Arabia would often turn up in Mosul or
Aleppo. So today the Bedouin are sometimes able to ignore even
the relentless frontiers of Israel, and cross from one friendly region
to another through the *kibbutzim*.

Just what constitutes a Bedouin tribe is difficult to define. Sometimes its members are scattered over immense distances, as members
of a Scottish clan are dispersed across the oceans. Often, for all the
invariably high-flown traditions, there seems to be no obvious
blood relationship or common place of origin. The only unifying
factor is some vague feeling of kinship, some sense of shared heritage. Tribes, it seems, create themselves like pearls, around small
and insignificant cores—perhaps about a leader who has given cohesion to a group of liegeless peasants, perhaps about the body-

guard of some celebrated camel thief, perhaps about the devotees of a remote and little-frequented holy place. Once established, the tribe can develop into one of the great tribal confederations which sprawl grandly across the Arab lands, or it can remain a little community of black, patched tents, huddled together in the wilderness.

Of these different tribal peoples, the true nomadic Bedouin remains the aristocrat, bound more firmly than others by the law of his kind, and contemptuous of those who toy with urban values. Mark Sykes once remarked (in the heyday of the Anglo-Arab flirtation, to be sure) that the Bedu's brain was as highly developed as that of any Englishman with a liberal education: there was no reasonable argument he could not follow, no situation he could not immediately grasp, nobody he could not understand—yet there was no manual act he could perform. I take these expressions of natural brotherhood ("Oh, the Bedu's nature's gentleman, you know. He and the English country squire have a great deal in common") with a strong pinch of salt. I very much doubt that the average Bedouin chieftain has so elaborate a mind as the Warden of All Souls, and the handling of camels in the desperate conditions of the desert seems to me a distinctly manual labor. Nevertheless, the Bedouin remains a figure of dazzling fascination, a man of ornate charm and subtlety, whose tents seem as distant from the frenzied bickerings of Amman or Damascus as Blenheim Palace does from Blackpool fun fair.

In the desert hills above Aqaba, one such Bedouin tribal leader lives in state. This great sheikh, son of a hero of the Arab Revolt, is a man of hospitality, and always welcomes strangers to his tents. He is nomadic, within the bounds of his accustomed grazing grounds, but any passing Bedu, leaning from his camel, will tell you where his encampment can be found; and soon enough you will see the tents in the distance, with a thin curl of smoke rising above them, and a camel or two tethered alongside, and a furtive scurrying of black-gowned women as you approach. No high-pitched Park Avenue hostess, with her eyes flickering over your shoulder to the next guest, can make you feel so honored by hospitality as can an old-school Bedouin leader. Nobody else, you feel sure, would be treated with quite such courteous condescension as this, though if you have time for reflection you will realize that

any destitute Central European student on a motor-scooter, passing
this way on some tedious marathon around the world, will find
a greeting just as lordly. Moreover, do not suppose that you are an
unexpected guest; somehow or other, by the peculiar desert intelligence of the Arabs, word of your coming has certainly preceded
you.

Here comes the old warrior now, stooping beneath the fabric of
his tent, followed and flanked by his henchmen. He straightens
himself nobly to await your arrival. There is nothing very ostentatious about his clothing—only the natural splendor of the Bedouin
costume, with its gold-edged *aba*, its white headdress, its brocaded
headcord, so wonderfully expressive of mood or manner, the
heavy, crossed bandoliers, and the thick leather sandals. But there
is something to the stance that is infinitely imposing. The chief
gathers his *aba* around him with a stately arrangement of its draperies, and tosses back his headdress with a slight movement of his
head, in a way that always reminds me of some great lady shaking
the folds of her silk brocade before sweeping into the ballroom.
At once you find yourself instinctively straightening your tie and
re-rolling the sleeves of your shirt; and when you step from your
jeep, probably tripping over the mudguard or getting the strap of
your camera inextricably entangled with the driving mirror, you
feel a most agreeable glow of flattered pleasure to find yourself
greeted with such attention.

So you recline on the carpets inside the tent, while the coffee is
prepared, and the conversation loiters from one subject to another
with plenty of laughter but not much momentum. The coffee is
served from brass jugs with a traditional elaboration of ritual that
may strike you as a trifle silly, but which certainly has an old-world
charm. The coffee-pourer serves you with stylized movements of
his pot; and there are one or two little formalities designed to convince you that you are not going to be poisoned. Sometimes the
weight of protocol will be relieved by the appearance, on an extremely distant horizon, of a couple of camel riders, and the company will compete among itself in identifying them first. Such
matters of fieldcraft are still dear to the Bedouin heart. Some tribesmen identify the hoof-marks of long-passed camels by methods
positively Holmesian. Some claim to tell, by the taste, from which

particular camel the milk has come. Some say, perhaps a little wildly, that they know by the texture of the mutton what color the sheep's wool was.

When the meat arrives, and is placed in its steaming bowl before you, with eggs and rice and sauces, the talk may well turn to matters of genealogy; for the old sheikh is not only an aristocrat, but also something of a snob. He loves to talk of his distinguished descent. He believes himself descended from Abraham, by way of Ishmael, and at the careless drop of a hat he will launch himself into the confused and dusty byways of pre-Islamic Arabia, his tribesmen picking their teeth in wonder, his women peering through cracks in the outside of the tent (they are not allowed inside), his guest, toying with the remains of his victuals, trying conscientiously to sort out the Khalids, the Ahmads, the Abdul-Rahmans, the Abdullahs, the Feisals, the Nasirs, and the Turkis, who seem to have recurred with breathless frequency through the tumbled centuries of the sheikh's ancestry.

This predilection for matters of heraldic tinge also colors the sheikh's political views. He does not view with much favor the run-of-the-mill politicians of the Arab world, and he is likely to regard the Egyptians as having gone to quite the wrong school. He is not by any means unreceptive to new ideas—the life of the Jordanian Bedouin has been transformed during the past quarter century—and he is, by the nature of the desert life, in many ways a thorough democrat. But he prefers things to be of organic growth, like the Great Mosque at Damascus, rooted in the soil or the heritage of the country. Ask him what he thinks of the Jews across the frontier, with their bright new concrete huts and their air services from Tel Aviv, and he will shake his splendid head and gather his cloaks around him with many a frowning, muttered "*Wellah!*" To him the Zionists are not only common thieves, as they are to the less high-flown Arabs to the north; they are also unspeakable parvenus. He speaks of them more with contempt than with hatred—an attitude that would certainly infuriate those clever young settlers who make experiments in advanced sociology in the *kibbutzim* of Israel, and who would probably either disembowel the sheikh or turn him into a tourist attraction. His associates murmur their equivalent of "Sure, sure, boss"; and when the meal

ends, and you prepare to leave, and the old sheikh rises gracefully
to his feet, these respectful people shoo away the little boys, and
can sometimes be seen surreptitiously rearranging the tentage, to
mask the curious womenfolk behind.

So you climb into your car and bounce away across the desert.
The sheikh stands there grandly, thinking genealogical thoughts,
until you are out of sight.

But Aqaba remains primarily a place of the sea. The Queen of
Sheba landed there, so the scholars seemed to think, when she came
in her golden fleet from southern Arabia to visit Solomon in Jerusalem. The Crusaders built a little sea fortress on the island of
Pharaoh, just in sight down the Egyptian coast. Renaud de Chatil-
lon, the Crusader lord of Kerak, based a fleet at Aqaba. His ships
ranged gloriously up and down the Red Sea, harrying the infidel
ports of the Hejaz, until the formidable Saladin first outfought him
and then personally beheaded him with a single stroke of his
scimitar. The Turks planned to build a big port at Aqaba, with a
railway to serve it. Lawrence saw it as a principal supply base for
the Revolt. The modern Jordanians optimistically hope that it will
one day be the channel for most of their imports, nowadays shipped
through Beirut. The world knows of it chiefly because of the
blockade enforced by the Egyptians at the entrance to the Gulf,
intended to hasten the throttling of Israel. Often enough there is
a small steamer lying offshore; and there is a little fishing industry;
and a white customhouse which the Turks built among the palm
trees. The place is impregnated with salt water, and almost everyone there understands the sea and knows his way about in a boat.
If you venture into the water wearing goggles you will find its bed
speckled with a gorgeous variety of strange sea creatures: parrot
fish and eels, urchins, sharks, chicken fish, one or two organisms
for which the Arabs have vulgar nicknames, and innumerable vivid,
indescribable swimming things. Above this unseen paradise Aqaba
stands, its back to the mountains, looking with a certain fixed and
glassy stare (for as a port it was not really a great success) towards
the Arabian Sea.

For a full-blooded taste of this marine flavor I once went out for the night with an Aqaba fisherman. We sailed at dusk from the quayside in an elderly motorboat called *Fred* (or it may have been *Alf*) and chugged away into the night down the coast of Saudi Arabia. Nothing we did, so far as I remember, was altogether legal. Our methods were strictly forbidden. Our fishing grounds were in foreign territorial waters. From time to time we landed illegally upon the shore of Saudi Arabia. I have no doubt that the market for which our catch was destined was not confined very firmly within the bounds of Jordanian fiscal law. Our crew was brash and swarthy, and our skipper was a roistering rascal with a bellowing voice and an enormous horny hand for slapping people on the back. Down the coastline we went, our stout engine echoing across the water. Towards midnight, keeping a wary eye open, we beached ourselves upon the sandy Saudi shore, and somebody opened a bottle of whisky. Our first task was to catch crayfish, one of the specialties of that coastline. Off into the night we waded, splashing through the shallows, leaving the *Fred* an indistinct hulk behind us. In front went a man with a big acetylene lamp, hissing furiously. Next went the skipper, wearing huge leather gloves and flexing his muscles for the fight. A young man with a red can carried a sack expectantly and the rest of us followed chattering behind. But suddenly an urgent whisper from the front told us to be silent, and we plashed on quietly with only the sizzling of the lamp and a few stifled mutterings from the crew. "There 'e is!" suddenly boomed the skipper, in the English he had learned from the British army; and with a bellow he threw himself headlong into the water. In the pool of the lamplight he threshed and struggled and spluttered among the rocks, with grunts and bubbles. "I've got 'im!" he shouted. "I've got the bastard!" And slowly, with such boisterous imprecations, he straightened himself in the water, grinning all over his face, still grunting and spluttering, the water pouring from his hair, until he was able to hold out in the glare of the lamp a gigantic dark armored crayfish.

After three or four hours of this, when the big sack was full of heaving protrusions, we snatched some sleep on the cool deck of the *Fred;* and when I woke from it we were at sea again, and the Saudi coast was dim behind us. Now we were after fish. Across the bay in Elath the Israelis could not maintain a fishing industry, despite the legendary richness of the waters, because none of their polyglot community wanted to be fishermen. Here among the Arabs of Aqaba the pursuit seemed to be at once a profession and a pastime, and we sailed out into the blue in a spirit of exhilaration. When the sun was well up and the sea was blue and pellucid, and we could see deep down into its depths, the skipper took up position in the bow of the boat. For half an hour we cruised slowly in the sunshine, looking for shoals; when we found one we slid slowly among it with muffled engines, like a tiger creeping among gentler creatures. Cautiously the skipper withdrew from his bag an old tobacco tin, packed tight with dynamite. Stealthily he drew upon his cigarette, and touched its lighted end gently to the fuse. Calmly and quietly he threw that bomb into the deep. The plop of its submersion was followed by a few seconds of silence.

But the explosion that followed was tremendous. A spout of water billowed high into the air, spewing up bits of bomb, parts of fishes, shells, coral and seaweed. The boat rocked. The captain turned and grinned at me. The engines stopped. In a trice we were all of us in that water, so unbelievably clear, tossing the stunned fish into the hold of the boat. A few hundred yards away the fins of sharks were circling expectantly, though not menacingly; and in a few moments a rickety little log boat appeared from the Saudi shore, paddled desperately by two half-naked scavengers. But most of the catch was ours, and we scooped it from the surface of the water and tossed it over the side of the boat with gay abandon. Soon the bottom of the *Fred* was piled high with fishes, blue and gold and spotted, like dogs or birds or nightmare animals, with eyes of porcelain and fins of nylon bristle.

We cooked a few of them for breakfast, on the Saudi shore; and the crew did a little wrestling on the sands, locked in brown silhouette against the sun; and the captain stretched himself out half-naked and slept; and presently, hoisting our gear aboard, we sailed slowly and contentedly home.

Such is the temperament of Aqaba, strange, gay and beautiful. There are people who dislike Aqaba, or who see it only as a hot, dull little village on the edge of a desert and on the shores of a blazing sea.

I have savored it in many circumstances, though—from the roof of Claridge's, from the comfortable tent of a cavalry mess, from the deck of a ship offshore, from the smart hotel at Elath, from a bumpy jeep breasting the last rise of the rough run down the Wadi el-Araba; and for me nothing can mask the truly exotic character of the place, nor dull the glamor of its setting. In the evening you can sit on its beach and see the hills of four Powers stretching about you, and watch Elath settle down to dinner surrounded by its implacable enemies. You will eat without a qualm or a raised eyebrow that green and orange fish with a face like an elderly hog, and at night find yourself lulled to sleep by the mythical murmur of sheikhs.

PART THREE

Miles
0   100   200   300

KUWAIT

Dhahran○ ○Bahrain
Hasa○   QATAR
Medina○   ○Riyadh   TRUCIAL OMAN. Buraimi
                                   ○Muscat
S A U D I   O   ○Nizwa
Jidda○   M
○Mecca   A R A B I A   A
                             N

Y
E
M   ○Shibam   ○Salala
E   ○San'a E.ADEN PROTECTORATE
N   W.ADEN PROT. ○Mukalla
    ○Aden

THE PENINSULA

SOUTH OF THE SYRIANS, east of the Egyptians, lies the
peninsula of Arabia, the cradle of Arabism, the Holy Land of Islam,
from which in the ninth century the irresistible Muslim armies
burst with pious battle cries to sweep across a quarter of the world.
Arabia is still mostly desert. The southwestern corner is hilly and
well-populated. Elsewhere there are patches of cultivation, pockets
of mountain country, scattered green oases, a few ancient cities.
But most of it is sand or gravel, wilderness inhabited, if at all, by
roaming Bedouin, enriched only by the presence of oil. The peninsula is almost as big as India, and contains perhaps as many people
as London, and around its perimeter are a number of interesting
political entities, ranging from a British colony through innumerable semi-independent sheikhdoms to the big and disagreeable
Imamate of the Yemen, a vocal member of the United Nations but
a state immured in the gloom and squalor of medieval autocracy, with head-choppings, public executions, slavery, witchcraft,
and all.

But the dominant force in this region is the Kingdom of Saudi
Arabia. It arose after the First World War through the energies of
its remarkable founder, Ibn Saud, and since 1932 it has comprised
nine-tenths of the peninsula. If its leaders had their way, it would
probably comprise ten-tenths, for their claims to sovereignty over
the coastal regions are strident and persistent, and their arguments
exceedingly intricate. Mecca is in Saudi Arabia, and gives it a special
position of sanctity and privilege in the Middle East; but so are the
great oil fields of Hasa, and the vast oil royalties issuing from them
have surrounded Saudi Arabia with an ambiance of arrogance,
avarice, hypocrisy and conspiracy. The Saudis, animated partly by
festering dynastic squabbles with Iraq and Jordan, are linked in
unnatural alliance with Colonel Nasser, and have often played the
part of his financiers (though there are signs, by the autumn of
1956, that they are beginning to shy away from the more inflammatory of his policies). I remember all too clearly one of the more
vicious demonstrations in Jerusalem, Jordan, in which this venom-
ous duality was clearly illustrated. It was evening, and I was having

a drink with the American Consul. His house had been stoned by demonstrators only a week or two before, and most of its windows were shuttered; nevertheless, when we heard the distant, familiar grumble of a political procession, we went out to the balcony to see it pass by. The marchers carried torches and beat drums and shouted praises of Nasser and abuse of the West, and their prancing figures streamed up the road beside the house with that awful half-crazed, drunken, ignorant roar of fury so characteristic of rioters everywhere. They took no notice of us as we watched them in the half-light, but made their way up the hill towards the Saudi consulate; and presently we saw a figure dart out of that building and hand something to the most inflamed and savage of the rioters. It was a furled flag. When those wild agitators came down the hill again, with their drumbeats and grimaces, they carried before them like a crooked talisman the colors of the Saudi kingdom.

It is difficult to escape the *nouveau riche* effrontery of the Saudis anywhere in the Middle East. So perverted is their society by the wealth of oil, so cramped their alleged contempt for the West, that the once proud name of Saudi is becoming all but synonymous with rudeness and intolerance. To be sure, there are still Saudi gentlemen graced with the old Islamic courtesies; but applying for a visa at a Saudi consulate in the Middle East is generally a trying process, in which the humble occidental, his mind very firmly on his visa, must endure in silence the slings and arrows of a truly outrageous fortune. The Arab in authority can be as deliberately nasty as any Turk, and at least as overbearing as the horrible British Consul encountered by Richard Burton at Alexandria. His technique is given subtlety by a clever exploitation of the slipshod, so that it is only when you arrive at Dhahrow airport that you find your visa is stamped with the wrong year, or expired last Tuesday, and that you must endure a night's uncomfortable confinement before being shipped back to Beirut again ("and that will be two dinars airport tax, thank you").

My own introduction to Saudi Arabia was less orthodox, though scarcely less characteristic. When the British army still had a Guards battalion at Aqaba, its officers often used to go swimming or fishing a little way down the eastern shore of the Gulf of

Aqaba. Somewhere along there was the frontier with Saudi Arabia, but it had never been demarcated, and nobody knew precisely where it was. However, the soldiers were nearly always interrupted towards the end of the afternoon by the arrival of a few Saudi policemen, festooned with arms and ammunition, who insisted that this was an international outrage, and wrote down everybody's name in laborious pencil script on grubby pieces of paper. The soldiery was not much perturbed by this formality, and the policemen often conveyed to their superior the information that Lord Nelson, Agamemnon, Helen of Troy, or Tennyson had infiltrated the kingdom; but the Saudis made an issue of it, and before long the bathing expeditions were officially banned.

Saudi law, however, is an elastic conception, and some time later I was surprised to be told that two army jeeps were going down the coast to a Saudi village some thirty miles across the frontier, and would I like to go? "There's a sort of prince down there, d'you see, with a nice flash Buick, and he likes our chaps to do a little maintenance for him now and then. Strictly on what they call the old boy net, of course, so don't breathe a word, will you?"

So off we went. The track down the coast is one of the pilgrim routes to Medina, worn by the feet of many pious generations, and still the last stretch of the journey for those many Muslims from North Africa who make the pilgrimage on foot. Nobody stopped us when we crossed the frontier area: the policemen had been warned. When we approached the village, a pleasant place upon a cove, four or five well-armed men welcomed us with respect. They were slaves. Slavery is still a well-established institution in Saudi Arabia. The law allows it, as does Islam itself, and there is plenty of evidence that Negro slaves are still imported from the east coast of Africa, often tricked into the journey by the prospect of pilgrimage. Ibn Saud, indeed, did his best to humanize the conditions of slavery with a decree, enacted in 1936, which was, by the standards of the environment, daringly progressive; but as an industry and a social institution, slavery is still important to the Saudis, unlikely though it may sometimes seem amidst the hygiene of the oil towns or the grand office blocks of Jidda. Among rich men a young slave girl is an acceptable gift. Among merchants a stout Negro is a useful piece of equipment. The

British Anti-Slavery Society believes there are about half a
million slaves in the Arabian Peninsula—about five percent of the
population; and four or five of them, looking cheerful and well-fed,
guided us through the village to the palace of the Emir.

It was not a pretentious structure, and looked more like a fort
than a home, but the Emir seemed to live in comfortable circumstances. We sat on fine rugs, ate some excellent food, and were
waited on attentively by household servants without number. I
was foolish enough to have a severe headache in the middle of the
meal and was promptly given a packet of Aspro, presented to me
with delicacy on a silver tray. The Emir, dressed a good deal more
expensively than our Bedouin seigneur above Aqaba, talked at
length. He was a member, I gathered, of the royal house (Ibn Saud
had at least eighty sons), established in this distant corner of the
kingdom as regent or khedive. He seemed very sure of himself.
He hoped his car would not be giving more trouble, smiled dis-
tantly when I mentioned the policemen on the seashore, swore a
few oaths of undying hostility to the Jews, and ate fastidiously but
with energy. When we left him, after protracted and ceremonious
goodbyes, he was crouching in the corner over an enormous radio,
his resplendent robes spilling about him, his long fingers twiddling
the knobs impatiently. At last he found his station, and as the slaves
saw us to the jeeps, we heard the booming voice of an announcer
emerging from the building behind us. It was Radio Israel, broad-
casting the news in Arabic.

The scandals of Saudi Arabia are so well known as to be a stock
joke throughout the Middle East. The national oil royalties are
about three hundred million dollars a year, but intermittent attempts to produce any kind of budget have not been a great success.
This is not surprising, for the educational system of Saudi Arabia
is so stunted that even its bureaucracy is practically illiterate. Moreover, since there is no kind of elected assembly, no sort of popular
representation whatever, the spending of state funds is entirely in
the hands of the royal family. There have been some public developments of worth, mostly conducted under American inspiration. A road now crosses the peninsula, and a railway with trim

diesel engines connects the capital city of Riyadh with the eastern coast. Jidda, a city still ennobled with Arab houses of the old style (shuttered, projecting windows and topsy-turvy balconies), has a new water system, new port facilities, and some public buildings of merit. There are a number of new hospitals (but hardly any doctors to run them). Some attempts at irrigation have been made, and one or two factories established. More is now being spent on education. Nevertheless, you do not have to be long within the frontiers of Saudi Arabia to realize that the pockets of the royal house must be extraordinarily well lined.

I am told that King Saud himself has tried to modify the extravagances of the monarchy. He is a tall and ineffectual-looking man, handicapped by extreme short sight, so that he wears the thickest possible spectacles, and weakened by the suggestion of protruding teeth. People say he is kindly, but seen at a distance, as he emerges from the recesses of his limousine or is greeted unctuously by some fellow ruler, he looks more sinister than paternal, like an ill-intentioned magician. Certainly he seems to have done little to restrain his personal expenditures. He now has twenty-four palaces in different parts of the kingdom. He is pulling down the old one at Riyadh, a delightful building (by no means a slum) with a handsome and unusual curved colonnade above its entrance. The new one will be nearly a square mile in area and will cost about forty-eight million dollars. It will have schools for his many sons, a zoo, a private mosque, and a hospital; there will also be quarters for all his wives, anything up to a hundred of them. Saud is said (nobody really knows) to have about twenty-five sons. Each, when he reaches the age of twelve, is provided with a personal Cadillac and a driver—a circumstance handsomely confirming the justice of that celebrated *New Yorker* cartoon in which the Arab sheikh's son, looking prodigal but penitent, confesses to his father that he has smashed a Cadillac—"one of the blue ones."

Nevertheless, as often in such oriental societies, it is chiefly the relatives of the King, rather than the King himself, who earn the royal house its reputation for excess. There are more than three hundred princes of the royal blood, each of them of some political importance because of the tribal origins of his mother. Each is now paid a salary by the state, but most are able to draw upon much larger privy funds. Those indeed who are members of the King's nominated council are officially paid about $300,000 a year; many of the others have invested heavily in real estate and business. Much of the fabulous building boom in Cairo is financed by Saudi royal funds; a big new hotel in Beirut is Saudi-owned; all over the Middle East, if you examine the financial structure of society, you will find Saudi money at work. This sordid plutocracy, sprung in two generations from the austere tents of the Arabian desert, stands totally above the law (except the indulgent laws of the family), and is often to be observed in all its dubious splendor, surrounded by scented retainers, coffee-makers, barbers, Cadillacs, incense, and an aura of bottomless and undeserved resource, lording it in grand hotels abroad. There has never been a ruling class of such glittering patrimony; and if you would see the Arab at his coarsened worst, observe some Saudi princeling in his vulgar car, emblazoned with the crossed swords of his blood, sweeping through the citizenry with a sneer upon his face and a total disregard of the traffic rules.

The biggest city of Saudi Arabia is Jidda, a relatively cosmopolitan seaport, which is the gateway to the cities of Mecca and Medina. Through this city pass those thousands of Muslims who make the pilgrimage each year by sea. Christians may not visit the Holy Places, and it is therefore in Jidda that the Westerner may best see these people approaching the culmination of their spiritual adventure, and the fulfillment of their most cherished ambition. This is the end of their journey; the beginning you can watch, at the time of the Haj, anywhere in the Muslim Middle East. In Cairo you will find the stationyard cluttered with poor pilgrims lounging the night away among their blankets or dancing to the watery music of pipes and drums. At Aqaba the pilgrim ships arrive to load their passengers—shabby old vessels diverted each year from their pottering voyages around the Indian Ocean, and packed to the gunwales with pilgrims, till they sail away down the Red Sea girded with heat and sweat and piety. From Basra the motor convoys set out; in the big airport at Beirut you may see rich pilgrims, already in the austere white robes of the pilgrimage, boarding their charter aircraft for the Hejaz. Those old Turkish tailors, their carpet finished, take a short holiday; those garage men in Damascus wipe their hands. During the weeks of pilgrimage the whole Muslim world has part of its heart in Mecca.

Until oil was found in Saudi Arabia, this annual rite was the economic mainstay of the Arabian Peninsula; and if the oil ever runs out it may have to be so again. It is therefore pertinent to consider how potent a force Islam remains in the Middle East, whether it is waxing or waning, whether it can ever be a basis of political unity or whether it is being slowly estranged from the secular affairs of the region. More than Christianity, Islam has been, in its great days, a rule of life, a complete submission to the will of God. All are equal under Allah, and every aspect of human conduct must be governed by the rule of Islam. There is an immense body of Muslim law by which the devotee can regulate with assurance his every act and thought. There are parts of the Middle East where life is still conducted on this strict Koranic basis; there are others where life is nominally governed by Islamic orthodoxy; there are some, such as Lebanon, where the presence of important Christian minorities has diluted the insistencies of Islam; and there are still others, notably Egypt, where Muslim thought no longer plays a very significant part in the running of the state.

Nearly everywhere the common people still observe the formalities of Islam, and most of them probably cherish the desire to visit Mecca. The Islamic feast days are lavishly observed. The mosques on Fridays are generally crowded. During Ramadan, the month of fasting, the entire Middle East is united in days of abstinence, nights of festivity, and an understandable flavor of suppressed bad temper. The festival of Bairam which ends it is perhaps rather more deeply embedded in religious thought than is Christmas. For what it is worth, the everyday language of the Arab world remains inextricably linked with Muslim sentiment, so that almost every sentence is uplifted by a reference to Allah and his mercy. The Muslim calendar is still used in the Middle East. The years are reckoned from the year of the Hegira, Mohammed's migration from Mecca to Medina, and are designated A.H.—*anno hegirae;* to convert Muslim years into Christian years the following formula is used: $A.H. - \dfrac{3 \ A.H.}{100} + 621 = A.D.$ The simpler manifestations of Islam—the kindliness that often goes with its piety, the haunting music of its muezzins, the generosity, the stateliness and resonance of idiom—are among the perennial solaces of the Middle East.

Politically the power of Islam is less deep-rooted, but not to be disregarded. There are several states, notably Saudi Arabia and Yemen, which like to regard themselves as theocracies, and several small principalities in which Islam is genuinely the yardstick of official conduct. In the more advanced countries it is less the established church, so to speak, which is a power in the land, than those fanatical extremist organizations so often engendered by Islam. It is fashionable nowadays to proclaim Islam the most tolerant of faiths, to compare the chivalry of Saladin with the frequent barbarity of his opponents, and to exalt the climate of opinion which allows so many minorities to flourish within the Muslim countries. I do not altogether accept this view, and I would suggest that one of the Western apologists for Islam make the journey (not in disguise) to the Holy Places of the Hejaz, where he would probably be tolerantly torn into a million pieces. No great religion spews up so many vicious extremist groups as does Islam, and no religion of my experience is animated by so constant an undercurrent of intolerance. A driving force of great malice and ambition characterizes such movements as the Muslim Brotherhood of Egypt and the parallel Fedayin el Islamin of Persia; and it is this very malignant dynamism that makes them politically important. Nasser's principal organized opposition comes from the Muslim Brotherhood. Except for the Communists, the Fedayeen form the most potent opposition group in Persia. I cannot believe that they represent any very widespread popular feeling, but it is just possible to conceive a Middle East united by a series of governments of this temper, as the disparate units of Arabia were united thirty years ago by the flaming puritanical zeal of Ibn Saud. If you think this fanciful, remember that in 1956 the most obvious alternative to military government in Egypt was government by the Muslim Brothers.

Extremism apart, it does not seem probable that the force of Islam can again unite the Middle East. The strongest binding factor in the religion has always been the Sharia, or Muslim Canon Law, at least as important to the development of the Middle East as

English Common Law has been to the Anglo-Saxon community. It is therefore interesting to see how many of the major Middle Eastern States still recognize the Sharia as the law of the land. In Saudi Arabia and the Yemen it remains supreme. In Syria and the Lebanon, Jordan, Iraq, and Persia it remains valid only in personal or specifically Muslim matters. In Egypt, the pace-maker of the Middle East, the Sharia Courts were abolished altogether in 1955. Among the intellectuals and the administrators of the region the movement is indisputably away from Islam as a code of state conduct. The idea of pan-Islam is all but dead. Who can conceive Pakistan merging her fortunes with Morocco? Or, even less likely, Persia with the Yemen? Most of the Arab progressives would, if they dared defy the influential orthodox and the simple faith of the innocent, be protagonists of secularism in government.

In 1955 there was a *cause célèbre* in Egypt which well delineated the tug-of-war between orthodoxy and liberalism. Nasser has been shrewd enough to foster even the more hidebound proponents of old-fashioned Islam, and the ancient university of Al Azhar still plays an active, if sometimes risible, part in Egyptian affairs. There was therefore an incredulous and violent reaction when one of its professors suddenly published an article expressing the view that fasting during Ramadan was not a *sine qua non* for entry into Paradise. Egypt (and the Islamic world) was staggered by this heresy. The brilliant Cairo cartoonists, all on the side of modernism, made caustic fun of the fogies of Al Azhar. The celebrated novelist Taha Hussein came out on the side of the heretic, but later recanted. The daughter of the Rector of Al Azhar let it be known that she disagreed with her father's conventional ideas on marriage. Al Azhar was described in one newspaper as "a cemetery for freedom of thought." The Rector summoned the lecturer before a disciplinary council, the nearest thing modern Islam can offer to the panels of the inquisition or the congressional committee. The lecturer sued the Rector for libel, in Egypt a desperate step indeed.

The denouement was especially interesting, for the brave sheikh, who had by then established himself in the popular mind as a young giant killer defying the ogres of orthodoxy, suddenly and completely surrendered. Perhaps the revolutionary government, with its eye on its allies in Saudi Arabia and the Yemen, had given him a discreet warning. Perhaps it was apparent, in some subtle way, that the powers of Al Azhar were still more formidable than the modernists. Perhaps the sheikh simply needed the money. Whatever the reason, he recanted absolutely. His original article had contained "printing errors"; he withdrew his action against the Rector; he had been, in short, wrong. "I am not infallible," said the sheikh abjectly.

Throughout this affair there was little doubt where the sympathies of the literate public lay. The faith of Islam, with its insistence on predestination and its origins in the paganism of Arabia, is perhaps proving less compelling to the young educated Arab than is Christianity to his opposite number in Europe. Before many generations have passed, we may expect to see a Middle East dulled by the familiar religious apathy of the West. Already Islam, in many ways a noble belief, has sunk into a slough of aridity, and produces no flowering of thought or craftsmanship, no grandness or freshness of inspiration. There are those who say, indeed, that the Arab renaissance can never come about until the shackles of this deadening religion are loosened; my own feeling is that it is decaying fast, and will soon no longer be a major political factor in the affairs of the Middle East (but I would prefer not to argue the point with the Supreme Guide of the Muslim Brotherhood).

No such brash young clerics are yet to be found in Saudi Arabia, and though the spirit of Islam can scarcely be described as inviolate many of its precepts are still firmly applied. For a taste of life under Islamic orthodoxy it is only necessary to visit the American oil camps and air base in the eastern part of the country, near the Persian Gulf. In most parts of the Middle East the foreigner and the Christian are excused the rigidities of Islam. The Saudis, though their wealth depends upon American enterprise and ingenuity, grant few spiritual concessions to their American guests.

In the usual American way, the oil and air-force families have established themselves very comfortably in Hasa. It is a desert region, hot and empty, but not altogether unlike parts of the American West; and in so sunny and dry a climate, in such immense landscapes, the American way of life, so continental in temper, does not seem out of place. The ranch houses are neat and crisp; the refrigerators are well-stocked; the suburban roads are so wholesome and ordinary that you may expect Junior to come whistling down the sidewalk with the newspapers; and in the dinette, as you eat your ice-cream, you may watch the Burns and Allen Show on television (there is a transmitter at the air base, an astonishing boon for every rich Arab within fifty miles). All the paraphernalia of Americanism is here, and the women, though indeed they do not seem to know very much about Arabia or the Arabs, home-perm one another's hair assiduously.

But if the Saudis depend upon the Americans for technique, the Americans depend upon the Saudis for oil, and in these spick-and-span communities you cannot escape the anomalous intrusion of Islam. If your hostess wishes to buy you a camel saddle in the bazaar, you must drive the Plymouth; for no American woman may drive a car in Saudi Arabia, except in the company compounds. If she belongs to a Great Books Discussion Group, she will find herself handicapped when she returns to Ohio; for no books may be imported into Saudi Arabia. If she wants a highball, she must build her own still in the kitchen; liquor is forbidden in Saudi Arabia. If she gets a letter from a friend in Israel, she is instantly deported; a Tel Aviv postmark will be sufficient grounds. She cannot go to church, for Christian services are forbidden in Saudi Arabia; the priest who sometimes flies in from Bahrain, in the manner of an early Christian evangelist, describes himself to the Saudi authorities as a teacher. "Oh, sure," says your hostess, "they'll have us all veiled before long—over my dead body!"

For so supreme is the authority of the Saudis in the peninsula, so vast are this country's deposits of oil, so blinkered (but often selective) its adhesion to Islamic orthodoxy, and so overbearing its instincts towards aliens, that even the most pervasive society on earth is not proof against its impositions.

QUEEN'S ARABIA

IF THE BODY of the Arabian Peninsula is thus dominated by
this antique plutocracy, many of the coastal districts are still, in
one way or another, controlled by the British government. Among
Westerners, this is a little-known paradox. Among the policy
makers of the Arab world, it is a running sore, and a situation that
they are determined, by hook or by crook, to end. In general the
British position in Arabia is assured by a series of agreements, of
widely varying import and effectiveness, with the innumerable
petty feudalists entrenched there. Most of these local rulers are of
little education and restricted vision; a few are adaptable and enlightened; none of them seem, in the present stormy circumstances
of Islam and Arabia, to have very much chance of surviving in
their present dignities. All over the Middle East the winds of
progress are sweeping, and even in the far fringes of Arabia they
are beginning to ruffle the gowns and rattle the sword-trappings
of feudalism. So far the British have not devised a satisfactory sub-
stitute for their system of alliances with petty potentates. There
is thus, even in the most idyllically unspoiled of the British-con-
trolled countries, a certain sense of tension and impending trouble.

The only British Crown Colony in Arabia is the bunkering
station of Aden, which lies near the southwestern corner of the
peninsula in a situation of startling discomfort. "To the newcomer
to Aden," says an official pamphlet, "this famous fortress and port
presents rather a forbidding aspect." This, I think, is an under-
statement. At first sight Aden strikes most newcomers as unmistak-
ably the most repellent city in the Middle East. During more than
a century of prosperous rule Britain has not brought one single
beautiful thing to Aden, and it stands there on its way, blasted
and despondent, as if life had become one long awful hangover.
Its streets are cracked and rubbish-blown. Its buildings are drab,
its shops slatternly. Its setting is infused with savage force, but there
is little sense of majesty or power to the vast rambling installations
which announce the faded presence of the British Raj. A hangdog,
shabbily mercantile feeling permeates the geometrical streets of the

colony, and only the great ships offshore, endlessly steaming in and out of the harbor, give it any sense of grace.

In the Middle East this is unusual. Almost every city has some mosque of dignity, some cool, austere courtyard, some endearment of manner. Aden, though, has none of the piquancy or spice of an Arab city. Its people are a hodge-podge of races—Arabs, Somalis, Hindus, Parsis, Jews, Egyptians, Syrians, Persians, Chinese, British —and its traditional purpose has been a grubby and graceless one: a coaling station. It is a great merchant center too, an air base and a naval station; but it is all too easy to equate the place, as you stroll its blighted boulevards, with one of those desolate coal yards that lie depressingly among the purlieus of English railway stations. Today it is mostly oil, but one or two coal-bunkering firms still survive, and do good business (so I am told), largely with Russian ships. There is no sense of aristocracy to Aden, no hints of gilded excess, no swaggering princelings, no imams of unspeakable sanctity. Its vices, you may feel, are squalid ones, tucked away in smutty backstreets; and its virtues, though very real, are a terrible bore. The old part of the Aden Colony is called Crater, because it is built inside the cirque of an extinct volcano; and in this dismal place there are some archaeological remains to which the unsuspecting visitor is sure to find his way. The famous cisterns, so we are told, were probably built in the millennium before Christ for the storage of rain water; and so important are they, *qua* cisterns, and so fresh a light do they throw upon the pre-history of Aden, and so lonely is the eminence they occupy among the sights of the city, that you will no doubt approach them with an interest not easily to be repressed. Calm yourself. Of all the archaeological remains I have ever seen, of all the unrecognizable ruins and battered bulls, the cracked water pots and lumps of lead, the bits of chariots and buttons and painted ostrich shells and rusty spears and headbands from the tombs of Bronze Age chieftains—of all these scholarly phenomena, the cisterns in the Crater at Aden are easily the dullest.

Melancholy, too, hangs heavily around the crags of Aden. When they talk nowadays of the empire on which the sun never sets, they are surely thinking of Aden. It is drenched with the mystique of empire. Its climate is atrocious, its manner garrisonic, and the visitor must climb about four hundred almost perpendicular steps to sign the Governor's visitors' book. Until 1937 the colony was administered by the government of India, and its character today is still masked by a façade of British India. Indian merchants and lawyers abound. Laborers are coolies here, Englishmen are sahibs, the *suk* is the bazaar. The spirit of the Indian Empire lives on, perhaps more potently than anywhere else, getting more tattered through the decades but not yet superseded by anything else. The old fans twirl slowly in the offices of the secretariat. The sweating bank clerks, in their shirt sleeves, write slowly in big ledgers above the go-downs. In the public gardens there are notices saying "For Parents and Ayahs Only," and up on the hill the Union Jack still flies all but imperturbably. If you would like a sad, nostalgic reminder of the British heyday, go to the Union Bar in Aden for your sundowner; the box-wallahs will be drinking their whiskies by the bar, wearing cummerbunds and talking about the price of hides or the boorish behavior of the brigade major; and their women will, with luck, be wearing those shapeless and respectable cottons which one used to see, labelled "Tropical Wear," in a magical window of Robinson and Cleaver's in Regent Street; and there will be copies of *Sporting and Dramatic* in the morning room; and from the verandah you will be able to inspect whatever spick-and-span and obsolescent cruiser happens to be showing the flag in the harbor. There is a certain somber attraction to this spectacle; and one can only wonder at the resilience of this fusty old organism, which has creaked on through the years like a steam train on some unhurried country line, and still has the same kind of determined strength as some crochety, but faintly twinkling, old relative who refuses to die.

It is a rich old body, too. Aden is a free port, and a great *entrepot* center. It distributes goods in many parts of Aden and East Africa; and through its wharves there pass to the markets of the world all kinds of eastern substances—skins, hides, coffee, mother-of-pearl— whose names on packing cases seem pungently anomalous among the drab Adeni warehouses. A vast new oil refinery seethes on one of the peninsulas of the colony. More ships arrive every year to refuel, and their passengers stream ashore to buy horrible handbags,

Leicas, watches, and Arab costumes for the fancy-dress ball with which the ship's captain plans, in desperation, to kill an evening on the long voyage home. Aden, for all its slatternly appearance, is very prosperous. Three or four merchant princes dominate the commercial life of the place. They have recently been having some labor trouble, for the trade-union idea (spiced with a strong pinch of nationalism) has caught on in Aden; but they seem to be still very comfortably enthroned. The greatest of these merchant families, that of Besse and Company, describe themselves as general merchants, importers, exporters, government and building contractors, ship repairers, refrigeration and radio engineers. They are agents for cars, oil engines, ropes, batteries, binoculars, dyes, citrus fruit, wire, gin, tires, cameras, exposure meters, beer, refrigerators, fans, radios, watches, and vitamins. They own a soap factory and a large garage; and until recently they were the proprietors of the Crescent Hotel, which they used to describe with telling ambiguity as "the only one of its kind in Aden."

The rambling, higgledy-piggledy shopfronts of the Crescent, near the harbor, hide reserves of substance and well-developed economic abilities. A big program of improvement is, none too soon, being launched—new houses, roads, roundabouts and government offices, and a new hospital to replace the ineffably gloomy, yellowish structure which now stands, with an air of exhaustion, near those significant cisterns in Crater. Outside the city a series of ungainly windmills provides motive power for the Adeni salt industry, which has recently lost its valuable Indian markets (the Indians have suddenly taken to making salt themselves) but is still reasonably important. Another source of revenue is a disagreeable narcotic called *qat*. Nearly everybody chews it, and your taxi driver or bellboy is almost certain to have an unsightly heaving bulge in his cheek. It comes by air every day from Ethiopia, and an eager reception committee awaits its arrival at the airport. The government, instead of banning this not very harmful drug, taxes the stuff, and earns something like $150,000 a year from it. A man I met in Aden told me that if it were not for *qat* he could think of no conceivable reason for continuing to live; and this (for he had spent his entire life working in an Aden coffee-shop) I could well understand.

Despite the nostalgia and the prosperity, you can feel the chill of change in Aden. There are the first bubbles of political tumult. Pan-Arabism is on the march. In the bazaars you will see many a portrait of Colonel Nasser (looking, one must agree, more compelling than Queen Elizabeth headscarfed at a point-to-point, and much more formidable than the good and conscientious public servants, counting the days to home leave, who represent British justice and administration). The sense of Arabism is a potent and insidious thing. Aden may not look like an Arab city, and many of its citizens have not a drop of Arab blood in their veins; but in the autumn of 1956 the most compulsive political force in the colony, more important by far than agitation for self-government or representation, is the hazy but not ignoble desire for Arab unity which is sweeping pell-mell through the Middle East. And, indeed, what Arab of spirit, sitting in Crescent Square while a Royal Marine band played "Nearer My God to Thee," would not think with thwarted longing of those magnetic Arab cities to the north —the great new highways, the glamorous film stars of Cairo, the phalanx of brilliant hotels along the seashore at Beirut, Riyadh, smothered in Cadillacs, Amman, with its intoxicating new tales of political ferment? If ever a city felt cut off from its affinities, it is Aden.

So inevitably the phenomena of frustration have made their appearance in the colony. There is nationalism, genuine and mercenary; trade unionism, cynical and constructive; seditious activity fostered from abroad; political chicanery and jostling; and a sensation of impending change, of eras ending and vistas opening. Sometimes I find this refreshing. Sometimes, after a protracted interview with some unusually kickable political opportunist, it is infinitely depressing. As always, political ambition has mixed allies. Nasserism, genuine liberalism, Communism, anarchism—you will meet them all as you wander, eyebrows raised in inquiry, through the streets of Aden. There is even a hardening of the rigid Islamic orthodoxy that is still a power in this provincial city. I met one Arab who told me that his brother had an English wife, whom he had met while being trained at a factory in the Midlands. I asked if I could meet her. No, he said, he was very sorry, but she was in purdah, like the other women of the family; she never left the house without a heavy veil, and she met no men at all except her husband and his close relatives. Was she happy? "Of course," said the man. "She is an Arab now, and a Muslim, and she loves our family very much. She is even," he added in an afterthought that opened for me prospects of desperate loneliness and despondency, "she is even learning to speak a few words of Arabic."

Faced by all these irrepressible emotional urges, the British can only fight a rearguard action in Aden. It is as obvious as the sequence of day and night that Aden will one day be emancipated, by one means or another, from its colonial status. Fortunately (for I am a believer in protracted rearguard actions) there exists in Aden a body of opinion admirably suited to British needs. A group of people calling themselves the Aden Association has presented a semi-nationalist program of probity and moderation. The group's leaders call themselves "The Queen's Arabs," and they have a soothing air of loyalty and restraint. Loyalty to the Crown, maintaining the British connection, reasonable progress towards responsibility—these are their policies; and they cooperate readily with the government in its arrangements for granting some measure of local self-government. Indeed they are the only political group which does not boycott the Legislative Assembly altogether. It is small wonder that the Aden Association is talked of with paternal affection in official circles. The Queen's Arabs are friendly and responsible, and to them political concessions can be made with dignity. Talk to some sensible, educated lawyer of the Association, with his happy memories of Coronation Day and his regard for the Governor and his respect for constitutional methods, and you will come away with the happy impression that Aden is advancing steadily and with mutual benevolence towards self-government, like some idealized African colony in the columns of the *Observer*. If you happen to have flown in from Cairo or Damascus, though, you will find the programs of this agreeable organization almost comically unconvincing. Compared with the bold, brash, invigorating scurrilities of Colonel Nasser, this kind of soothing talk is hollow stuff indeed. So long as the maelstrom swirls outwards from Cairo, no counsels of moderation can be very effective in Arabia.

When the coolies strike, they are striking *au fond* for Nasserism, and the more visionary of the politicians probably see Aden as the southern outlet of a vast united Arabia (and themselves as controllers of its southern trade). Some of the political pressures come inevitably from Saudi Arabia and the Yemen, for Aden has a large Yemeni population, and strong commercial ties with Sanaa. The keenest minds behind the ferment, though, certainly do not envisage an Aden engulfed in such reactionary societies; on the contrary, they want to see the old-style potentates of the Middle East overthrown to a man and replaced by a federation of republican administrations. Do not laugh at them. It may very well come true.

So the Aden Association, alas, is far less representative of the state of Aden than are the passions of the rioters and the maddening quibblings of the barrack-room lawyers.

For the truth is that there is no compromise, no point of negotiation, between British rule and Arab nationalism. One is dynamic, one static. One has glamor, one only integrity. One is indigenous, one benevolently alien. Even the conservative Englishman visiting Aden in 1956 must feel a conflict of sentiments. He will have some sympathy for the routine nationalist creed. He feels instinctively that there is something unnatural and unhealthy about the present status of Aden. He wonders, looking at the barefoot illiterates around him, whether Britain could have done more for the inhabitants. He has a hazy suspicion that there is something noble to the idea of real Arab unity, unconvincing though the concept may sound; he is not inspired by the spectacle of an impoverished empire clinging to its outposts with the ageing jets and second-rate cruisers that leave it impotent in a wider sphere of diplomacy.

On the other hand, he suspects that, on the whole, British control of Aden is a good thing for the rest of the world. It bolsters the British economy, and keeps the port out of the hands of Powers that seem to be inimical to the serenity of nations. The flag may be tattered and the streets cracked; but on the whole perhaps it is right to hang on to Aden as long as possible, if cruelty is not required to do it.

PROTECTORATES

W H E N   T H E   B R I T I S H   seized Aden in 1837, they also had
the good sense to take control of the huge and generally disagreeable tract of desert that forms its hinterland. They retain control
today, thanks to a complex series of protective treaties with the
extraordinary army of little potentates who govern the tribes and
peoples of the region. The Aden Protectorates, eastern and western,
cover an area of 112,000 square miles, and if you stick a pin anywhere in the large-scale map of the country you are almost certain
to pierce a potentate. There are sheikhs and emirs and regents and
sherifs and sultans and people for whose titles there is, as an Englishman once told me with a pedantic smile, no very precise English
equivalent. Many and obscure are the states they govern—Fadhli
and Audhali, Shaib and Lower Aulaqi, Yafa and Lahej and Dathina.
Goods travelling from Aden Colony to Dhala, a distance of
seventy-six miles, have to pass through six different states and are
subject to six different custom dues. Some of the potentates are
entitled to be called "Your Highness," some distinctly are not.
Some have their own armies. One used to hold the hereditary title
of Zamindar of the Nizam of Hyderabad's Army Levy. One is
entitled, so I am creditably assured, to a salute of one gun. The
average Englishman has heard of none of them; but to the exchequer of each he makes, through the dark medium of the tax
collector, some small but welcome contribution.

Most of these people are capricious governors at best, and often
seem unconscionably addicted to the pleasures of violence and deceit. Nevertheless, government remains largely in their bejewelled
hands, for only a handful of British advisers roam these territories,
and some of them have two or three oligarchs to deal with. The
Protectorates produce almost nothing and are in general a fearful
nuisance; but their control is important to the British for three very
different reasons. First, they act as a buffer between Aden Colony
and the difficult states of Yemen and Saudi Arabia to the north,
both of whom are only too anxious to prise these territories away
from the British Crown. Secondly, there is the prospect of oil in
the Protectorates, especially in the east, and British companies are

diligently prospecting there. Thirdly, and most remarkably, a persistent sense of altruism pervades the British attitude towards the
Arabs of the Protectorates. Ask one of the advisers why he thinks
Britain should maintain the *status quo* there, and he will probably
say that the standard of living must be improved, that the Arabs
of the place must be protected against aggression, that some sense
of serenity must be induced into these quarrelsome and self-destruc-
tive tribesmen. A cynic might find this posture goody-goody, but it
is, happily, perfectly sincere.

The British government therefore helps the potentates with
technical advice, subsidizes (though not very lavishly) their development schemes, and has got itself embroiled in a depressing
tangle of intrigue and procrastination concerning their future—
whether they should unite in a federation, as London would like;
whether they should be incorporated in the Yemen and Saudi
Arabia, as Riyadh and Sanaa and Cairo would like; or whether they
should continue their present erratic relationships with Britain and
one another, as (or so it seems) the impenitent potentates would
like. Another problem concerns oil royalties: who is to benefit from
the oil if it is ever found, individual rulers or the Protectorates as
a whole? The reactionary visitor may feel inclined to suggest that
all the money should go to the British Treasury, which can use it
better than most; but the advisers would probably be shocked at
the very thought of it.

When I was in the Eastern Protectorate I stayed with the most
remarkable of these devoted officials, Colonel Hugh Boustead, adviser to the Quaiti Sultan of Shihr and Mukalla. He lives in the
seaside capital of Mukalla, perhaps the most beautiful small city
in the whole of the Arab world. It stands on the shore of the Indian
Ocean like a little oriental Venice. Its buildings are pale and delicate, and a single minaret stands like a majestic sentry on the harbor
front. There is a jostling fish market beneath tattered awnings; and
a barber's shop where men are bled with queer, crab-like instruments fastened to their necks; and a harbor with splendid high-
pooped dhows beached upon the sands. Offshore a school of porpoises makes its appearance regularly each morning, patrolling the

shore with exuberant splashings and bubblings; and outside the town a miniature army called the Hadramaut Bedouin Legion drills indefatigably, looking rather like the Arab Legion in the days of the British.

This delectable place, under the guidance of a succession of wise administrators, has achieved a fair measure of political responsibility. There are already a few incipient fires of subversion—Sultan and British advisers being equally anathema to the progressives of the Arab world. In general, though, its progress has been admirable, and it now has a successful local administration, run with a minimum of British participation. There is the prospect of oil in Quaiti State, and in a delightful whitewashed house near the customs shed a young English manager sits with all the paraphernalia of overdrafts and credit notes, waiting for the money to start flowing. The town feels prosperous enough, relatively stable, and purposeful; and it is worth recording that its nextdoor neighbor, the shadowy territory of Qishn, is practically unknown, all but uninhabited, subject to a testy Sultan called Isa bin Ali bin Afrur of Hadibu, and has no kind of administration whatever.

The presiding dignitaries of Mukalla are a young Sultan and Colonel Boustead. One lives in a big house on the south side of the city gate; the other in a big house on the north side of the city gate, and there is a fairly well-marked path across the intervening street. Boustead is one of the last, and one of the best, of the marvellous British patriarchs of the Arab world, a dying breed. He is shortish, brownish, and immensely tough, and he speaks fluent and knowledgeable Arabic, having once been commander of the Sudan Camel Corps. In the First World War, as a midshipman on board the cruiser *Hyacinth*, he deserted his ship in South Africa and joined the South African Horse, in the hope of seeing more action. After a brilliant military career on the western front he was officially pardoned, and is thus, I believe, the only deserter to be publicly forgiven in the history of the Royal Navy. Boustead captained the British Pentathlon team in the 1920 Olympics, and went to Mount Everest with Ruttledge's 1933 expedition. After all these wonderful adventures, and a distinguished career in the Sudan, he came at last to Arabia.

Boustead is a bachelor, and lives alone with two or three servants.

It is a queer experience to stay in his house, for the place is at once an unconventional home and a sort of public meeting place. Household affairs are conducted with brusque efficiency. If Boustead wants some more fish at breakfast (he lives almost entirely on fish) he reaches a hand inside his jacket and gives a piercing blast upon a silver whistle; this has no cataclysmic effect upon the servants, but sooner or later they arrive with the haddock, and as they serve the colonel they give you a cheerful and affectionate smile, amounting almost to a wink, as much as to say, "What a truly wonderful old eccentric he is!" On the other hand Boustead has all the time in the world for visitors. At any time of day you may walk into his drawing room to find the City Council sitting there, eight grave-faced men in white linen hats or turbans, talking seriously and drinking tea, and rising courteously when you stumble into the room. Often some grand old sheikh will be buried in the cushions of an armchair, his stick in front of him, discussing a problem of appalling personal import with the Resident Adviser. Once I walked into the house to hear angry bellowings from the drawing room. I ran upstairs and found a very old man in rags sitting all alone on the sofa. He was banging the floor with his stick and his face was contorted with fury. He paused for a moment to take a quick look at me, and then hastily resumed his declamations. "There's no justice under Allah!" that angry old man was shouting in the drawing room. "There's no justice under Allah, and I *demand* justice under Allah!" I left him bawling there, and in a moment or two the servants, without batting an eyelid, brought me my lunch.

Every afternoon Boustead goes for a walk along the glorious sands on the eastern side of Mukalla. His Land Rover drives him a few miles down the beach, and he then dismounts and walks very fast, his hands behind his back, in the direction of the city. The car follows respectfully a few hundred yards behind. I found this an exhilarating exercise. The sands are level and hard and golden, and the sea always sparkles. In the distance the towers of Mukalla stand shimmering. Sometimes there are people digging for crabs on the beach, their heads down in the hole, while small boys hold sacks. Sometimes a string of camels lopes down the sand, urged on by a wiry Bedouin of jerky locomotion, with crows picking away at the harsh hairs on the animals' humps. Sometimes a man will pass carrying a lump of fish on a string, and sometimes a party of small boys will be playing with a dead turtle on the foreshore. Through this fascinating milieu Boustead strides, speaking kindly to everyone he meets, greeted with affection, talking incessantly, walking faster and faster as the hours pass, while the car lumbers along behind and the panting guest, now and then breaking into an uneasy trot, keeps a hopeful eye upon that distant minaret. If you would understand British colonialism at its very best, take an afternoon walk with Colonel Boustead.

He is successful in Mukalla because he, and a number of predecessors, have had a genuine respect for Arab pride. They have lived as the people live; no suggestion of patronizing superiority has tainted their attitudes; and disgruntled old men have always been welcome to march into their drawing rooms, sit upon their sofas, and shout. In many ways the effect has been astonishing. The states of the Eastern Protectorate now live in harmony, honoring an arrangement named, after its British creator, Ingram's Peace (the document of accession contained 1,400 signatures). There is a good hospital in Mukalla, and some excellent schools. I met a young man in the city who was being sent by the government to study art in Khartoum (Quaiti maintains strong connections with the Sudan, thanks partly to the British link); some of his paintings hung in Boustead's house, and colorful, vigorous pictures they were. I also watched a gymnastic demonstration at a school which has been started for Bedouin boys. Children flock from all parts of the desert to attend this school, and they evidently attend to their instruction with energy, for the demonstration was one of the liveliest and funniest things I have ever seen. The boys were all very small, lithe, and barefoot, and had the traditional long hair of the Bedouin. They ran helter-skelter on to the field, trying to restrain their grins, and plunged into a routine that reminded me irresistibly of the silent films, so unbelievably abrupt were their movements, and so breakneck the speed with which everything was done. The field was a mass of violently flaying arms, legs jumping up and down like humming-bird wings, flapping hair, jigging small bodies. Sometimes there were sudden disconcerting changes of direction; and sometimes, to heighten the Keystone Cops illusion, the whole sequence was reversed, and all the little legs, all the

arms, all the flying hair performed their frenzied gyrations backwards. The audience was limp with laughter and even Colonel
Boustead, thanking the instructor, allowed some small flicker of
amusement to cross his face. As for the Bedouin boys, they thought
it was a riot.

   The hinterland of this place is not all tranquil. To the west the
petty states of the Western Protectorate are themselves fractious
and unruly; and in both Protectorates the frontiers are constantly
under pressure from the Yemenis and Saudis, who are tirelessly
trying to subvert the tribespeople with bribes of rifles and money.
Here and there in the desert there are isolated forts on the Beau
Geste pattern, manned by a couple of British officers and a platoon
of Arab soldiers; and from time to time the R. A. F. has to disperse
concentrations of tribesmen with jet fighters, or even scare the
populace into good behavior by the use of some old black Lincoln
bombers, inexpressibly sinister in appearance, which are to be seen
any day brooding gloomily upon the airfield at Khormaksar. Life
can be quite exciting for these servicemen, especially in the more
jungly states in the west. When I was visiting a fort on the Yemeni
frontier, an Englishman drove in with two or three trucks and said
quite casually that he had been ambushed over the hill. Nobody
took much notice, but one of the officers remarked genially that if
he could have his way he would dismember that bloody sherif (or
emir or regent, or whatever the local quarrelsome autocrat happened to be), and another said that if nobody else was going to use
the shower, he would. There is an almost constant state of emergency on these northern frontiers, fluctuating according to the
general political weather of the Middle East, but reflecting all
kinds of ingrained issues and rivalries—some modern, arising from
nationalism and oil, some as old as the hills, with their roots in
ancient tribal animosities.
   One or two centers are more advanced in culture and education.
One is Lahej, not far from Aden Colony, which has become a hot-
bed of political agitation; another is Mukalla, on the whole a model
of what an Arab town in such a state of development can be; a
third is the fabled valley of the Wadi Hadramaut, hidden away in

the cruel hills near the Saudi frontier. This is the home of an old culture and the cradle of merchant-adventurers. It has a respectable Islamic literature of its own, and a well-developed social hierarchy ranging from Sayids by way of sheikhs and slaves to people called Akhdam, permitted only such "untouchable" tasks as the sweeping of streets or the playing of music. The original fortunes of the Wadi Hadramaut were made by the production of frankincense, conveyed along the trade routes of remote antiquity to India and the temples of the Mediterranean. The incense market has shrivelled, though, and much of the water which used to fertilize the valley has dried up; so for the past century the Hadramaut has subsisted largely on the enterprise of its adventurers. They have sailed across the world, built their businesses in Hyderabad, Singapore, East Africa, and Indonesia, and faithfully sent back their remittances (in the honorable Arab way) to their dependents at home. Like the Lebanese, they nearly always stay abroad for twenty years or more, but like the Lebanese they nearly always come home in the end; and if they have prospered they build themselves splendid homes and live a retirement of great ease and dignity. Alas, events have blunted the grandeur of this way of life. It is no longer so easy, it seems, to cable a million dollars from Djakarta to the Hadramaut, or to take with you, when you leave Hyderabad, all the rich trappings and luxuries you have accumulated during your thirty years of acquisition. Times have been hard for the Hadramaut, and it is chiefly British help that has staved off disaster.

Nevertheless, the Wadi Hadramaut remains one of the glories of Arabia, if only because of its architecture. I had of course seen photographs of the great city of Shibam long before I went there, but my first sight of the place, from the air, remains one of my most memorable experiences. The wadi is a great gash in the desert running from east to west, shut off from the north by the immense wilderness called the Empty Quarter, in the east and west by mountains, and in the south by the drab waste land that runs away to Mukalla and the sea. Until a few years ago it was largely unknown and there are still no roads to take you there. An enduring sense of mystery accordingly surrounds the Hadramaut. The first European to explore it thoroughly, Adolph von Wrede, eventually committed suicide in Texas, chiefly because he simply could not persuade people that he was telling the truth about it; and before I went there I was prepared to believe that its remote brilliance had been exaggerated. I was therefore unprepared for my first sight of Shibam. The aircraft had flown laboriously across the boring solitudes from Mukalla, and had now turned eastward into the wadi. There were high cliffs on either side, and touches of green in the valley, and crumbled rectangular patterns of derelict irrigation works. I had my eye on the northern side of the wadi, which was dark and precipitous; but somebody leaned across the aircraft and touched me on the shoulder, and there through the other window was Shibam.

If you can imagine a little Manhattan, aged by five centuries or so, mellowed by the touch of Islam, and deposited in a remote valley in the Arabian desert, then you can imagine Shibam. As we approached it shakily through the air currents of the wadi, it stood there tall and proud and cluttered, a thicket of skyscrapers beneath the cliffs. Most of the buildings were seven or eight stories high, and they were pressed tightly together on a small hillock in the valley bed, so that the city was at once an island and a towering fortress. Six hundred soaring houses were jammed together like this, and around them was only the wadi bed: the thing stood there suddenly, teeming and angular, savagely forceful and intense, and with all the power of some great engineering work, a Boulder Dam or a Krak des Chevaliers.

In a moment we had passed it, and when I looked back the town was in shadow, and had lost this sense of mastery, and was more like some wasted esoteric symbol of the past, the field of obelisks at Byblos or one of those forgotten pyramids that lie, encrusted with sand, forlorn beside the Nile in Egypt.

DHUFAR

T H R O U G H O U T these little-known territories, all around the southeastern perimeter of Arabia, Britain maintains a series of airfields. They are not vast strategic bases, like the American field at Dhahran. Their airstrips are small, their facilities limited, and they have never seen an intercontinental bomber in their lives. Only a handful of R. A. F. men is to be found at most of these airfields, stripped to the waist and cheerful, and doing the job with that almost demure correctness so characteristic of the postwar British serviceman. They seem to like the austere isolation of such outposts, and generally get on well enough with the local Arabs, within the limits imposed by difficulties of taste and language—that is to say, the British think the Arabs are likable "wogs," and the Arabs think the British are passable infidels. Hardly any of them know exactly why they are there; and indeed, even when some outmoded transport aircraft comes wheezing in from Aden, it is difficult to define very convincingly the prime purpose of these stations—whether they are important strategically or politically; whether, as people sometimes suggest, the entire British strategic system would collapse without them; or whether it is simply that they are handy for quelling tribal impertinences and neighborly aggressions.

One of the best-known of these strips is to be found at a place called Salala. This is the capital of a delightful seaside territory called Dhufar, adjacent to the Eastern Protectorate and falling under the sovereignty of the independent Sultan of Oman, who treats it as a kind of Balmoral, spending rather protracted holidays there between bouts of statesmanship at Muscat, his capital. The town has none of the beauty of Mukalla, and little of the austere fascination that characterizes other seaside places in Arabia; but it is memorable because it lies in a crescent of country so fertile and fresh, so astonishingly green and fecund, that it is perhaps the happiest place in the whole peninsula. The monsoon, by a fortunate quirk of fancy, chances to strike Dhufar on its way from the Orient to East Africa; and this gives the province a tolerable rainfall, be-

sides plunging it for a few months every year into a thick pall
of deep cloud.

I knew nothing of this when I flew into Salala, and I was therefore astonished to find the little capital encouched among lush
groves of coconut palms, fields of wheat and millet, plantains, sugar
canes, indigo, and cotton. Behind the town stretched a wide and
friendly plain, and across it two streams ran generously. Here and
there were irrigation wells, with ancient camels groaning round
them, and the bare gleaming backs of Negroes tending them, and
a creaking of wood and harnesses. A little way along the coast the
Sultan has a summer palace almost theatrical in the delicacy of its
setting, with pools and streams and white walls, old retainers cracking coconuts for you, Arab bucolics cooling their toes in the water,
a soft smell of burning wood, and sometimes even a white-sailed
dhow beyond the palm trees, idling its way to Dhufar with a load
of dates.

The town itself did not quite live up to this background. It had
once been rich and famous, in the days when this southern shore
of Arabia was the Incense Coast, and aromatic convoys set out from
here with treasures for the temples of India and the Mediterranean.
Fabulous and exotic were the merchandise that then passed through
Dhufar—monkeys and peacocks, slaves, spices of all kinds, ivory,
silks, ostrich feathers, sword blades, pearls from the Persian Gulf;
and unusually well-upholstered were the homes of the great Salala
merchants. Now, to be honest, the houses of Salala needed a lick of
paint, and their half-hearted ornamentations (rather in the Petra
manner) called for the attention of craftsmen who had, I suspected,
long since become extinct. From a distance some of the bigger
buildings looked vaguely reminiscent of the great Hadramaut skyscrapers; but in fact the only structure of much dignity in Salala,
the only symptom of present prosperity, was the Sultan's palace
beside the Indian Ocean, dominating the town conclusively. From
Mukalla in the west to Kuwait at the head of the Persian Gulf, the
rulers of Arabia have their seaside palaces, varying in style and
comfort chiefly in accordance with the state of the oil royalties.
The one at Salala is perhaps the nicest of all. Its courtyards stretch
to the water's edge, and often a couple of dhows stand lazily beneath its windows. High walls surround it, with a meshwork of

courtyards and alleyways, and an avenue of palm trees leads to
the big double gate tower at its principal entrance. Around this
thoroughfare the life of Salala revolves. Sometimes a big bearded
Sikh can be seen leaning from a window of the tower, or playing a
protracted chess game with some white-robed dignitary; he is an
important member of the Sultan's household, and one of the most
influential figures in Dhufar. Sometimes a young Englishman
marches into the palace for a conference with the Sultan; he commands the local army, and lives with his young wife in a comfortable house he has built for himself along the shore, complete with
nursery. Sometimes the commander of the R. A. F. station presents
himself at the palace with compliments; the Sultan is always very
kind to him, and allows the airmen to have strong drinks and ciga-
rettes (two commodities forbidden to the local inhabitants of this
old Islamic paradise). Outside the gates those locals in search of a
job parade each morning to be chosen, rather as you pick sides for
netball, by the representatives of the Sultan, the air force, and the
American oil company which is operating down the coast. And
from this gatehouse, when the Sultan wishes to journey in his desert
hinterland, the trucks of his convoy emerge roaring and jolting,
with the big red flag of Muscat streaming in front, and the attendant turbaned sages bouncing in their seats, and the slaves at the
gates bowing low, and the bondsmen on the backs of the trucks,
holding their rifles, chanting a loud unison *fatiha:* "In the name of
Allah, the merciful, the compassionate! Praise be to Allah, Lord
of the worlds! The merciful, the compassionate! The king of
doomsday! Thee do we worship and of thee do we ask aid!"

The people of Salala bow respectfully when such a cortege
sweeps past, for this is still an oligarchal society. The Sultan is
supreme, and indeed runs this particular province of his domains
more or less as a private estate (it once impertinently seceded from
the Sultanate, and was recovered by the intervention of the British). Below him, too, society is distinctly layered. There are the
Arabs of the town, settled and dignified, though often emaciated;
they live lives of rigid orthodoxy, and their poor women are stifled
with hideous black, beak-like masks, rather like the spiky-nosed
iron helmets worn by medieval knights. There are Bedouin from
the desert hinterland, splendid swaggering men, attended by clouds

of tribesmen and armed to the teeth. Slaves and freedmen abound: they are all Negroes, of fine physique, and their lively and flirtatious wives jingle with ornaments. Occasional sailors wander through the streets, and soldiers in khaki, and a few Indians; and finally there are the people from the hills, as queer and compelling a stone-age survival as you will find anywhere in the Middle East.

Far behind Salala, separating the fresh province of Dhufar from the Arabian deserts, there runs a range of hills unique in Arabia. The Qara Mountains are not very high and not very extensive, but they act as a startling corrective for anyone who supposes all Arabia to be sandy aridity, and they are inhabited by tribespeople of most peculiar characteristics. To enter these hills you must cross the plain and climb up one of the several tracks that lead into their shuttered valleys, still largely unknown to the Westerner. At first the journey seems unexciting. The foothills are dry and rocky, enlivened only by a few wild olive trees and stunted bushes, and the coastline behind you, with its bright fields and palm groves, looks infinitely more refreshing. Before long, though, an astonishing transformation overcomes the landscape. Everything grows greener and fresher and kindlier; the air brightens, the breeze freshens, and presently you emerge among wide green highlands, dressed in meadows, for all the world like Sussex downs or Housman's Shropshire hills. There are groves of thick, shady trees studding the fields, and lavish clumps of a bush like rhododendron. Blossoms of many kinds decorate the track, as primroses embellish English lanes in calendars. The grass is a lovely yellowish green, infinitely soothing to contemplate in the peninsula of Arabia; herds of fat, rich cattle stand about, and the hills roll away into the distance, gentle and serene. Because of the miracle of the monsoon, these highlands carry a foliage richer than anywhere else in Arabia. You might be a million miles from Aden.

Two places in the Qara Mountains would be described by the American publicists as "scenic wonders." The first is the abyss of Dahaq, from which (so some scholars say, without much fear of contradiction) Ptolemy's city of Abyssapolis took its name. I approached this place all unsuspecting, and a marvellous surprise it was. The track there winds its way along the escarpment, through groves of sapless trees and round innumerable rocky corners; the only living things about are herds of cattle which scatter recklessly at your coming; the country feels lifeless and uninviting. But the unheralded appearance of Dahaq is spectacular. Round yet another corner you go, clutching the windscreen of your jeep; and all of a sudden there stands before you an enormous precipice, stern and sheer, instantly reminiscent of Boulder Dam or Grand Coulee. At this spot a stream running out of the mountains above suddenly splits into rivulets and plunges over the precipice, five hundred feet deep. Above the cliff and below it the valley is narrow and severe; but the abyss itself stands there like some huge and sententious symbol of transition. Below it everything is dry and inhospitable, only relieved by the splashing of the stream; above it the narrow valley is crammed and vivid with vegetation. There are crops of cotton and chile, palm trees, a mass of streams, herds of cattle and goats. In the middle of this little Shangri-La stands a village of hive-shaped huts with straw roofs, inhabited by gaudily-dressed Negro freedmen; and their plowed fields run down to the very edge of the precipice, and bulge over it ominously like a rich red cornice.

The other show place of the Qara Mountains (though there is nobody in particular to show it to) lies higher than Dahaq, just below the meadows. Through the centuries the peoples of the desert, always thirsty for water and fertility, have dreamed of Damascus as their ideal of all that is green and luscious. Tucked away in these mountains, though, is a place infinitely cooler and more seductive than any shady corner of the Ghouta. Hidden among the hills, unvisited by Europeans from one year to the next, lies a wide greenish lagoon, surrounded miraculously by reeds and rushes and languid trees. Soft grass runs down to the edge of the water, and little green moor hens, fussy and scurrying, ruffle its surface delectably; hills stand all about; there are flowers to pick and long green stalks to suck and soggy water meadows to squelch through. In Arabia this enchanted lake has an air of wild unreality, and I know no better place in the whole of the Middle East for a long, cool lemonade and an afternoon of innocence.

The steep hillside above the lagoon is pocked with a warren of caves and crannies, like the tunnelled colony of some giant Arabian marmoset. Rush mats are suspended over some of them, and out-side others there are rickety structures made of palm fronds. These are the homes of the Qara mountaineers, who keep their herds of cattle in the highlands and come down to the plain only for an occasional visit, or during the period of fading sunshine which precedes the monsoon. They are a strange and beautiful people. If you chance to meet them in the mountains, you will find them oddly stiff and self-conscious, as if they are desperately afraid of making fools of themselves; but you will also sometimes discover them to be of a truly classical perfection of profile. Their features are often delicate and exactly molded. Their attitudes are graceful. They wear leather thongs around their foreheads and robes slung carelessly around their middles like bathtowels, and belts with daggers in them. Thick streaks of indigo disfigure their faces, and they carry ancient rifles, knobbly sticks, and sometimes comical crude weapons vaguely related to the boomerang.

There are four distinct tribes of these hillmen. Each speaks a different language, unwritten, unintelligible, and unrelated to Arabic. Each has its own obscure rituals and taboos, often derived (like those of the southern Sudan) from the respect the tribesman owes his cow. Each, I gather, loathes the other, and occasionally attacks it with screams and undisciplined hurling of throwing-sticks. Nobody knows where they came from or why, and hardly anybody understands their languages, and only one or two determined scholars (notably Bertram Thomas) have tried very hard to master their prejudices. For myself, I viewed them as I might view some community of neolithic men, encountered in one of those time transitions popular in space fiction; that is to say, I frankly stood and gaped at them. They stood and gaped at me too. Once an old woman pressed a pigeon upon me; to these opinionated people all kinds of birds, hyenas, foxes, and eggs are taboo—though they gratefully accept toffees. Elsewhere I gave an unusually neolithic old man a handkerchief, the only possible gift I had on my person. First he put it over his head; then he tucked it in his waist, beside the dagger; and then he gave it back to me with a courtly gesture. I sometimes noticed these people saying their evening prayers (they are nominally Muslims, and observe the fast of Ramadan). They did so with obvious devotion, but it seemed to me that either I was confused about the whereabouts of Mecca, or the Qara people were not praying in that direction at all, but were prostrating themselves before an even older sanctity: the sun.

But only a few such indigoed primitives wander into Salala; and it is the easiest thing in the world for the time machine to whisk you back, through the Middle Ages of the town, to the huts where those cheerful airmen, wearing only shorts and gym shoes, thumb through the tattered pages of their magazines as they drink their beer.

SULTAN'S PROGRESS

NOT ALL ARAB RULERS are as capricious as the chiefs of the Protectorates, as grasping as the princes of Saudi Arabia, or as medieval as the Imam of the Yemen. A good example of old-fashioned Islamic kingship, governed by generally kindly and constructive autocracy, is provided by the Sultan of Muscat and Oman, Said bin Taimur, whose territories march with the Western Protectorate but extend all around the southeastern horn of the Arabian Peninsula. The Sultan was educated in India, and is a man of grave but enterprising outlook. He takes his position solemnly, but his character is enlivened by a streak of adventure, so that he loves desert journeys, helter-skelter motor travelling, nights in the outdoor, navigation and surveying. I once undertook a journey with this ruler across the unknown interior of his Sultanate. I have never travelled under more dashing or skillful leadership, and I always think of the Sultan as a man of the desert, bouncing merrily up and down in the front of his rugged American truck, delving into a blue canvas shopping bag for his compass or his aneroid, or stepping from the cab for midday prayers, dressed in a simple fawn *aba*, with a sword at his side, a pair of binoculars around his neck, and a noble turban on his head.

But for a glimpse of his kingship, it is perhaps better to have an audience with the Sultan in his palace on the harbor front at Muscat, his capital, an ancient seaport hidden modestly away among rocky coves on the Gulf of Oman. The Sultan's family have been rulers here since 1744, and their position is very firmly embedded in heredity and tradition; the palace stands there, as it has since the days of the Portuguese Empire in Arabia, with rather the comfortable paternal manner of a minor French château. The waterfront at Muscat is narrow and crowded, jammed in by high cliffs at the end of a cove. In the middle of it the palace stands, foursquare and assured, guarded on each side by fine Portuguese fortresses built upon bluffs. Everything is solid and well-built, and merges easily with the rocks, and the place feels, in many ways, more like India than Arabia.

The Sultan, too, has an air of inherited assurance. His has been a distinguished dynasty (once it ruled Zanzibar, too, and it still has a colony on the shore of Pakistan). Though the affairs of Muscat and Oman have long been linked with those of Great Britain, he is still a ruler of independence; and indeed it is instructive to see with what cautious prudence the British representatives in the Persian Gulf handle their relations with Said bin Taimur. The Sultan is also one whose life is governed by the rigid disciplines of Islam, and this gives him a calmness and serenity not common among rulers of less devout instincts. There is no longer a Caliph of Islam (though sometimes Colonel Nasser gives the impression that he is ambitious to revive the office) but among a few Arab rulers the strict rules of conduct laid down for that office are considered applicable to the conduct of modern kingship. The king must be a free man; be sane and virile; possess physical integrity; have some knowledge of divine law; be wise and brave; and lead a life of morality, according to the ethics of Islam. Upon these lines, more or less, the Sultan has obviously trained himself. He observes the edicts of his faith with care; does not smoke or drink; leads a life of continence; takes an active and intelligent part in the affairs of state; and seems to do his best to further the condition of his people. He is not a rich man, and his Sultanate is, by and large, one of the most backward places on earth; but compared with most of his colleagues in the field of Arab dominion, he is an advanced liberal.

He is, of course, helped by the fact that in Muscat, cut off by the whole of the Arabian Peninsula from the fountainheads of Arab dissension, there is no political activity at all and no challenge to his authority. He certainly does not encourage the development of democratic practices, and he is as determined as the next sultan to retain his hereditary dignities; but in Muscat there are none of the barbaric survivals of feudalism that you find in Saudi Arabia or the Yemen, and in general it feels a kindly and contented country. There is undoubtedly some slavery still, but thanks partly to the unremitting watch of the British Royal Navy, slave trading as practiced in Saudi Arabia seems to be all but dead. It is sometimes said that the Sultan is a little too jealous of his royal dignities, but there is goodwill to his tinge of pomposity, and the suspicion of a twinkle to his severities. One of the pleasures of the Arab world is its persistent sense of natural democracy. Nobody is master of the true

Arab, and though it is often a good idea to shout at an Egyptian, if you particularly want something done, in Arabia every man is your brother and you must ask him kindly. Theoretically, anyway, Islam is a community of equals. In Muscat, despite the recognizably monarchical flavor of the state, this egalitarian instinct is agreeably present, and you will meet no cringing tradesmen or greasy subservience.

Even the servants who greet you at the great gateway of the palace do so with cheerful smiles, and they usher you pleasantly up the wide staircase to the anteroom of the reception chamber. They are all Negroes, all agile and strapping, and they give an impression of well-fed athleticism. In the anteroom you may find others waiting for an audience. Perhaps the Sultan's English wazir is there, in his ceremonial costume of a black *aba* and a Breton beret. Perhaps, if it is a day of ceremony, the British consul-general will be wearing his uniform, a sort of yachting kit not without a certain bold raciness. Perhaps the director of the customs department, a portly Egyptian of the old school, will be sitting there with his tight-trousered legs wide apart, the tassel of his tarboosh hanging comfortably over his left ear. Or it may be only a deputation of country sheikhs, in complicated gowns and turbans, with the inevitable ornate, curved daggers thrust ostentatiously into their belts. Whoever is there, a quiet murmur of politesse will run around the room as you enter, and you will be undecided whether to bow, or clear your throat and say good morning, or pretend not to have heard it.

Presently your turn comes to enter the presence. The audience chamber is a fine long room with windows opening on to the harbor. You can see the cove outside, and one of the great forts (it is now a prison, in which you may easily be incarcerated if you forget to observe any of Muscat's complex laws, such as the one insisting that you carry a lantern if you ever step outside after dark). There is probably a bustle of country craft in the harbor, and perhaps a white packet boat, from Basra or Karachi, moored in the roads. On the rocks all around the crews of innumerable visiting vessels have painted their ships' names, and the whole cove is blotched with their patches of white, some fresh and clear-cut, some all but faded away with time. "My visitor's book!" says a

gentle voice; and there is the Sultan, courteously following your
glance out of the window. "Some people say they disfigure the
harbor, you know, but I like them. They are a record of my callers,
you see. Your own Lord Nelson, you know, once visited Muscat.
He was a midshipman at the time, on board the frigate *Seahorse*,
and he spent a month here, I believe. I am very much interested in
historical matters, you see."

There is a slight Indian lilt to the Sultan's voice, and perhaps a
touch of the Negroid to his face. He wears a gold-hilted sword and
he has a string of amber beads in his hand as he surveys you calmly
from his elevated chair. His face is composed and unwrinkled, and
his beard (all good Islamic rulers have beards) is luxuriant. His eyes
have a hooded and sleepy look to them, his mouth expresses both
humor and ruthlessness, and his fingers are a trifle podgy. He sits
there in shadow, an impressive figure, and though there are long
silences in the conversation, he will answer all your queries with
friendly intelligence, and only say goodbye to you when you have
drunk a sweet ceremonial coffee and been given the opportunity to
perfume your beard with incense. People say the Sultan is of a
miserly turn; but I believe there is generosity to his spirit, if not
to his purse, and I hope he prospers.

Up to now his rule has certainly not been without anxieties.
Until 1956 you could enjoy a peculiar experience in Muscat, or
better still in its twin city of Mattrah, which well illustrated the
extraordinary schisms and rivalries that plague the Arab world. If
you stood beside the gate of the city (closed every night at sun-
down, as in medieval Europe) you could look to the west and observe a range of hills. They were only thirty or forty miles away,
and you could see them clearly. The caravan of camels likely to be
grazing in the clearing beside the walls had almost certainly come
down from the highlands that morning, bringing loads of obscure
fruit and vegetables in return for the merchandise of the port. Yet
those hills were as totally forbidden to you, as unknown to Westerners, as fanatically secluded and shuttered, as Tibet at the beginning of the twentieth century. Westerners had lived and worked
in Muscat for years, and the Sultan's dynasty has for generations

enjoyed relations with the European Powers; yet only five or six Europeans had ever penetrated the hills, and some of them only in disguise.

It was a queer feeling to stand there among the rickety taxis, the Union Jack waving on the consulate-general behind you, and contemplate those unknown mountains. There were two reasons for the situation. First, the hills were inhabited chiefly by adherents of an Islamic sect called the Ibadhi, of xenophobic inclinations, and travel there for a Christian had always been startlingly hazardous. Secondly, since the end of the last century most of the hill country had not been under the control of the Sultan. Many of the tribes had rebelled against his authority and paid a hazy allegiance to a theoretically elected functionary called the Imam of Oman. This meant that, although in the general opinion the Sultan was the ruler of the hills (loosely called Oman) his writ did not run there; his passport would afford no security; he had no officials in the territory; and indeed, he had never been there.

Until a few years ago this strange political schism of the Sultanate scarcely engaged the attention of the world. Hardly anyone knew where Oman was, let alone who ruled it, and it was extraordinary how few people cared. In the past few years, though, all the disputed and undemarcated frontiers which separate Saudi Arabia from its neighbors have become important. Just as the Saudis looked greedily, if myopically, towards the Aden Protectorates, so they began to cast covetous eyes upon the hills of Oman. Helped by Cairo radio, they revived old (and not unreasonable) arguments to prove that the Sultan of Muscat had relinquished his legal control of Oman; and they conceived the idea of setting up the Imam, who lived in a remote and improbable fortress-city called Nizwa, as a puppet ruler of an independent Oman. This understandably displeased the Sultan. It also displeased his British allies, if only because His Highness had granted an oil concession for both Muscat and Oman to a predominantly British oil company.

At the end of 1955 the Sultan accordingly seized the interior of Oman by force and sent his troops (looking very British in equipment and leadership) to occupy the fortress of Nizwa. The Imam climbed down the walls of the fort on a rope and ran away on a donkey, and has scarcely been heard of since; and an administration was promptly installed by the Sultan. For the first time a European looking up at the hills from the streets of Muscat could contemplate paying a visit to them with a reasonable chance of survival; and for the first time in this century Muscat and Oman, one of the three biggest states of Arabia, was a political entity.

I was in Nizwa, hitherto practically unknown to Europeans, on the day of the Sultan's triumphal entrance. The town stands among rich palm groves in the very heart of the mountains, a place of terraced houses and wadi beds, dominated by the great, rotund keep of the fort. Its people struck me as being urgently in need of care and protection, so emaciated were their frames, so froward their appearance, and so overpoweringly delinquent their attitudes. Listlessly they crowded the streets of the old town, beak-nosed and hollow-cheeked, holding sticks or long antique muskets. Behind them there billowed a huge crowd of women, unveiled and wearing bright, if grubby, orange costumes, vivid in the sunshine. Through this welcoming assembly the Sultan drove splendidly, with a string of dusty, travel-worn trucks. He had made an unprecedented crossing of the highlands from Salala on the Indian Ocean, and he swept up that rough highway with his red banner waving, his black bondsmen clinging to the backs of the trucks, his soldiers in proud escort, and a general manner of adventurous but regal panache. Shattering explosions now rang out from the battlements of the fort, filling the blue sky with smoke and disintegrating some of the looser bits of the structure; and these welcoming cannon shots were supplemented by a series of *feux-de-joie* from the Arabs lining the route; so that what with the cannons, the spasmodic peppering of rifles, the squeaky murmurings of the women, the roar of the trucks, and a little throaty mumbling from the male bystanders, something approaching pandemonium ruled in Nizwa that morning.

But there is always dignity in Arabia. Nizwa was, of course, doing its best to convince the Sultan of its undying loyalty. Machine guns and trucks and Europeans had never been seen there before, in all the turbulent history of the place; and it no doubt seemed to the citizens, once the Imam had disappeared on his donkey, that this was a moment for discretion. Nevertheless, the magnificoes who waited in official poses beside the great doorway of the fortress managed to look both grand and decorous. Their faces were grave (though alas, in a few cases almost irresistibly comic) and their turbans were wound loosely around their heads with the ends hanging down over their ears, making them look rather like popes in medieval portraits, or ski instructors. They all had daggers at their belts, and nearly all had beards, and as the Sultan approached they stepped forward in a stately flurry of draperies.

The Sultan emerged from his truck with grandeur. His many-colored turban was impeccable. His robe was gold-encrusted. His sword hilt was of gold, and as he stepped out with composure, he laid upon it, to keep the blade out of the way of his legs, a well-manicured hand with a ring upon it. Those standing near His Highness (that is to say, the strongest and most determinedly respectful of the sheikhs) were able to enjoy the faint scent of frankincense that exuded from his person. His face, though, was excessively severe, and did not even twitch when the masonry around us reverberated again under the impact of a cannon shot.

All the sheikhs of that country had gathered to pay allegiance to the Sultan and to recognize the new unity of the Sultanate. They came from the distant corners of the highlands, some on foot, attended by a shabby servant or two, some in splendid camel caravans, surrounded by armed men on prancing animals. One, the closest confidant of the discredited Imam, was even to arrive in a Plymouth convertible, with a slave sitting on the boot like a footman; it was undoubtedly the only car in Oman, and was almost certainly a little present from across the frontier. The most important of these tribal leaders, some of them Bedouin, some from settled areas, had assembled in the fort. The place was bright with bunting and flags. Some of the sheikhs sat in hollow squares, grunting at each other spasmodically and drinking coffee; some sat on parapets, dangling their legs; some wandered about; some battered at a big wooden door, studded with nails, in unsuccessful attempts to enter the interior of the keep. There were many hunchbacks and cripples, and nearly everybody seemed to suffer from some eye disease.

Inside the Sultan sat in state, and his grave eyes flickered for a moment in my direction when I peered into the dim great hall of the fortress. The most distinguished of worthies sat mutely in a long rectangle, their legs tucked underneath them. Not a word was uttered. Coffee-pourers padded up and down, pouring coffee from long-spouted pots with florid ritual; and a man passed round with a big bowl of sticky sweet stuff, but nobody said anything. They sat there still as stone, sometimes fingering their beards or adjusting their robes, sometimes twiddling their canes, but never murmuring. The silence was awful. Awful, too, was the look on the face of the Sultan. He sat there rather like an Arab sphinx, crosslegged, immobile, and into his eyes there had entered an expression of tremendous hauteur and authority. His head was held autocratically high. The faint suspicion of a sneer curled the corners of his mouth. His attitude was one of unshakable command. No wonder those penitent sheikhs sat there subdued.

This was the remotest part of Arabia, and one of the least-known places in the world. Such is the importance of the Middle East, though, that events even in these backwaters can be of shattering world importance. Fabulous oil royalties might depend upon the Sultan's ascendancy over those picturesque chieftains; the fortunes of corporations were at stake; the wealth of empires; and the whole Western position among the Arabs was intimately linked with such coups, intrigues and ceremonials. Many a watchful eye was focussed on Nizwa that day, in the chanceries of London and Washington as well as in Cairo and Riyadh; and it was surprising how soon the news of the Sultan's success was flashed back to Whitehall, and heartening to see how skillfully the two young soldiers of the British Royal Signals handled their transmitter on the plateau outside the city of Nizwa.

To the northwest of Nizwa, beyond the mountains, there is a small oasis of equal interest to the Foreign Offices and the State Departments. Buraimi is one of those places which crop up hazily but regularly, over the years, in the columns of the world's newspapers. Most people, perhaps, have vaguely heard of it, just as they have heard of Okinawa or the Johnston Plan; but not one Briton or American in a thousand could say where it is. A glance at the map, nevertheless, will soon convince you of the importance of Buraimi to the politics and strategies of Arabia.

It lies in desert country about a hundred miles inland from the Persian Gulf, at the northeastern extremity of Oman; and among its palm trees are the only substantial water supplies for hundreds of miles around. Every important caravan route of this region accordingly passes through Buraimi, and it is the chief staging point in Saudi Arabia's lines of communication with the southern Persian Gulf. From here routes splay off to the Omani highlands, to the Muscat coast, to the series of Anglo-Arab sheikhdoms that line the Gulf shore. In the course of their intermittent attempts to extend their dominion in the Arabian Peninsula the Saudis often have cause to send agents or moneybags into the countries along the Gulf shore; and much the easiest way to do this is to send them through Buraimi. What is more, Buraimi is a key to all that country in and around the Omani highlands that is thought to contain vast quantities of oil. Whoever controls Buraimi has a very good chance of controlling Oman too.

Unfortunately the British (suzerains still of the Persian Gulf) and the Saudis have never been able to agree on a defined frontier for these regions of Arabia, and this has given rise to a protracted difference of opinion about the status of Buraimi. The Saudis, quoting precedents historical, genealogical, diplomatic, military, and moral, claim that the oasis is theirs. The British believe part of it belongs to the Sultan of Muscat and part of it to the Sheikh of Abu Dhabi (agreeably pronounced "Abu Dubby"), which is the next state to the north. There was a celebrated arbitration attempt in Geneva, which broke up in confusion after everybody had accused everybody else of bribery; and in 1955 the British seized the place by force and handed it over to the jurisdiction of the two friendly potentates. They are very different in character—the one, as we have seen, earnest and high-minded, the other so volatile and inquiring as to verge upon the eccentric—but for the moment, they have agreed to this division of possession (there being, indeed, no very obvious alternative).

I was in Buraimi soon after this British coup, which had inspired some marvellously bloodthirsty diatribes on the Cairo radio; and a very queer place it proved to be. Far from being, as I had imagined, a shady oasis of the chocolate-box kind, it was a straggling series of wishy-washy villages, sprinkled with palm orchards, that seemed to have no very recognizable center. Where Muscat began and Abu Dhabi ended, nobody seemed to know; and I found myself quite hopelessly disoriented, so that all the palm trees, all the scrubby houses, all the crenellated, tumble-down forts seemed to blur into unity, and nothing was very precisely in focus.

This may have been, though, because I dined on my first evening there with the British political agent, who had an adequate supply of whisky in the tall and imposing fort he occupied. He was an example of the younger breed of British Arabists, no longer paternal in their approach, but level-headed and suffering from no romantic illusions. Few of them, alas, are in the Foreign Service; and even the political agent at Buraimi, I learned without surprise, was only on secondment to Her Majesty's Government from an oil company, which had, indeed, a rather more direct interest in the place than anybody else. "Kill me a dozen sheep!" said the agent to his servant with a lordly flourish, as he invited me to eat with him. The servant did not take the hyperbole very seriously, but splendid, nevertheless, was the meal he brought us, and golden the whisky we drank, and bright and clear the stars which winked at us through the narrow slits of the fort. There are times when the British Raj still has its moments of nobility; and when, later in the evening, Arabs came seeping into that dimly lit room, to squat on their haunches with us and exchange gossip, to pick at the victuals with their fingers, to raise discreet but tolerant eyebrows at the whisky, to treat us, in short, as friends rather than aliens or educationalists, it seemed to me that there was still a good deal to be said for the Pax Britannica.

THE BRITISH

BY THE AUTUMN OF 1956 the Persian Gulf was the chief center of British power in the Middle East. Since the war the record of Britain in the area had been one long withdrawal: from Cairo and Alexandria; from Palestine; from Persia; from Iraq; from the Suez Canal Zone; from Jordan. Her strongholds now, if they could be described as anything so virile and assured, were the territories we have examined along the southern shores of Arabia, and the oil-bearing sheikhdoms of the Gulf. With all of them she had treaty relations, no more; but she remained the effective suzerain of the area, and an imaginative cartographer, stretching a point, could color most of the southern and eastern coasts of the peninsula a watery but recognizable red.

This is not to say that Britain had vanished, like an unwanted jinn, from the rest of the Middle East. It was, after all, only a few years since she had been the effective mistress of almost the whole of it. During the war she had all but succeeded in imposing a kind of unity upon the Arabs. There were thus echoes of her manners and methods everywhere, from Aden to Kurdistan. Her position was unique. She was implacably hated by a large proportion of the Arab population, yet she still retained their respect; and in 1956 an Englishman, for all the vituperations of Cairo and the moneybags of Riyadh, could still feel proud of his passport. Britain was accused of last-ditch imperialism, of political manipulation, of Zionism, of multitudinous atrocities; yet even Colonel Nasser admitted sometimes to an admiration of the British character, and the more resolutely British you were among the Arabs and Persians, the better you fared.

Britons were still thick enough on the ground. Predominantly British oil companies were active in Iraq, Syria, and Lebanon, and in many parts of Arabia; Britain held majority shares in the Persian oil consortium. Despite the thrusting competition of Germany and the bludgeon blows of the Communist trade departments, British goods and contractors could still be found in most countries of the Middle East. English culture was successfully peddled by the British Council. More to the point, both Jordan and Iraq were still

members of the sterling area, and you could pay your hotel bill
in Baghdad with a check on a Pall Mall bank.

Politically, though, Britain had sheathed her claws. Outside
Arabia, by late 1956, there were virtually no British troops on the
ground. The great Suez military installations had been transferred,
as far as was practicable, to the ill-suited island of Cyprus. The
rumbling barracks at Gaza were full of refugees. British officers
no longer led the Arab Legion, and though Britain was a member
of the Baghdad Pact she had handed over her air bases in Iraq.
Without these disciplinary aids, impotence had overcome the British embassies of the Middle East, so recently the powers behind the
thrones; there was no capital, except possibly Baghdad, in which
the exertion of British influence could affect the conduct of the
nation or alter the flow of history.

This process was generally regarded in England with consterna-
tion, on grounds of national pride, necessity, and obligation. For
myself, I think the criterion must be whether what replaced
British power was good or bad, stable or erratic, and that each
stage of the British departure must be examined on its merits. What
was the purpose of each of these old footholds? What would be
the advantage of retaining them? What, indeed, did Britain want
of the Middle East? Was it either necessary or desirable for her to
bear so many responsibilities? Britain's vast prewar political hold-
ings in these countries were established because of her unquestioned
status as policeman of the world; because of the need to secure her
communications with her Indian Empire; and because the interests
of her oil companies required political stability. Of these three
considerations, only the last remained valid in 1956.

First, it was becoming apparent to the most resolute Westminster
reactionaries that Britain was no longer the supreme defender of
the Western faith. The Mediterranean had become, if anything,
an American lake, and Russian armies poised in the Caucasus could
sweep aside the British forces in the Middle East in a matter of
days. The bases in Jordan were, by modern military standards,
useless. The Middle East Air Force was equipped only with aging
and second-rate aircraft. The Mediterranean Fleet was a sad
shadow of its great forebears, and when the Admiral visited Alexandria in 1955 he did so in a cruiser so weak and obsolescent that

his predecessor Lord Fisher would have consigned it instantly to the scrap heap. The army in Cyprus, transferred there from the Canal Zone, was not only heavily engaged in anti-nationalist operations on the island, but also dismally lacking in the parachute formations, transport aircraft, and landing craft that would enable it to strike swiftly and effectively on the mainland. In any case, it was so obvious to everybody that Britain could not resist a Russian aggression by herself that the military policy of "going it alone" in the Middle East rang hollow.

Secondly, Britain no longer had any vast empire in the East. It was poppycock to talk of safeguarding Commonwealth communications with a squadron of elderly fighters upon an airfield in Jordan. When people talked in the imperial tone of voice they were thinking, as often as not, in terms of the overland route to India; they envisaged, as the Victorians did, a Russian drive to the Persian Gulf which would cut us off from our Indian possessions; they vaguely supposed that the passage of the P & O liners to Sydney depended upon the efficacy of the British embassy in Teheran. Not only was this patent nonsense—in wartime the Mediterranean is virtually closed to traffic anyway—it was also a dangerous misrepresentation of British needs and duties.

So we come to the third supposed purpose of the British presence —the maintenance of stability. It is clear enough that the operations of the oil companies can be disrupted by political unrest in the Arab countries or Persia. Mossadegh's coup proved how easily the passions of an ill-governed country could overcome both logic and self-interest. Extracting oil from the ground, buying it at a reasonable price, shipping it safely to the markets of the West, depended above all upon some degree of responsibility or permanence in the local administrations. By 1956 this was the crux of Britain's problem in the Middle East. She was no longer the guardian of the general peace; no longer mistress of India; but she depended for her prosperity, if not her very existence, upon the oil of the Muslims.

How best to ensure it was the riddle—whether to rely upon physical strength which would enable her to sway the policies of the local powers, or whether to bend before the winds of nationalism and hope for the best. Neither course seemed very promising, in the prevailing mood of the Arabs, and in the event British policies fluctuated madly (as indeed is inevitable in a state where public conscience still has some influence on political action). The new regime arose in Egypt, but nobody knew whether to encourage it or resist it, and it was only after a wave of terrorism and the withdrawal of labor that the British government agreed to the evacuation of the Canal Zone. A flood of nationalism and pan-Arabism poured across the Middle East, encouraged by the Egyptians and the Saudis; but the Foreign Office seemed undecided whether to ride it or stanch it. Social dissatisfaction was rampant and virulent; but the sympathies of Britain were torn between the friendly old despots and the angry young men.

So by 1956 the British position in the Middle East was an ambivalent one. We had quit Sudan and the Canal Zone in good grace, turning the other cheek to endless rebuffs from Colonel Nasser, including the shelling of a pilgrim ship at the entrance to the Gulf of Aqaba. We had abdicated our special position in Iraq. We grumbled and hissed at the expulsion of Glubb Pasha, but reconciled ourselves in stages to the extinction of our position in Jordan. In Persia we had accepted, willy-nilly, a settlement of the oil dispute that drastically reduced our share in the exploitation of Persian oil. Only in Arabia, where conditions were more primitive, political circumstances were more primitive, and Cairo more remote, did we stand fast. The oilfields of the Persian Gulf, though largely American-exploited, and the putative fields of southern Arabia remained firmly under British political control. Elsewhere our policy might be described as swallowing, rather than exploiting, the inevitable.

Whatever the merits of this progression, forced upon the British by economic and material weakness, it had a profound effect on the outlook of individual Britons. It would be both foolish and arrogant to pretend that only the Arabs were responsible for the weakening of Britain in the Middle East. The fault was often in ourselves. Successive applications of "divide-and-rule" had left an inevitable residuum of ill will against us. Many an act of political chicanery was remembered with bitterness. The procrastination and ambiguity of our later policies in Egypt had made us distrusted, and the shady dealings of some postwar British business houses and contractors had besmirched our commercial reputation. The story of Palestine, of our ill-advised attempts to placate both Israel and the Arabs, and of our eventual ignominious scuttle, was engraved on every Arab's heart (or so they liked to claim).

What is more, the British persisted, all too often, in a stand-offish, holier-than-thou aloofness that could be almost unbearably irritating. A century before, Britain had enjoyed a privileged position in the world perhaps comparable to the ill-defined eminence of *The Times* among British newspapers. By the 1950s all had changed; but it was difficult for any Englishman, however liberal his sympathies, to resist the illusion that he was somebody special in the Middle East, somebody to whom the normal rules did not apply, a being apart and divinely favored. I knew this sensation well. I worked constantly among Arabs and Persians, respected and liked them in many ways, interviewed their statesmen, reported their manifestoes, even paid, in a desultory sort of way, their income taxes; but however hard I fought against the instinct, I always felt obscurely insulated from them. We were not of the same species. For that matter, since the heart has its unreasonable reasons, it would have annoyed me to admit that the Dutch, the Spaniards, the Peruvians, or the Japanese had just the same rights in the Arab world as we had, and were just as much entitled to send their protests to Colonel Nasser or their warships on courtesy visits to Beirut.

This was a deep-rooted imperial instinct, an instinct of responsibility which was not without merit. The British did not generally view the Arabs with arrogance or greed. To be sure, they often stayed well away from them, as the old truisms about cocktail parties and company compounds demonstrated; but their instinct was patronizing rather than dominating. They felt themselves teachers, administrators, advisers, or simply good examples.

By 1956 this complacency was beginning to disintegrate. It was becoming clear that, whatever we thought ourselves, the Arabs would not tolerate us in our old capacities of superiority. In many parts of the Middle East, British advisers and experts were being dismissed. Dr. Hurst, the Nilologist, was the last Briton in the employ of the Egyptian government. The British director of the Jordanian Antiquities Department had been replaced by a Jordanian. The British pilot who guided our frigate through the Suez Canal had himself sailed for home. Only one or two British officers remained as advisers to the Jordan army. Only in the areas of Arabia under British control were the Colonel Bousteads still in office, and the Arabists sitting lordly in their starlit forts.

So for the first time Britons began to see themselves as other men saw them: as people making money, or extracting oil. For the first time they envisaged a relationship with the Arabs based upon the normal give-and-take of business, untrammelled as far as possible by politics or strategy. The Westminster diehards, indeed, shouted of gunboats and ingratitude; but a growing number of Englishmen saw the British connection as one primarily of trade and technique. It might be wise and even altruistic, such people thought, to sustain the British power on the coasts of Arabia, not only because of oil, but also because the withdrawal of the British would probably lead to anarchy and strife, and possibly to the extinction of the smaller sheikhdoms. But even there the British presence need not be permanent; with luck the heyday of oil was passing, and in fifty years we might live in an atomic world.

All in all, there were many Britons in the Middle East who did not view events with complete despondency, and were even able to shrug off the vagaries of Colonel Nasser and his friends; their only grievance, in fact, was the reluctance with which Britain accepted the obvious, and the tenacity with which she sometimes clung to her outmoded positions.

Indeed, the step-by-step withdrawal of Britain was logical enough, in view of her weakened circumstances; but then, if she withdrew, somebody of equal strength and parallel sympathies would have to replace her. If the policeman was retiring, a successor must be found to take over the beat. Logic demanded that either the United Nations or the United States should fullfill this role, should step with decision into Britain's shoes and impose some degree of authority upon a community of potential delinquents. Nothing of the sort happened. As Britain left, the political vacuum was filled by the malicious energies of Egypt; and soon the Russians, lumbering onto the scene at last, became a Middle Eastern Power for the first time.

Turmoil inevitably resulted. With the British armies withdrawn from the canal, Nasser would with impunity mass his Russian weapons against Israel. Jordan, without the restraint of Glubb and his officers, became a constant threat to the stability of the region. The Russians became ever more influential in Cairo and Damascus. The friendly pro-Western government of Iraq was threatened by the contagious examples of neighboring states. The cauldron of the Middle East, its British lid removed, seemed about to boil over.

In itself, it might be argued, this was no business of the British. If Britain had no privileges, she had no responsibilities either. But the United Nations proved powerless. The Americans, who had done so little in the past to bolster the British position, were hamstrung by commercial interests and electoral issues and hopelessly confused by the issues of the area. And when the decisive crisis came, it was as dangerous to Britain's national interests as it was to the peace of the world; Britain was concerned both as a retiring trustee of security and as a business corporation. For in June, 1956, Colonel Nasser nationalized the Suez Canal, and thus laid his hand upon the oil supplies of Europe.

It was in pathetic desperation that the tired British acted that autumn, not in arrogance. I hold no brief for the methods of the Conservative Government, for the web of deception and secrecy that surrounded their policies, for the successive shifty excuses with which they explained away the half-cock invasion of Egypt. As I talked to my Israeli colonel that day beside the desert road it seemed to me that a nasty air of dishonesty infused the operations. But I believe there was a despairing, pitiful dignity to the part the British played in that forlorn campaign, as of a thoroughbred gone wild among mustangs.

TRUCIAL COAST

DESPITE ALL THESE ANXIETIES, the peace of the British remains especially effective and memorable in the string of little sheikhdoms that lies between Muscat and Bahrain. There are eight such sheikhdoms, of varying wealth and magnitude, and the life of each of them is governed largely by its treaty relationship with Great Britain. This system of agreements, which grew up during the nineteenth century, has done much more for the region than you might suppose from the generally blighted and blasted appearance of the place. Trucial Oman, as the coastline is generically called, has always been an area of bloodshed and turmoil, and often still is; but it is largely because of the presence of British authority that the petty sheikhdoms and peoples have been able to preserve their identity at all. Piracy has been stifled, slave traffic reduced to a minimum, the ambitions of predatory neighbors held in check. "It is no exaggeration to say," wrote Lord Curzon in 1892, "that the lives and properties of hundreds of thousands of human beings are secured by this British Protectorate of the Persian Gulf, and were it either withdrawn or destroyed both sea and shore would relapse into the anarchical chaos from which they have so laboriously been reclaimed." It remains more or less true today.

Take, as a prime example of these sheikhs, Sultan ibn Shakbut, ruler of Abu Dhabi, who shares sovereignty of Buraimi with the Sultan of Muscat and Oman. Shakbut combines in his own experience the medieval and the modern, the age of feudal bloodshed and the age of oil. He is described in one reference book as a "quiet, nervous personality," and he is certainly highly strung, sensitive, and inquisitive. His face is humorous and quizzical and constantly in motion; and his figure is slim and a little bowed. He has dignity of the desert kind, and gives me the impression of being well able to take care of himself. Shakbut is the scion of a tribe called the Al Bu Falah, and rules (with British support) an area of 25,000 square miles of desert inhabited by Bedouin tribes, with settlements only on the coast. Constant and intricate are the feuds and rivalries in which he and his family have traditionally been involved, and fluctuating the fortunes of his dynasty. There were fourteen ruling sheikhs of Abu Dhabi before Shakbut. Eight were murdered, four of them by the agency of their own brothers. Four were deposed or expelled, one by his brother, one by his son. Only two died peacefully in their palaces. It is small wonder that Shakbut has rather the air of a man keeping his fingers crossed. To this day, in these Persian Gulf principalities, family rule is the practice, and there are often rivalries among brothers and sons both for the manipulation of power and for the succession. Shakbut himself has three brothers, and the youngest of them, Sheikh Zaid, is probably the strongest character in Trucial Oman; a few years ago, it is said, he actually refused a bribe of sixty million dollars to perform a piece of skulduggery for the Saudis, and when I met him at Buraimi he struck me as a man who might well, if born into some other sphere of society, have achieved tycoonship or honors lists.

One of the tasks of these feudal rulers is to consolidate relations with the roaming tribes of the interior, who meander about the undemarcated frontiers of Arabia and are often the key factor in some obscure struggle for power. (And obscure, indeed, they often are. One of the fundamentals of the political situation in Oman is an immemorial feud between two misty factions, the Ghafiri and Hinawi, which I am totally unable to understand; I am far from clear as to what the two factions are, and as their squabble arose from an eighteenth-century indiscretion of exceeding complexity, I suspect that even the participants are hazy about the causes of their undying antipathy.) Shakbut's family has been successful in this activity, and is probably more respected among the Bedouin than any other of the sheikhly clans. Abu Dhabi is thus assured of support in the interior when it has one of its periodical differences with its neighbors. When I was last there relations were good with Muscat, to the south; poor with Dubai, to the east; middling with Sharjah; and excellent with Ajman. Even now there is a war occasionally, and sometimes a tribal raid. Until recently the very town of Dubai was split into viciously hostile factions, living on opposite sides of a creek. Someone once told me of a duel fought with ancient Portuguese cannons, abandoned on the coast centuries before, which was enlivened by the frenzied efforts of the combatants to recover the cannon balls during the night in order to shoot them again next morning.

Amid this confusion Shakbut lives in a palace in his capital, a village built chiefly of mud and palm fronds on a disagreeable little island offshore. There is hardly any fresh water, and hardly any stone, and hardly any place to grow anything. Even food is scarce, and the Sheikh depends for his income (oil apart) chiefly on pearl fisheries and on the date gardens he owns at Buraimi. No steamers go to Abu Dhabi, no aircraft land there, there are no roads and few public services of any kind; and the scanty water supplies of this begrudging coast are slowly drying up. The ancient shipping industry of the region was based upon piracy, and its economy was inextricably linked with the wars and tribal raids which the British have done their honest best to discourage. The standard of living is thus almost intolerably low; Othello's various occupations have nearly all gone.

To this extent the Sheikh of Abu Dhabi still lives in the Age of Ignorance; but he is chiefly known to the world because of the impact of oil. In 1951 he was involved in an international arbitration case of great importance. He had granted an oil concession for his territories to a predominantly British company, but the question arose whether it covered deposits under the sea-bed off his coasts. The company claimed that their concession extended beyond the Sheikh's territorial waters. The Sheikh claimed that it did not, and that he might therefore grant another concession to somebody else. Since no oil has ever been found in his domains, onshore or offshore, and since such concessions usually entail a substantial down-payment on the part of the company, the matter was of some importance to Shakbut. One problem was that since the whole of the Persian Gulf is fairly shallow, there is really no such thing as a Continental Shelf—a litigious conception which was the subject of contention throughout the oil industry—any more than there is in the North Sea. The arbitrator, faced with this problem, decided that the original concession covered territorial waters, but not the sea-bed outside them. Shakbut promptly granted another concession to a different company, establishing a significant precedent.

Thus do these strange Arabian princelings find themselves embroiled in the affairs of the industrial era, firing a flintlock with one hand, briefing Sir Hartley Shawcross with the other. In many ways Shakbut bears more than a family resemblance to the founder of his dynasty, fourteen sheikhly generations ago; but thanks largely to the influence of the British (who have generally left the rulers to themselves in the handling of their internal affairs) he has had an adequate education in the ways of the West. My last glimpse of Shakbut was memorable. He was bouncing westward across his sheikhdom in the back of a flamboyant yellow Cadillac convertible, with two attendant jeeps bumping along behind; and he sat there in its springy recesses, bouncing slowly up and down with the vagaries of his terrain, like some wily, brightly-plumed bird, or perhaps the Gryphon in *Alice in Wonderland*, so improbable was the environment, and so imperturbable and unfathomable the look on his face.

Oil is the hope of the Trucial Coast, and several companies are working hard to find it. Their difficulties are increased by the peculiar political conditions of the region, which make concessions and rights extraordinarily difficult to define. The only unifying factor in Trucial Oman is the British connection; for the rest, it is a place of semi-anarchy, in a constant state of uneasy motion. The British recognize seven independent states on the Trucial Coast proper—Abu Dhabi, Sharjah, Dubai, Ajman, Umm el Quwain, Ras el Khaima, and Kalba. Some of these, to be sure, are simply towns; but they are recognized by the British government as being of equal sovereign status, subject only to the paramountcy of Great Britain. There are, however, several other places along this testy coastline which believe themselves to be just as independent. There is an almost indistinguishable village called Al Hirah which claims such status; and an infinitesimal settlement called Hamriyah; and a minute hamlet called Fujairah. You must have a fairly large-scale map to find these villages at all, but each of them stands firmly enough upon its fancied dignities; and as we have seen, the wise oil company must bear in mind all possible claimants to concessionary areas. Sometimes the oilmen must woo a sheikh or a princeling simply because of his influence over the tribes; for like the sheikhs themselves, the oil company depends partly upon the goodwill of the wild men of the hinterland, and must assiduously foster all those elements which will allow it to work safely in regions not (to put it kindly) under very direct administrative control. The interior of Trucial Oman is, politically, a fearful muddle. The frontiers marked on the map are largely imaginary, and over them rambles a succession of tribes and nebulous Bedouin alliances, any one of which may be important to the oil company's cause. There are (to illustrate the point) the Beni Qitab, who dispute the sovereignty of the Sheikh of Sharjah; and the Naim, who are divided into two hostile sections; and the Al Bu Shamis, who hate the Naim; and the Beni Kaab, who hate everybody; and the Baluch of Mazam; and the Duru; and the Wahibah and Janaba; and the Harasis, who live in the Learish region of Hugf. One tribe of this region is possibly more primitive than any other in Arabia, which (as we saw in Dhufar) is saying a good deal. These are the Shihuh of the Shamailiya Mountains, a range of hills running down to the sea at the entrance to the Persian Gulf. They inhabit caves and pits dug in the ground, only intermittently emerging from the gloom to do some fishing on the coast, and they speak a dialect peculiar to themselves. The other Arabs believe them to be the direct descendants of Sinbad the Sailor, whose memory still persistently haunts the shores of the Gulf; and with this theory I would feel it presumptuous to disagree.

None of these fraternities are firmly subject to any of the sheikhs, and oil prospectors must establish friendly relations with all of them, if they are to explore and drill in safety. The peoples of Trucial Oman, underfed and under-endowed, are a difficult and avaricious lot, and the task of the oil man is often trying. Alas, for all the hard work of the oil companies, whose representatives in the field now know more about the Oman tribes than anyone else, no oil has yet been found in these petty sheikhdoms. Most of them are therefore sinking slowly, despite brave efforts by the British to improve their agriculture and enrich their bloodless economies. The town of Dubai is prospering more than most as an entrepot center for the whole coast; but more typical is the case of Sharjah, a little way to the east. There was a time when Sharjah was a flourishing pirate center. Then it made a comfortable income from pearls. Before the war the ponderous biplanes and flying-boats of Imperial Airways used it as a staging post, and cloche hats and silk stockings enlivened the guest house beside the sea. The war came, and with it both the British and American air forces. After the war some civilian air traffic was resumed. Nowadays, though, nobody loves Sharjah. It still has no oil wells. The R. A. F. station has dwindled almost to nonentity. The Americans have long since gone. The modern airliner needs no staging post, but flies direct from Cairo to India. Most conversations in Sharjah accordingly seem to revolve about negatives: no oil, no rain, no airplanes.

At the northern end of the coast, however, is a rather larger political entity, enjoying more or less similar relationships with Britain, which has been blessed with oil. I first landed in the sheikh-dom of Qatar, a peninsula protruding into the Gulf, at a small port on its eastern shore, some miles from the capital city of Doha. I asked a local taxi man to drive me to the capital, and we set off along an excellent tarmac road. Presently we approached a small Arab city beside the sea, with high walls, palm trees, and some of the big square wind-towers (rather Italianate in style) with which the wise Arabs ventilate their houses. Was this Doha? I asked the Arab with a conversational smile. He looked at me as music-hall comedians sometimes look at their vacuous stooges. Could he have heard aright? he seemed to be wondering. Surely he misunderstood me? Was *that* Doha? That crumbling, broken-down, derelict, un-hygienic, archaic, decrepit old travesty of a slum? *That* Doha? By God, I must have forgotten that *oil* had come to Qatar.

I saw what he meant when we did reach Doha, for that old seaport was in the condition of ear-splitting convulsion. They had found oil in Qatar in 1940, but during the war all the Persian Gulf wells were plugged in the supposition that within a month or two they might be in German hands. It was therefore only within the past few years that oil royalties had been flowing: Pygmalion had not yet tamed his Galatea's accent, but was already buying her mink. Such was the din of the cement mixers in Doha, and such the vibrations of the electric drills, that I was never certain pre-cisely what was happening; but there seemed to be some all-embracing program of reconstruction in progress, and the entire city felt topsy-turvy. The Sheikh's palace, a sprawling structure

beside the sea, bore such obvious signs of internal modernization
that it reminded me of one of those New Mexican hotels in which
every device of modern comfort is squeezed into a shell of Pueblo
mud-brick (indeed, it was related; Spanish-American architecture
has Arab antecedents, thanks to the Moorish conquests in Europe).
Offshore there stood a lovely steam yacht. It had been presented
to the ruler by King Saud of Saudi Arabia, complete with an
Italian captain and stocks of champagne, but it had never once
been out of the harbor. It simply stood there in the sunshine, with
the crew sunning themselves happily on deck and the champagne
hopefully chilled in the galley.

The Arabs, contrary to popular fancy, are astute businessmen,
and there is always someone to take advantage of such a situation as
this, in which great supplies of new money are poured into a
basically medieval town. In Doha the prince of entrepreneurs is
a notable called Abdullah Dawish, and his influence is all-pervasive.
Scarcely a signboard does not bear his name, scarcely a new-
sprouted company, with an officious title and wide-ranging functions, does not mask his enterprise. Everyone, Sheikh, British, oil
company and all, must pay court to Abdullah Dawish; and when
his huge American car sweeps through the churning concrete
mixers, even the bulldozer men look respectful.

So it is towards Qatar that the seven hungry sheikhs of the
Trucial Coast, Sharjah and Ajman, Abu Dhabi and Dubai, Umm el
Quwain, Ras el Khaima, and Kalba, cast their envious eyes.
This is the metamorphosis they would like their own slatternly
capitals to undergo, and they would even put up with the pre-
tensions of a Dawish and the attentions of those greasy adventurers
whose homing instinct guides them infallibly to the sources of oil.
It must be agreeable to rule an oil sheikhdom. Ignorant, mean,
irascible, autocratic, stubborn, dishonest, ugly though you may be,
everyone is nice to you. The British agent calls you Your Highness
and gives you medals and probably invites you to Coronations.
Abdullah Dawish painlessly procures your Cadillacs. All kinds of
unsuspected gadgets blossom in your palace. Yachts await your
pleasure in the harbor, oil magnates flatter you, your old rivals
and enemies accept with obsequies the largesse you occasionally
scatter in their direction. In the desert of your hinterland, and

among the shoals of your repulsive coastline, the drills and pumps work incessantly to augment your royalties. No problems of income tax need obsess you (you are the tax collector); no threat of rising prices (you are the exchequer); no covetous neighbors (the British will protect you). Nor need you abandon altogether the old sheikhly pleasures. There is still room for intrigue and hocus-pocus, even in Qatar. The present sheikh came to the throne as a result of an old-fashioned family squabble. The previous ruler succeeded his father in 1913 and ruled happily enough, with frequent political stimulations, until 1949. He then received a down-payment for some offshore concession, and rashly refused to share it with the other members of his family. A small war followed, and Ali ibn Abdullah ibn Qasim al Thani, present ruling sheikh of Qatar (1955 production 110,000 barrels a day) emerged the happy winner. He recently imported a pair of elephants just for the fun of it.

Indeed, my own most tenacious memory of Qatar remains an image of traditional character. I was once strolling through the *suk*, within sound of the drills and within sight of one of Dawish's emporia, when there emerged from a doorway beside me the smallest man I have ever seen. He was about two feet high. He was a stout and prosperous-looking dwarf, and was dressed in all the resplendent regalia of the Arab gentleman—splendid brown *aba*, milk-white *khuffiya*, black headband, dagger, and beads. With a flourish and a toss of his head this marvellous figure strode down the steps of his house and swaggered away down the *suk*, as bold and assured and magnificent as any gigantic African chieftain or Renaissance aristocrat. His proud head bobbed away among the packing cases, and a breath of the incense that perfumed his beard hung in the bazaar behind me.

BELGRAVIA

THE HEADQUARTERS of British authority in the Persian Gulf is the archipelago of Bahrain, a sheikhdom bound by treaty relations with Great Britain (that is to say, a sort of protectorate). I was once taken to a fireworks display on this island, organized by the local motoring club. The principal guest was the ruler of Bahrain, Sheikh Sir Salman ibn Hamad al-Khalifa, a friendly person who was once unkindly (but accurately) likened by the Duchess of Westminster to Miss Elsa Maxwell in fancy dress. The program was long and elaborate, and the rockets illuminated half the island and sometimes soared uncontrollably towards the Saudi shore, the lights of which twinkled two or three miles away; but during one of the lulls, while we ate excellent hot dogs and the ruler distributed apples from some hidden privy purse, somebody chanced to tell him the tale of Guy Fawkes, and how he tried to blow up the British legislature. His Highness thought for a moment about this cautionary tale, and then, taking another bite at his apple, commented with a wry smile, "Just what we need in Bahrain!"

For the first political tremors were then beginning to shake this trim but rather tedious little state, under the unavoidable mutations of the British connection. The ruler had been troubled by an organization called the Higher Executive Committee, and there had been an annoying general strike and some riots. With the boisterous support of the Egyptians, the committeemen had already forced some concessions out of the government, hitherto a purely family affair. They wanted a legislative council, a revision of the legal system, trade unions, and a high court of appeal which would be superior in authority to the government itself. They had managed to get popular representation in some departments of the administration; and the ruler had reluctantly agreed that the island's judges, who were all relatives of his, should in future have professionals sitting on the bench beside them. Everybody knew, though, that these were only the beginnings of the agitations of Bahrain—agitations that would certainly be aimed both at the ruler's well-upholstered palace and his easy-going relationship with the British. It was small wonder that the Sheikh, as he sat there munching, was dreaming of a pile of Catherine wheels and penny crackers ignited beneath the High Executive Committee.

When I began to investigate the activities of this reformist group, however, I was surprised at the bourgeois respectability. Most Arab experts in progress or subversion are lawyers, or Palestinians, or students, or ne'er-do-wells, or professional politicians, or ill-orientated intellectuals, or Egyptians, leavened and toughened by a sprinkling of genuine liberal thinkers. In Bahrain, though, these activities were being organized by people of almost unimpeachable worthiness. Most of them were solid merchants. None was less than 40 years old. There was not a student, not a reader of Kafka, not an attorney, not an argumentative refugee, scarcely a shabby opportunist among them; they seemed to me the least rapacious progressives I had ever met. Indeed, the very fact that they were agitating was a testimonial to their quality, for Bahrain was still governed on generally old-fashioned lines, and the astute merchant usually did his best to please the establishment.

The governors of Bahrain did not often see things in this light; and they perhaps did not realize that the nature of their troubles was a direct tribute to their administration. For thirty years Bahrain has been one of the best-governed little states in the world. Its modest oil royalties (it is not one of your Eldorados) have been wisely used. Its progress has been steady and unostentatious. Its educational systems are enlightened, and one of the more hopeful spectacles in the Middle East is break time at the big girls' school at Manama, when the girls of every social background, wearing trim blue uniforms and hair ribbons, troop into the playground in an atmosphere far removed from the black prison of the veil. Bahrain indeed is a model example of Anglo-Arabism; and if you are tempted to think that such sensible progress, built upon a traditional or monarchical foundation, is not precisely exciting, well, no more is the London County Council. The important thing is that it works, in the sense that it is a system that is improving the lot of the island's citizens and doing its best to preserve their modest prosperity. It is also, inevitably, a system that must lead eventually to reformist demands, Egypt or no Egypt, nationalism or no nationalism, as surely as the Education Act in England led to government by Socialism. What is more, the oil of Bahrain (extracted by an American-owned company) is drying up. Part of the state's oil profits have been sensibly invested all along, but the island's income will soon decrease, all the same; a high standard of education, a fundamentally liberal tutelage, a well-fed and relatively energetic populace will then be allied with a slowly declining standard of living and an ever more galling foreign connection. His Highness may be tempted to take the fireworks down to the cellar himself.

In 1956 Sir Charles Dalrymple Belgrave, the prime begetter of the island's fortunes, was still in office in Bahrain. This elegant man was officially adviser to the ruler; but in effect he was prime minister and cabinet as well, and Lady Belgrave enjoyed the beguiling title of Directress of Female Education. For thirty years he had guided the destinies of Bahrain, one of the most successful of the Anglo-Arab patriarchs. My own opinion is that he should have retired earlier, just as Britain should have realized earlier that the time for paternalism was past; but in his genre Belgrave was superb, and it will be many a long year before Bahrain and Belgrave can easily be disassociated in the mind.

The influence of this Mikado was all-pervasive. The people called him "Mr. Charles" and a mere mention of the name Belgrave would have its immediate impact upon almost any merchant or taxi driver. A request to send a pair of socks or a carpet or a sleeping bag to "Beit Belgrave" would instantly bring the price down. Belgrave's son, James Hamed, was the state's public information officer; Lady Belgrave played the part of an energetic lady of the manor (the ruler's own wife being totally immured in the palace); there was a street called Belgrave Road; and there was not a soul in the place, not a grand merchant nor a guttersnipe, not a sheikh nor a tailor nor a man picking his teeth on the high curved poop of a dhow, who could not direct you to the house where the Belgraves live.

Sir Charles Belgrave, however, was no stuffy, self-satisfied little autocrat such as Britain has sometimes imposed upon the Arabs. He viewed his own eminence with a trace of dry amusement, and his home—above his office—was a gay and racy place. The social life of British Bahrain was, in general, heavy going. Fairly rigidly segregated, only moderately enlightened, no more than fairly well-off, the British lived their island lives with a ponderous gentility, only occasionally enlivened (so far as I could see) by some minor matrimonial scandal; so that I used to wait in torment, through the thick, sweet custard that surrounded the canned apricots, for the party games that would, as surely as night follows day, follow the last tired flickers of the dinner conversation. But the Belgrave ménage was very different. For one thing, Mr. Charles had a splendid and eclectic library, and some good pictures. For another, he was a man of esoteric tastes, addicted to (for example) roulette, cigars, painting, swords, and pantomimes.

His was not the normal background of colonialism. Indeed, he was not an employee of the British Crown at all, but of the ruler; and he was not always (so I was assured) altogether *en rapport* with the British political resident in the Persian Gulf, who lived up the road. Belgrave, moreover, had not come to Bahrain by courtesy of the British government. He had seen an advertisement in the personal column of *The Times* asking for an adviser to the Sheikh, had answered it at once, and had been in Bahrain ever since.

It was a queer partnership, the chubby and saturnine ruler and the tall and startlingly handsome *bon vivant;* and it is paradoxical that this quixotic alliance should have fostered so worthy and rather pedestrian a state. Riots and strikes apart, there is an air of modest order to Bahrain—in its way a self-assertive air, smacking slightly of the sanctimonious. "How good our roads are," the island seems so say, "and how sensible and excellent our schools, and how thriftily we use our oil royalties—nothing extravagant, you know; our budget isn't large; no squandering here, I hope. Mohammed, stop picking your nose in front of Lady Belgrave!" Nothing is dramatic or feverish in Bahrain. The oil wells are unspectacular, and the oil company has built a town for itself strongly reminiscent of one of the less expensive suburbs in one of the medium-sized cities in one of the more moderate Middle Western states. The roads are indeed good, and the harbor, which handles some entrepot trade through and from Saudi Arabia, is well equipped. In short, it is an example of good, steady, level-headed British administration, something only the wastrel or the anarchist will scoff at.

There are, however, one or two odd things about Bahrain that help to alleviate its manner. For example, if you want to go from Bahrain to Persia, you must have two passports, just as you must have two if you wish to pass from Israel to the Arab world. This is because the Persians, who were the intermittent rulers of Bahrain from 1602 to 1785, claim that it is still theirs, and from time to time complain to the British when they make some new agreement with the usurper sheikh, whose family, after all, has provided rulers for the Bah archipelago only since 1816. British passports entitling travellers to enter Bahrain are therefore, in jaundiced Persian eyes, illegal documents. It is difficult at the moment to see how the Persians are going to implement this hoary claim; but there are a good many Persians living in Bahrain, and sometimes you will see, tacked to the wall of a cobbler's shop or protruding from behind a commercial calendar, a fading colored portrait of Dr. Mossadegh, still the hero of many Persians overseas.

Another gilding factor is the pearl industry, for centuries the basis of Bahrain's fluctuating fortunes. Up many an old rickety stair in the *suks* of Bahrain, in many a low-ceilinged, littered room, the pearl merchants will still unlock their safes for you and show you their treasures. The pearls of the Persian Gulf are the finest of all, and they once gave Bahrain the highest per capita income on earth. Nowadays cultured pearls and revolutions have together gravely weakened the market. Only the Indians and the Americans remain important buyers. The profit on the genuine pearl has been cut, so they say, by at least eighty-five percent; and the artificial product is now so good, so the story goes, that the Bahraini pearl divers themselves sometimes take a few to sea with them and throw them in to augment the catch.

The princes of the pearl industry, the juvenile leads, are of course the divers, and when the big pearling dhows put to sea you may see these men swaggering aboard like buccaneers. They are slim, wiry people whose trade seems to suit them; they go down to ninety feet with only a nose-clip to protect them, the use of diving suits being forbidden by Bahraini law. The divers, once sadly exploited, now earn reasonable money and are carefully protected by law, though the long days and nights they spend on the pearl banks are obviously demanding.

Just as the tank is a carriage built around a gun, so the pearl ship is a vessel built around the diver. Husky Negroes pull it to sea; a stately owner-captain guards the catch and gives the orders; a cook prepares the frugal meals (dates, coffee, fish, and rice; it is a mistake, as any mother knows, to dive on a full stomach); and out at the banks, in the blue of the Gulf, the divers plunge down with a weighted rope and a basket just as the film star, with a last smoothing of his hair and a twitch of the mustache, strolls like a monarch before the cameras. After a few years of this, the diver often buys a boat of his own, and then acquires a new kind of dignity, enabling him to supervise operations from a rope cot slung to the rail of the poop. But though there is glamor to the pearl diver's life, there is still insecurity. The pearl is a treasure without much future. The government has done its best to devise alternative work for the divers and their kind—in particular, by encouraging the breeding of a species of white donkey peculiar to Bahrain. But it seems a sad transition, from the limpid waters of the Gulf, the barracuda and the sponge beds, the boxes of pearls and the rope cot on the poop, to the propagation of small white donkeys.

Two other circumstances spice the staid atmosphere of Bahrain and temper its sanity. One is the presence on the main island of a multitude of mysterious tumuli. There are said to be fifty thousand of them, forming perhaps the largest graveyard on earth, and in Damascus they would no doubt be accepted without question as the graves of prophets, martyrs and apostles. In Bahrain the theories entwined around their origins are hilariously contradictory. For all expeditions that have come to the island, with their reference books and microscopes and devices for measuring the specific gravity of dust, nobody really knows what these tombs are. Persian, says one scholar; Arab, says somebody else; the work of nomads from the mainland, says a third, with an endearing flourish. But nobody knows. When a recent expedition announced that it would be opening on the following Thursday the tomb of a king, probably complete with all his accoutrements, the tumulus turned out to be an ancient lavatory, complete with watercloset. It seems unfair that so neat and logical a state should be burdened with such eccentric antiquities.

Finally there are the parrots. Many a roving sailor has, at one time or another, brought a caged parrot back to Bahrain; and many a caged parrot has, over the generations, escaped and mated. Do not be alarmed if a vivid flash of blue or yellow dazzles you among the drab sandy flats of Bahrain, or a harsh croak emerges from a palm grove. When an entrenched feudalist of the island once told me, with a sniff, that the deliberations of the Higher Executive Committee were "as the chatter of silly parrots," he knew what he was talking about.

BOOM TOWN

THE MIDDLE EAST is a place of contrasts (as the reader of travel books knows all too well); but nothing could be more surprising than the transition from Bahrain to its neighbor sheikhdom, Kuwait, one hundred and fifty miles up the Gulf. My own most enjoyable approach to Bahrain was by sea, in a sedate little steamer going to Basra, when I was met, after the usual efficient formalities, by James Belgrave and whisked away to town on a neat, gray motor launch. But I first went to Kuwait in the company of a sheikhly hawking party, who had been down to the Trucial Coast to practice their sport. Splendid were the caparisons of those haughty Arab sportsmen, and their eyes were cold and heavy-lidded. They wore magnificent flowered gowns, and crossed bandoliers, and daggers, and spotless headdresses, and gilded swords; and big black lackeys carried their peregrine falcons, hooded upon their pedestals; and a brass band puffed away upon the airfield at Kuwait when this gorgeous crew, looking slightly airsick, staggered on to the ancestral soil.

In 1954 Bahrain earned about nine million dollars from its oilfields; Kuwait in the same year earned about two hundred and forty million. It is by far the richest place, per capita, on earth. It consists simply of a seaport and a desert hinterland, and the dollars are packed so tightly into this enclave that they burst its frontiers and spill out into the stock markets of the world. The Sheikh of Kuwait is, I believe, the richest of all men. He is the most important single provider of new money for the London investment market. His income has increased twenty-fold since 1950. When he paid a recent visit to Paris, I am told, he gave his two new Cadillacs to his French chauffeur when he left. He earns more money every hour than most British Cabinet Ministers do in a year. If you laid his bank accounts end to end . . . but no superlatives can do justice to the fabulous resources of this Arabian sheikh, whose grandfather was responsible for the mud wall that surrounds the city of Kuwait, a protection against marauding tribesmen.

There has never been a Belgrave in Kuwait, and the Sheikh has had a succession of British advisers, in one capacity and another, and some unfortunate experiences with opportunist British businessmen. There is thus none of that sense of orderliness so apparent in Bahrain. The ruler, partly with altruistic intent, partly as a hostage to fortune, has lavished large sums of money on social services; but it is as though he had opened his mullioned window one morning and scattered bank notes to the streets outside, so wildly extravagant are some of the projects, and so grossly ill-suited to the environment. There is, for instance, a vast technical school, built in the Festival of Britain manner, all airy-fairy colonnades. Cost plus was the general rule in postwar Kuwait, and the machinery shop had parquet flooring. The corridor lights go on automatically at sunset, in theory, anyway. Each pupil, extracted from the tents of the desert or the cluttered backstreets of the town, has his own dainty cubicle; and the kitchens, I feel sure, could turn you out a *crêpe suzette* or a *fondu* in the twinkling of an eye. A caustic Egyptian engineer had been imported to preside over this marvellous establishment; but alas, he told me, shivering in his raincoat (they forgot to put in any heating) he only had twenty pupils for a school as big as Eton, and remarkably few of the gadgets seemed to work.

Innumerable other gaily-colored schools brighten the skyline of Kuwait—girls' schools and boys' schools, infant schools and adult schools, technical schools and social schools and secondary schools and elementary schools; these had been halcyon years for those many British architects who make a specialty of rambling, pastel-shaded, peelable, rustable, fadable places of education. There is a splendid communal kitchen for supplying these places with food. It is run by Lyons under contract, and is the biggest and grandest kitchen I have ever seen. An army of cooks works at its vats and ovens, an ocean of milk percolates through its pipes, and a fleet of trucks distributes its products to the fortunate children.

There is also an astonishing new water filtration plant, the greatest in the world. Kuwait is a place without fresh water, and in the past has always been dependent upon supplies brought by dhow from the Shatt-el-Arab in Iraq, about fifty miles away. It would be very easy to pipe this water to Kuwait, but the ruler does not relish being beholden to the Iraqis, and possibly suspects that one day a hostile Iraqi government might cut the water off. He has therefore commissioned this vast machine, built by British engineers. It is brightly painted, each channel of water, I suppose, being marked by a different color, so that it looks like one of those dismembered motor cars used for instruction. The control room is silent, spotless, and opulent, like the switchboard rooms of the great American dams; and the whole thing stands beside the sea foursquare and glittering, gulping the salt water in, pouring the drinking water out, night and day through the years. (It puts a little salt back into the final product, just to give it tang.)

All this has, of course, greatly altered the character of Kuwait, once the most Arab of the big Gulf ports. They still build the high-prowed, ungainly dhows along the waterfront, observing the immemorial taboos and shibboleths of the Arab shipbuilder; each dhow carries a muezzin to sea, who utters the call to prayer each morning from the poop. And there is still a big, rambling, jumbled old quarter of Kuwait, in which many a woman is held in such strict purdah that she may not even climb to the rooftop to see the view. If you stroll along the seashore in the evening, among the shipyards, with a smell of wood and oil and fish, and a murmurous Arab hubbub arising from the coffee-shops, you may imagine the Kuwait of two decades ago, when it was still little more than a petty sheikhdom, living on pearls and shipbuilding and entrepot trade, and supported, believe it or not, by a small British subsidy.

But most of Kuwait is now brash and noisy, and exemplified best, perhaps, by the yacht presented to the incumbent ruler's father by an American oil company. That remarkable vessel was of course air-conditioned and equipped with every kind of modern navigational device; but it also had a throne room of elaborate magnificence, a sheep pen on the upper deck, and a galley designed especially for the roasting of three whole sheep at a time. The present Sheikh seems to be a man of relatively abstemious tastes; but, as in Saudi Arabia, some other members of the ruling family are less self-disciplined, and set an example of profligate spending and improvidence that is eagerly copied. Huge, noisy, and thoughtless are the cars that speed through the rackety streets of Kuwait, themselves a turmoil of demolition and reconstruction. The old, flowery courtesies are dying fast, and of all the cities of the Middle

East Kuwait is now perhaps the rudest. There is an air of get-rich-quick to every corner of the place. The shops are cluttered with expensive things, thrown in the window willy-nilly, or stacked in trays as toys are displayed at Woolworth's. The names of a few big Kuwaiti merchants crop up in every commercial conversation, and around the fringes of these magnates there hovers an unprepossessing company of foreigners, obsequious as any pasha's eunuchs. I know of few cities more impregnated with shadiness, and the steely impatience of Kuwait *suks* is a most disagreeable phenomenon.

This is a change of values as complete and as significant as any contemporary social transition, even including the metamorphosis of Communism; but though it is distasteful to watch, good is coming from it as well as evil. Not all the Kuwaiti public monies are being squandered, and the presence of oil in this dry little state gives it hope and energy, as well as this new squalid commercialism. There is, for instance, a fine National Health Service, totally free to all comers. There is a mental hospital, a magnificent tuberculosis sanatorium, and a new general hospital, all in a special hospital area (like the great medical centers of the United States) a little way outside the city. There are also mobile clinics and a dental center. All is free. I was ill in Kuwait once, and found myself looked after by a New Zealand doctor of very high caliber. Any Kuwaiti has the same treatment, and people come to the sheikhdom for attention from many parts of the Middle East, if they find the air fare costs less than a first-class doctor at home.

The most far-sighted people in Kuwait welcome this influx of shrewd patients, for they optimistically see their city as a kind of international technical center for the Middle East. Already a few students from other Arab countries come to school at Kuwait; and there is no logical reason why the great technical schools of the place, with their fabulous and largely wasted equipment, should not prove as potent a magnet to the young scientists and technicians of the Arab world as the universities of Beirut have been to the thinkers—except that in the Arab countries, as in other fundamentally aristocratic societies, hardly anybody wants to be a scientist.

Power and momentum, too, are certainly apparent in Kuwait. Everything is moving, and moving fast. There are always ships offshore, and the four-engined airliners of Kuwait Airways stand gleaming on the airfield, for almost every pocket-state of the Middle East has its own airline, not excluding the Yemen. Some of the new roads, sprawling over the surrounding desert, look splendid from the air; and the red flag of Kuwait, which flies boldly from many a white-washed rooftop, is so thickly cluttered with white Arabic lettering, vertical and horizontal, as to be excitingly cabalistic in its appearance. The British element, fitting so easily into the sedate stability of Bahrain, here feels swamped by the pace of it all; you could spend a week in Kuwait without noticing the British political agency, or observing any particular manifestation of the British connection. (But all is well so far: the ruler is still investing his millions in London.) Kuwait has all the attractions of a genuine boom town: gusto, vivacity, shifting, wary relationships, new faces, enterprises galore, and a sometimes invigorating sense of no-holds-barred. It is a young man's town, brash and scurrilous. If you stand on one of the sixty-seven towers of the city wall and look across the variegated rooftops of the town, the grasping vitality of Kuwait hits you like a slap in the face—unless of course it is the heat of high afternoon, when the motor-scooter factory goes to sleep like any other Arab institution.

Above all, you can rarely forget in Kuwait that you are above the greatest reservoir of oil on earth. The oil reserves of the entire United States (area, three million square miles) are estimated at twenty-four billion barrels; the reserves of Kuwait (area, five thousand eight hundred square miles) are estimated at twelve billion barrels. The Anglo-American company which exploits this unbelievable wealth has built itself a handsome oil city outside Kuwait proper, in which you can enjoy an excellent meal in a clubhouse that reminds me of Roehampton. From a hillock near this town you can see all the processes of the oil industry within the space of a few square miles. To the south, in the desert, they are still looking for oil, and on a distant horizon you may catch sight of an exploratory rig and the little caravan of trucks that goes with it. Nearer, there are the productive wells of the oilfields of Burga, the richest in the world: each has its pump, like a crooked old man, working away tirelessly through the years; and each has its pipeline to the plants where the waste gasses are burnt, flaming away, night and day, like beacons in the sand. There is a small refinery and a bitumen plant, near the sea; and finally, on the coast of the Persian Gulf at Mina el-Ahmadi, there is a new oil port that is the most exciting engineering project in the Middle East.

It is a single pier, made entirely of steel, running parallel to the shore at the end of a causeway. Ten big pipelines run down this causeway to the pier, and at the end of them there are berths for eight big ships. There are always tankers at this pier. Throughout every minute of the year oil is being pumped into ships at Mina el-Ahmadi, and a greater tonnage of merchandise is handled there annually than at the Port of London. The pier, however, is spotlessly, almost clinically, clean. There is not a sign, not a smear, not a sniff of oil. The great tankers simply slide alongside; pipes are screwed into them; and the oil is pumped into their bunkers. It takes only a few hours, and the tanker crews, who have often sailed direct from the United States, generally do not bother to come ashore, but sail directly back to America again. A tremendous sense of controlled power dignifies this process; and the most beautiful things in Kuwait are the tankers that come to Mina el-Ahmadi, with unlikely flags (Panama or Liberia) and adventurous owners (Niarchos or Onassis) and superstructures that look like vast white refrigerators, and hulls like sleek black whales.

It is easy to sneer at the Coca-Colonization of the Middle East, which is indeed hideous to observe; but it is difficult to carp at the advent of new pleasures for a people whose lot has been, in the past, not without monotony. Thanks to oil many a Kuwait housewife now has piped water, something, until a few years ago, outside the range of her imagination, let alone her aspiration. For the first time she is being prised free, bit by bit, from the tyranny of the veil, so muffling that even today many Kuwaiti women cannot even sew, but while away their lives, cloistered in their quarters, in desultory gossip and childbirth. The ill-mannered young Kuwaiti at the cinema is certainly less agreeable to meet than his forebear, courteous and hospitable in his goathair tent; but it must be a fearful bore being a Bedu for long, and who would begrudge such a youth his evenings among the cowboys? There is less honor in Kuwait than there used to be, less beauty, less moral certainty, less sense of glory and decorum; but for the local inhabitants there is certainly more comfort, and there may well be more fun. If you agree with Jefferson that education is the first duty of government, and believe that any widening of horizons is, per se, a good thing, then you must regretfully reconcile yourself to the ghastly phenomenon of the new Kuwait. For myself, loyal Jeffersonian though I am, I prefer the goathair to the chromiumplate.

PART FOUR

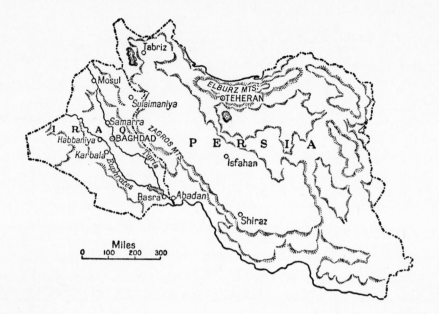

OIL AND ABADAN

THE SOUTHERN GATEWAY of Persia, at the head of the Persian Gulf, is more a machine than a city, more a thing than a being, more symbolic than animate. We have travelled through the oil states of Arabia, through some countries where oil is already gushing, through others where only the hope of it glimmers fitfully. Now we reach the country where the first of Middle East oil was extracted and we stand in a town whose name is synonymous with the power and the anxiety of oil: Abadan. When the Persians nationalized their oil industry, and the British technicians from the Abadan refinery sailed despondently away down the Shatt-el-Arab, a shudder ran through all the oil companies, and the germ of an ambition was engendered in the chanceries of the Arabs. It was a watershed in the geography of Middle East oil: on one side of it oil was pseudo-politics, on the other it is simply business. Since then nothing has been quite the same in the oilfields and refineries of the Middle East. The threat of seizure, the pressure of politics, the peril of nationalism color the thoughts of the oilmen; the prospects of blackmail excite the instincts of the Arab politicians.

Abadan remains symbolic of the old days, before oil and imperialism were finally divorced. It is vast, gleaming, and very pompous. Its tall chimneys stand in twos beside the hot, muddy river, and a slow stream of vapor issues from them insolently. Tankers load in the shimmering heat; launches chug across the water to Iraq; the catalytic cracker stands in ungainly majesty among the storage tanks. Everything is functional, metallic, big, aloof. It is also foreign. Around the geometrical confines of the refinery there straggles a dingy, higgledy-piggledy Persian quarter, jerry-built bazaars and littered alleyways, and women sitting on the pavements in grubby flowered blue; but the oil city of Abadan remains uncompromisingly alien. It has no affinities, shares no point of communion with the spirit of the country, and a barrier of high mountains separates it physically from the Persian heartland. It lies there between the mountains and the great river, in a shuttered enclave at the edge of the kingdom. Teheran is five hundred miles away; the Zagros Mountains bar the way to the interior; Abadan is almost as foreign to its hinterland as the pariah state of Israel is to its implacable Arab neighbors.

This pernicious sense of insulation was a prime factor in the debacle of the Anglo-Iranian Oil Company, and by 1956 it was the aim of every Middle Eastern oil company to "integrate" its activities with the local life around it, and to scotch (with an ingratiating gesture) any suggestion that the company played an independent role, political or economic, in national affairs. "*Our* company?" the oilmen used to say to the natives gushingly; "just yours and ours!" In this exercise, as we have already seen, the Americans were especially adept. In Saudi Arabia they fought so strenuously against any charge of political manipulation that they were sometimes manipulated themselves. If ever the Saudis planned some political hocus-pocus upon their remote and disputed frontiers, they knew they could rely upon the oil company for the necessary transport. Saudi political claims were dutifully accepted by the oilmen; maps published by the oil company show the whole of southeastern Arabia, except for a narrow coastal strip, within Saudi frontiers.

The British, though at least as hungry for the mess of potage, had not yet sold their birthright so unconditionally. Nevertheless, in their efforts to please the Arabs they were often so greasily flattering as to be dishonest. Blatantly undeserved credit was lavished upon local employees, especially those who, wearing expensive suits and expressions of genial vacuity, were installed in grand offices as tangible evidence of integration. Whatever you did, you must never imply that any Arab was incapable of doing anything that a European could do. If you had to have a picture of a refinery man in your house magazine, make it Gamal Hussein, who cleans the wash basins, rather than Henry Jones, who has spent a lifetime mastering the intricacies of gravity flow. If you were foolish enough to refer to the British pioneers who had explored and mapped those waste deserts, you must be sure to qualify your admiration with some fulsome reference to the Bedouin tribesmen who had, it need scarcely be said, been crossing those trackless wastes for centuries before, and in whose spirit, my dear Hussein, the Arab love of adventure was still so gloriously apparent.

As a necessary corollary to all this, the oil companies worked with well-publicized zeal to train Arabs and Persians for technical jobs. Huge and expensive were their training schools (though much more economical than the ones at Kuwait) and their programs of education were often ambitious. But it was a tricky business. If they neglected these activities, the oil companies were accused of suppressing the natural talents of the Arabs in order to keep more foreigners on the payrolls. If, on the other hand, they allowed them to blossom too lavishly, they were accused of interference in the internal affairs of the state. If they pursued the mean, half their apprentices learned all they could at company expense and then ran away to the capital for comfortable city jobs. In Saudi Arabia, as may be imagined, any precipitate extension of education, any broadening of horizons, could be construed as a threat to the royal house; to avoid employing too many Americans, the company imported more than a thousand Italians, classed in the context of the Middle East as semi-Europeans, or pseudo-Levantines. (If you think this unfair, compare the way of life of a Sicilian hill farmer with that of his Lebanese counterpart.) But striking the balance in a matter so delicate is a task of infinite difficulty, and whole departments of the oil companies, designated by resounding titles and staffed by young men of urbanity, devoted themselves warily to the problems of integration.

Whether it did any good is open to question. Perhaps it made everyday relations easier, perhaps it helped governments to restrain the nationalist fervor of their populaces; but it is difficult to believe that the Arabs, any more than the wandering Englishmen, took these sophisms very seriously. Certainly they did little to modify the naturally acquisitive approach of the Arab governments to the oil companies. In the Finance Ministries of the oil states life was a constant struggle for extra royalties. For months, for instance, the Syrians threatened to block the passage of oil by pipeline across their territories from Iraq to the sea. They wanted a much higher fee for this privilege. Moderates in Damascus wanted the charge to be instantly tripled; others, of wilder inclinations, demanded a higher share of the profits than was earned by Iraq herself, where the oil came from. The Syrians did nothing to speed the transit of this oil; they already profited greatly from the presence of pumping stations; but so strong was their position of stranglehold, and so disruptive and contagious the force of nationalism, that the company, smiling sweetly, doubled their fees. When the British launched their attack on Suez, a few months later, the first repercussion in the Middle East was the blowing up of that very pipeline, royalties and all.

Other countries were scarcely less trying and illogical. The Egyptians, for a variety of ill-explained reasons, were almost uniformly unhelpful to the British and American companies operating within their frontiers. They had virtually no oil and were always hoping to find some, but they so irritated the prospectors with their constant pinpricks and hindrances that one great company packed up and left, and the others operated with a notable diminution of enthusiasm. Even the Lebanese, at our particular moment in history, had caught the habit. They, too, had no oilfields, but oil from Saudi Arabia and Iraq crossed their territory in pipelines to the Mediterranean, and fired by the Syrian example they were demanding higher transit dues; indeed, at one time they were claiming the same dues for their twenty-five miles of Iraqi pipeline as the Syrians were for two hundred and fifty miles. Reason and friendship played little part in the oil politics of the Arabs, and scarcely more in the business negotiations of the West. The relationship between states and companies was, in general, one of uneasily stanched blackmail. The Arabs, for the time being, wanted Western technical help anyway; the companies, it need hardly be said, wanted the oil.

The shift in ownership, indeed, has generally been within the Western community. British, French, and Dutch companies were all represented in the Middle East, but the most important producers had long been Americans. They exploited the Saudi and Bahraini oilfields outright, had a half-share in Kuwait and a substantial cut in the Iraqi, Persian, and Qatari fields. Britain, on the other hand, had only a half-share in Kuwait and a major share in the Iraqi, Persian, and Gulf fields. In 1939 the American share in Middle East oil production was thirteen percent and the British sixty percent. By 1956 the American share was sixty-five percent and the British thirty percent. This was partly the result of diplomatic pressure—American interests were first admitted to a share of Iraqi oil as a result of State Department intervention, and no doubt the same is true of Persia. It was chiefly, though, because of direct commercial competition, in a sphere of industry not noted for its altruism. Nowadays the competition chiefly concerns the marketing rather than the extraction of oil; but in Arabia, where most exploration was being done, the lingering sense of contest between American and British companies, and the natural rivalry between the pound sterling and the dollar, was unhappily linked with Saudi ambitions, so that the oil companies found themselves fighting dynastic battles far removed indeed from the struggles between the service stations.

But if the oil cauldron was simmering in the autumn of 1956, and stirred only by Colonel Nasser's Suez Canal coup, the threat of ultimate seizure still lay heavily over the companies. It was obvious enough that one day the Arabs, whether separately or in unity, would become the owners of their means of production. It was only a matter of time. In many other technical spheres the Arabs were now their own masters. They ran their own railways, produced their own electricity, sailed their own ships, wove their own textiles, built their own roads. The technical progress of Egypt, in particular, had been impressive, and in industrial skill that country was already the equal of more than one European state. Arabs often made excellent mechanics and machine workers, and adapted themselves all too easily to the industrial life.

Sooner or later, they would master the production of oil, too, and unless atomic power had by then replaced the internal combustion engine as mankind's principal motive force, they would then hold the Western world in fee. The Suez Canal can be bypassed—the biggest tankers are doing it already—but oil is irreplaceable. The Arabs were slow to realize this portentous possibility, just as they were often strangely slow to comprehend changes in the balance of world power. Colonel Nasser, however, had it constantly in mind, and was no doubt thinking of it when he seized the canal. He saw oil not only as a means of transferring power to the Arabs, to the underdeveloped peoples, to the Bandung spirituality; he saw it also (in his more lucid, less blinkered moments) as an instrument for welding together the Arabs. Steadily, over the months, Cairo radio had been educating its myriad

listeners in the meaning of oil. "Oil is for the Arabs! Why do you
not exploit your lost wealth, which is being plundered by aliens?
Remember that the oil which flows from your land is seized by
your enemy! Remember oil, your lost wealth! Oil is for the
Arabs!" In Cairo the League of Arab States, under Egyptian inspiration, set up a committee specifically to study the Arabization
of oil. The Egyptians even began to cast about for tankers, for as
the Persians found, lack of the means of distribution could be as
decisive as the lack of oil itself. The first dribble of Egyptian technicians, so it was said, had gone to Russia or eastern Europe for
training. Three sources of power bound the Arabs in hope, Nasser
wrote in his booklet, *The Philosophy of the Revolution*. One was
the common heritage of the Arab peoples, spiritual and historical.
The second was the strategic situation of their lands. The third was
oil. "Oil is the vital nerve of civilization, without which its
great works, its weapons, its communications would be motionless,
lifeless things. We can consider ourselves powerful, powerful in
our thorough understanding of the strength of this bond which
links us and makes our territory one."

Who can doubt that any Arab visionary, with his mind on the
renaissance of his peoples, must see this fabulous resource as the
basis of their prosperity? And could such a man be content with
the prospect of a half-share, with Mrs. Harris, the General Manager's wife, presenting boxes of chocolates at sports meetings, and the
company magazines doing their unconvincing best not to feel
superior? It will be many a long year before the Arabs can extract
their own oil, ship it to the markets of the world, and sell it for
the currencies they want. They will need thousands of trained
technicians, a competent managerial class, a tanker fleet, a marketing agency. Above all they will need unity, to prevent this great
industry from subsiding into that bog of suicidal bickering so characteristic of the region. But one day, no doubt, they will achieve
it, and the blackmail will be over.

With this idea simmering in the mind of the Middle East, no
wonder there are frayed nerves and ulcers in the oil industry. As
the great Western empires have wilted and withered, so the oil in-

dustry has, in parallel, adapted its manners to the demands of the time. In Abadan this process will be made poignantly clear to you. It is no longer one of the world's vital refineries, for it is out-of-date both in technique and in style. There are newer, better ones, more compact, more efficient, and much more integrated. Abadan is a nostalgic white elephant of the industry—an object lesson in which the developing maneuvers of the oil industry are piquantly demonstrated.

Nowadays it is run by an international consortium, but in its heyday it was a show place of Britain overseas, a product of the supreme confidence of an empire. No concessions to local sentiment were made when they built Abadan. There was no obsequious shuffling of feet, no bowing towards Teheran, no disguising of the fact that this was a British refinery, run by Britons, intended to bolster the British economy and bring comfort to the King's subjects. Abadan was as bold and British as the flag, and as bluff as the warships of the Royal Navy whose bunkers it resolutely filled.

Much of this Englishry remains, even in the anemic circumstances of today. There are London taxis, British buses, genteel gardens, clubs, and signposts. An air of old-style British orderliness still pervades the place. There are men in bars talking about cricket averages; and an Old Etonian who says diffidently that he is something to do with Public Relations, and that sort of thing; and a guest house with notices of church services and airmail editions of *The Times*.

Ghostly you may find it, pathetic it certainly is; but it throws a revealing, retrospective light upon the problems of the oilmen, and it serves as a curious introduction to the Imperial Kingdom of Persia, where the Shah-in-Shah, King of Kings, successor to the dynasties of the Qatars, the Afsharids, the Safayids, and the Ilkhans, still lives in imperial splendor in the Palace of Marble.

GARDEN OF THE SUN

And on from thence to Isfahan,
The golden garden of the sun,
Whence the long dusty caravan
Brings cedar and vermilion.

A LAST GLIMPSE of the chimneys is your farewell to Abadan,
a last blur of the vassal bazaars beside the water, a last faint suggestion of the smell of oil, before your aircraft plunges rocking into
the Zagros Mountains. A violent transition then occurs. You look
out of your window, all unsuspecting, and suddenly there are
rocky crags high above you. The man in the next seat clutches
your arm for support and the elderly Muslims invoke the protection of Allah and prepare their paper bags. The aircraft is probably
not young, and its American pilot is both skillful and daredevil;
so your passage through that unfriendly range is, if you like that
kind of thing, hilarious. This is your way to the imperial city of
Isfahan.

It is a different world across the mountains, with the taste of
Asia to it, and a flicker of India; but when you land at last in
Isfahan you will feel yourself easily enough at home. The architecture is different, and the language, and even the race; but you are
still adjacent to Arabia, and the extraordinary potent radiation of
the Muslim faith still permeates every activity and flavors the very
air of the city. Like Damascus, Isfahan is an oasis. The desert that
surrounds it is moonlike and mysterious, punctuated by small
pimply hills; the landscape is alive with constantly shifting colors;
and Isfahan stands amid the aridity, domed and pinnacled, in a
posture of welcome. It is one of the most famous and most beautiful
cities on earth; but I find it graced also with a marvellously beguiling eccentricity that seems to me characteristic of the Persian
nation.

At first you will be struck only by the astonishing beauty of the
place. Isfahan is a planned city, laid out by Abbas Shah at the end
of the sixteenth century and retaining an orderly perfection of
form that makes it, compared with most of the jumbled and cluttered cities of the Middle East, infinitely calm and restful. There

are some textile factories scattered about the perimeter of the place, and the suburbs are beginning to intrude into the surrounding desert; but the center of Isfahan remains very much the same as Abbas Shah left it, and it is easy to accept the legend that this fabulous oriental city, glimpsed by the ambassadors and couriers of the seventeenth century, was the inspiration of the Champs-Elysées. The gorgeous heart of Isfahan is Imperial Square, which the Persians sometimes claim, though they are by no means a boastful people, to be the biggest square on earth. In this great space, called in Persian "The Design of the World," the glittering court of the Safavid monarchs played its polo and mounted its magnificent military parades. At one side of it is the Shah's own pavilion, a high grandstand directly related to Ascot or Churchill Downs, where even now a gray top hat or a flouncy parasol would not seem out of place. Opposite is the delectable mosque of Lutfallah; to the north the bustling entrance to the bazaars; to the south the unbelievable Blue Mosque—a structure as blue and perfect as an eastern sea, grand and delicate at the same time, a kaleidoscope of pools, blue tiles, and shining Islamic script.

So genuinely magnificent is this spectacle, so vast and almost Kremlinesque in concept, so grandiose but graceful in style, so wide and airy, that it might well be unpleasantly pompous. But such is the temperament of Persia that it is redeemed by a singular circumstance: it is crooked. Not only is Imperial Square "out of true," so to speak, with the rest of Isfahan, so that it is not parallel with the two great thoroughfares that intersect the city; it is also asymmetrical in itself, because the great Blue Mosque is twisted towards the southeast so as to be in the correct relationship with Mecca. If you therefore stand at the entrance to the bazaars and survey the square before you, there stands the Shah's pavilion, dominating one side neatly enough; and there is Lutfallah's mosque, opposite; and there are tidy, symmetrical gardens in the center, where the polo ground used to be; but the masterpiece at the other end is all askew, its gateway facing one way and its great *iwan* another, so that it looks like one of those quixotic attempts, by architectural draftsmen of the eighteenth century, to draw buildings in two perspectives at the same time.

The Arabs, with their flair for formality in architecture, would never have countenanced this quirk of design; but Persia makes its own rules. There was never such a tortuous, inside-out, back-to-front way of thinking as the Persian way; never such a fascinating, will-o'-the-wisp, unpredictable community of peoples; nowhere buildings so inexpressibly lovely as these dreams of Isfahan; nowhere a landscape more peculiar than the wide Iranian plain, sometimes bleak beyond description, sometimes warm and multi-colored, often queerly criss-crossed with the big round craters that mark the passage of underground water channels. And there was never a language more immediately unintelligible than Pharsi, the predominant language of the Persians, so that you will readily sympathize with the old Englishman's commendation of his English-speaking servant: "He speaks a known language, don't you know!" Ask a Persian which is his right ear, and he will put his left hand behind his head and point out the ear from behind.

In Isfahan you are never far from expressions of oddity. Here and there English notices are stuck on the walls: they always have the letter "N" printed backwards, and somehow this little aberration hauntingly reflects the flavor of the city. Not far from the Blue Mosque there is another building which the people of Isfahan regard with almost equal favor. It is called, I think, the Quivering Mosque, and its claim to fame is that if you stand inside one of its two little minarets and shake it with your shoulders, the other minaret quivers too. Earnest and determined is the expression on the face of the caretaker as he performs this curious duty. Ponderously he climbs to the roof, past the tomb of the fourteenth-century divine who is buried in the mosque, and worms his way inside the minaret. You stand in the sunshine expectantly; and presently there is a sound of heaving, squirming, heavy breathing, and grunting, as the caretaker, now jammed hard inside the tower, sets the phenomenon in motion. At first nothing at all seems to happen; but after a moment or two, sure enough, a faint but just perceptible rocking motion overcomes the roof, and if you concentrate very hard you can see those two little minarets swaying together in queasy motion. When you climb downstairs again there stands the caretaker's wife, rubbing her palms on her skirt, to tell you with an air of ineffable astonishment that, miracle of miracles, while you

were up there on the roof the tomb of the fourteenth-century
divine began to quiver too!

It is impossible to escape the pleasant suspicion that she thinks
this rather funny. Life in Persia is largely governed by a sense of
humor, and depends for its continuity upon a series of *non sequiturs;*
so that affairs there progress bumpily but soothingly, like an opiate
with grits in it. It has long been so, for through centuries of despotism the Persian has erected around himself an indefinable screen of
humor, slipperiness, and oddness, a smoke-screen or camouflage,
a false trail, a tear gas, behind which he can dive when trouble
approaches him, to the bewildered chagrin of his tormenters. It
was so in the great days of the Persian imperial dynasties, when a
monarch might decapitate you at the drop of a hat, and if anything
it is probably more so now. Everywhere among the glories of
Isfahan you meet quiddities and irrelevancy. When I was visiting
the Palace of the Forty Pillars they were repairing the roof of its
great audience chamber. On the floor, among the frescoes and
glass cases, all was solemn and in earnest; but high above us a workman on a scaffolding was clowning away in the shadows, with
dances and funny faces and quaint buffooneries, for the amusement
of his fellow craftsmen. (The palace really has only twenty pillars,
but the Persians, who like high-sounding titles, include the reflections in the great pool outside.) On the opposite side of the road
there is a photographer's shop, in which you may expect to see the
usual faded display of picture postcards. You will be agreeably
surprised, for the *pièce de résistance* of that respectable window is
a series of brownish photographs of local criminals at the moment
of apprehension. Wonderfully bestial are the faces that peer at
you from behind the dusty glass, and proud and stern the looks in
the eyes of the successful constables, who have generally clamped
an enormous chain around the neck of the criminal, shackled his
hands and feet, and caused him to sit on the ground in front of
them like some ugly and ill-bred dog.

Over the river at Isfahan there are three fine bridges, the best of
them almost Florentine in splendor. When I was taken to see this
structure my guide told me that Shah Abbas, its builder, had taken
a particular interest in its design. There had to be a rest room for
tired travellers, comfortably furnished; and a retreat for holy men;

and rooms where jugglers and singers could entertain the travelling public; and a place reserved for wedding festivities. "And the
strange thing is," my informant added seriously, "that it is also
exactly right for the washing of buses!" I looked over the edge as
we approached the bridge, and indeed, two rickety buses had been
driven beneath the inner arches, where the water was shallow,
and were being energetically washed: the bridge might have been
made for them, so exactly did they fit. Why did the buses have
to go under the bridge to be washed? I asked the guide. In case it
rained, of course.

In the bazaars this tang of Isfahan is very potent. Of all the
splendid bazaars of the Middle East, I enjoy these most. They are
winding and rambling and mysterious, lit by shafts of sunshine
streaming through the roof, full of fabrics and carpets and jewelry
and vegetables, with exotic turbaned figures wandering through
them, and a constant pushing and tumbling and shouting and bargaining; the whole conducted in a series of vaulted corridors of
faintly ecclesiastical character. Women get short shrift in this
Islamic mart, and are pushed out of the way with donkeys or
sworn at mercilessly; and sometimes the vivid gusto of the place
evolves into the macabre or the eerie. I was once walking through
the bazaars when a young man fell off his bicycle; a package
wrapped in newspaper, fastened to the carrier rack, came undone,
and on to the pavement rolled the complete head of a horned sheep,
its eyes glassy, a thin trickle of blood oozing from its neck. On
another occasion I was taken to a cavernous room in the bazaars
to see a dozen young Persians, stripped to the waist, engaged in
exercises with staves and dumb-bells, which combined athleticism
with a strain of the mystic: such clubs are common in Persia, but
it was none the less creepy to move out of the extrovert life of the
bazaars and see them contorting themselves with an air of such
queer fanaticism, their eyes glazed and their mouths unsmiling, as
if they were addicts of the black art. Obscurely disturbing, too, is
the antique camel mill which still works in a kind of dungeon near
the entrance to the bazaars. You enter it down a flight of worn
steps, and find yourself standing in a windowless, subterranean
cavern. There in the middle of this awful place two aged camels,
their eyes covered, lope round and round a grinding mill in the

half-light, with a smell of dung, hair, straw, and burning wood, and the flicker of a flame from a distant corner where three old camel men in rags are cooking themselves an improbable meal.

In such places you can clearly hear the beat of the Persian heart— old, shuttered, wily, erratic; there is an edgy feeling to the crowds that shuffle and barge through these draughty arcades. If you meet the eye of an Arab in the *suks* of Aleppo, Sidon, Aqaba, or Kuwait, there is likely to be lurking in his glance the suspicion of merriment, the suggestion of something jovial and Christmassy, however over-laid it is with politics or rapacity. In the Persian's eye, though he has a gaudy streak of the clownish in his make-up, there is a differ-ent look, keener, more calculating, deeper, darker, more introspec-tive. You never feel remote from the desert in Isfahan; you are never divorced from Islam; there are many reminders that the city stands on the brink of wild, unworldly territories, inhabited by roaming bands of tribesmen and colored by many a lingering taboo and superstition. But this is the home, too, of the Zoroastrians and the great Persian mystics, and the nurturing-place of the fragile Persian poets of antiquity. To this day, up more than one winding and rickety staircase in the bazaars, in the dust and the sweet smoke of the hubble-bubbles, you will find the miniaturists still at work, squatting cross-legged on their benches with their pupils around them.

Isfahan is both bitter and perfumed; and if you are ever lulled into sentimentality by the charm of it all, there will soon come swaggering by some figure of glorious insouciance, dressed in turban, cloak, fur hat, sheepskin boots, cummerbund, limpid gown or tight-belted jerkin, the very personification of the perennial Persia. His astringent image haunts the Persian scene, and breathes a spiced breath upon most of its activities.

WEST UNTO CHINA

IN TEHERAN you may observe the impact of these dry peculiarities upon the conduct of government and diplomacy. Dr.
Mossadegh was, of course, a virtuoso of the Persian technique:
pyjamaed and hypochondriac, now twisty, now forthright, sometimes astute and intelligent, sometimes almost certifiably dotty, he
achieved his dubious ends rather in the manner of one of those
semi-animate creatures which slither, billowing and distending,
among the shadows of the sea-bed. I shall always remember the
appearance of this masterly camouflage artist at the International
Court at The Hague, where he had gone to help plead his country's
case in its dispute with the old Anglo-Iranian Oil Company. For
several days he had been in a state of recumbency at his hotel, his
spokesman from time to time making statements of delightfully
comic pungency; and when at last the time came for his speech
in court, he arrived there gasping on the arms of innumerable at-
tendants, theatrically pallid and unkempt. Most of us expected
something funny from him, if not actually farcical, after such
effective preliminaries. But you never know with the Persians, and
when at last he was lifted to his feet, mopping his brow with an
enormous handkerchief, he delivered a perfectly sensible, well-
phrased, and competently argued speech. In Persian dramatics, as
in the Imperial Square at Isfahan, there is often a twist at the end.

For a century or more the affairs of Persia have been governed
by the need to play off the several great Powers anxious to control
so strategic a territory; and at the same time to maintain those
positions of hereditary feudalism which still set the tone of Persian
social life. These demands are so insidious and persistent, and the
channels of the Persian character are so tortuous, that political life
in Teheran has an unusually misty and dreamlike quality. At the
head of the state, in an ornate palace with his beautiful wife, stands
the Shah-in-Shah, whose predecessors once ruled the mightiest of
empires, but whose father was an obscure army officer. Beneath
this resplendent monarch there moves in a mazy motion a bewildering succession of figures and influences. I was in Teheran in 1956
when Dr. Mossadegh was studying medicine in a gloomy military

prison outside the city; the current Prime Minister, a nice little Harrovian, had a big patch of plaster on his head where somebody had hit him with a revolver butt; the fanatical Islamic fraternity, the Fedayin Islamin, was threatening all kinds of horrors, secure in the certainty that death in the cause resulted in instant and painless transference to Paradise; and the outlawed Communist Party (Tudeh), which had only recently attempted a *coup d'état*, was still secretly publishing its daily paper and impudently sending it through the public post to the British embassy. Yet this was a period of relative stability, in which governments dominated by the pro-Western landlord class managed to keep the forces of violence in check. Persia remains a country of latent extremism and of sudden fluctuations in fortune; in many a fancy-goods store, muddled up with powder puffs and nail files and children's pencil boxes, you may find a selection of knuckle dusters.

Even today, this capital seems to be walking a loose and precarious tightrope between Westernism and Orientalism—not a tightrope between cultures, as in Lebanon, or between ideologies, as in Egypt and Syria, but a tightrope between atmospheres. As Sir Thomas Browne remarked in one of his more obvious aphorisms: "The same Countrey is sometimes East and sometimes West; and *Persia* though East unto *Greece*, yet is it West unto *China*." Teheran is a dull but handsome city, well-planned and embellished with grand government buildings; and the snow-capped Elburz Mountains which overlook it have an Alpine rather than a Himalayan grandeur (though Mount Demavend, northeast of the city, is the highest mountain in Eurasia west of the Pamir). On the surface this is the most Westernized of Muslim capitals, and it sometimes reminds me of Salt Lake City. Even in matters physical, though, there are some strange discrepancies. Those slimy gutters of liquid, for example, which you see running sluggishly beside the boulevards, represent the only water supply for a large part of Teheran. In the past couple of years they have begun to install proper water pipes; but the best-known source of good drinking water in Teheran remains a conduit installed in the British embassy compound, and to this day the word "British embassy" means, in the argot of Teheran, "drinking water." Then there is the vast Opera House which has stood unfinished for many years in one

of the principal streets of the capital; and many a poster with
backward N's; and one or two restaurants, probably run by White
Russians, which specialize in caviar and sturgeon from the Caspian;
and the countryside itself, all around Teheran, a drab and dusty
landscape pierced by the queer round holes of the water channels.
"Why is your house No. 7, when it is on the corner of the street?"
I asked my host in Teheran. "It had no number, so we just gave
it one." "Well, then, how does it happen that your neighbor's
house is No. 8?" "Why, he's next door to us, isn't he? What silly
questions you do ask!"

Some people say that this trait of inconsequence in the character
of Teheran was strengthened by the policies of Reza Shah, the
present Shah's father, who tried to Westernize Persia by the simple
imposition of laws. Not only did he change the face of the country,
making railways, rebuilding towns, erecting great official buildings
and esplanades; in 1936 he also made it illegal to wear the traditional
Persian dress. Women sheltering behind the all-embracing Persian
version of the Muslim veil found it stripped from their faces in the
street, and there were many Muslim ladies, I am told, who preferred not to venture into the streets at all during the period of
this regulation. (It fell into desuetude during the war.) This was
rather like forcing a left-handed child to write with his right
hand. Many an anecdote is told to illustrate the consequent clash
of manners and instincts. For example, it is said that when Reza
Shah once paid a visit to a small town on the Caspian the local
dignitaries were so anxious to observe the new proprieties that
they caused the local tinsmith to knock them up a few top hats
to go with their best suits; the monarch arrived in a hailstorm,
and the clattering of hailstones on the hats of the reception committee sang the song of the unchanging Persia, while the tinsmith's
black paint dripped heavily over the brims. Again, they say that
when Reza Shah was once making a ceremonial journey down the
new trans-Iranian railroad a preceding locomotive was derailed and
turned upon its side near the track. The railway workers, fearful
that such a sight would enrage the irascible Shah, tried desperately
to put it back on the tracks, or at least to stand it upright. Failing
to move it an inch, they thereupon hit on a characteristic Persian
expedient: they buried it in sand, and the last shovel-load was

placed upon its boiler just as the dread puffs of the royal train appeared upon the horizon. It can scarcely be said that Reza Shah's
policies were a complete success, despite these evidences of enthusiasm. We have seen how vividly Eastern Isfahan remains; and
even among those Teheran women who do wear European clothes
there remains a strange, unnatural uniformity of taste, so that at any
one street corner there will be seven or eight people dressed all
but identically in head scarfs, trim dark coats, and pumps. By a
paradox that would sadden the intemperate reformer, this gives a
pungent sense of the harem to many Teheran shopping expeditions.

It is small wonder that the political life of Teheran is not marked
by any great sense of decision or straightforwardness. It takes
courage simply to *be* a politician in Persia. I once asked a perfectly
respectable Teheran journalist if he had ever visited the central
prison. Certainly, he replied casually, for as a young man he had
unfortunately murdered a general, and had therefore spent some
little time inside it. In a country where life can be so easily dismissed, and where the cross-currents are so intense and befuddling,
it is only to be expected that men of affairs will often be of cautious
inclinations. And if you must be a brave man to be a Cabinet
Minister at all, you must be a stout one to combine office with
honesty; for nobody will deny that the Persian capacity for prevarication and subterfuge is often allied with corruption of grandiose proportions. Teheran is a terrible place for getting things done.
Nobody is ever there for another hour or so, but please join us
in a glass of tea. Resolutions, laboriously arrived at, somehow trail
away hollowly down the long hours of inaction, or are securely
enmeshed, once and for all, in the familiar Persian web. It is very
remarkable how little had been done with the immense oil
royalties that have been pouring into Persia for several decades—
far longer than in any other Middle Eastern country. There remain extremes of rich and poor as hideous as anything in the bad
old Egypt, and you have to search hard for any project of development or improvement financed by oil. Old Anglo-Iranian employees often remark piously that things would have been very different
if the Persians had known how to use their royalties properly;
certainly it must have been galling for the refinery men at the old
Abadan to be accused of sharp practice and hypocrisy when every

penny of the oil royalties were frittered away in nepotism and corruption. The long night of Dr. Mossadegh's leadership is over now, and there are brave new schemes of development; but over the years so many such plans have faded away into oblivion, like the colors of proud ensigns running in the wash, that not many Persians seem to expect much from it. "Is there not an English saying," an amiable cynic once remarked to me, "do not be kidding yourself?" (The opium monopoly of Persia, a profitable affair, is invested in the Department for the Prevention of Cultivation and Consumption of Opium.)

But in one respect Persia has recently belied her tradition. She has become, formally and practically, an ally of the Western Powers. Persia has always been an arena for power conflicts, and in particular for the perennial rivalries which animate relations between Russia and the rest of the world. She therefore procrastinated successfully for several generations in deciding where she should stand—with the West, whose ways she at once coveted and suspected, or with the East, which stood so formidably upon her borders, whether she was east of Greece or west of China.

For most of the nineteenth century and the first half of the twentieth, the opposing magnetisms were those of Russia and Great Britain. Many were the intrigues and dark initiatives that riddled Persia in the great days of Anglo-Russian rivalry, and skillful was the age-old technique with which Persia played one off against the other. The Russian menace was plain to see. In the old days it was the threat of military force, and in particular of a thrust to the warm-water ports of the Persian Gulf. Since the last war it has chiefly been the danger of subversion. The Soviet frontier is only three hundred miles north of Teheran and the Tudeh Party is the most disruptive force in political affairs. In its heyday, in 1953, the Tudeh had a host of subsidiary "front" organizations, including the Peace Partisans, the Democratic Women of Iran, the Democratic Youth, the Society for the Protection of Children, the Society against Illiteracy, the National Society against Colonization, the Society to Defend the Rights of Villagers, and the Muslim

Socialistic Association. Among them these eager institutions published sixty-five newspapers and magazines.

The Persians' worst suspicion of all these activities were confirmed when the Communists fostered a separatist revolution in the northern province of Azerbaijan; but even as late as the 1950s the British were often regarded as almost equally threatening. Many a Teheran innocent was firmly convinced that the British government, through the agency of Anglo-Iranian, was actually occupying, as a political force, the chunk of Persian territory that surrounded Abadan. All over southern Persia, indeed, Britain was considered a subversive influence. The territories lay adjacent to British spheres of influence in the Persian Gulf (until 1946 the British political resident in the Gulf lived at Bushire, on the Persian coast). British agents enjoyed long-established relations with the tribes of the region, and had great influence over some of them. The several British consulates in the south, closed under Mossadegh, were regarded as the dangerous outposts of those old "Persian hands" who still wanted to manipulate the affairs of the state. (Persia is still very touchy about the prospects of subversion, from any quarter. It is not always easy for a British journalist to get an entry visa, certainly not without reference to Teheran; and what with stamps of arrival, police permits, permission to land and permission to leave again, the shortest visit to Teheran uses up, with many a rampant imperial lion, four full pages of a passport.) To be frank, there had been a good deal of British hocus-pocus in the country, and the wariness of the Persians was understandable.

So until very recently Russia and Britain weighted the equilibrium of Persia. When Anglo-Iranian was nationalized, so was the predominantly Soviet company which exploited the fishing along the Persian shore of the Caspian. If a rebuff was hurled at the British, a snub was prepared for Russia. At first America was only a balancing force. Point Four aid was accepted, and a big military mission came to Teheran, but in most Persian minds the United States was still a neutral in these traditional antagonisms. Slowly, though, as the full implications of the cold war became apparent, the Persians realized that a new kind of struggle was now being fought in the Middle East. This was no mere rivalry between empires for control of the passage to India; it was a war between societies, from which no Power could remain easily or safely aloof.

So much the most decisive action in recent Iranian history was the adhesion to the Western system of alliances, which came about in 1955. It is said that the Shah himself was responsible for this decision. He certainly has a taste for things American. In Teheran I was given a publication which referred to a recent visit by the Shah to the United States. It said, without a flicker of a smile, that His Imperial Majesty had spent some time studying agricultural methods in Palm Beach. Cynics might also suppose that Persia's sudden conversion to Western political sympathies had something to do with land tenure. Persia is still largely owned by a smallish group of very rich landowners. The Shah has, with a jab in the ribs from his American advisers, set an example of reform by distributing parts of his estates to the peasantry; but the conservative forces now in control of Persia's destinies certainly do not relish the idea of reform on the Communist pattern. For them, even democracy is preferable to the Peasant Cooperative.

All the same, there are plenty of people in Persia to oppose this stout orientation of foreign policy. The powerful religious leaders, for example, are as uncompromisingly entrenched as the landlords and are afraid of any Western influences which might weaken their position or corrode the faith of their followers. The dominant Islamic sect in Persia is the Shia, on the whole a more militant group than the Sunnis predominant in Egypt and the Levant. If you pass through the Shia center of Qum, for example, especially on a feast day, you are quite likely to have a mud brick hurled through the window of your car; and there are mosques even in Teheran where the unsuspecting visitor, all sweet smiles and Leicas, may find himself confronted with symptoms of a disconcertingly virulent fanaticism. This temper of thought has bred, especially since the ending of Reza Shah's Westernizing ordinances, a number of extreme Islamic organizations of violent tendencies—the Fedayin Islamin, for example, and several other groups of similarly vicious piety. (Soon after the Prime Minister of Persia announced adhesion to the Western alliance, he was assaulted at the entrance of a mosque by a young man dressed in a green shroud shouting Islamic slogans; but this is a fairly normal occupational hazard of Prime Ministers in Persia.) None of these reactionary elements likes the idea of an alliance with the secular West. Nor, it need scarcely be said, do the Communists; nor the dogged admirers of Dr. Mossadegh, who include many intellectuals; nor the enemies of the royal house; nor the political have-nots; nor the fierce orthodox nationalists; nor those ubiquitous supporters of Egypt and Saudi Arabia who oppose the Western link per se or pro rata. All in all, it took courage to contract the alliance, even with the American stage managers, check books in hand, smiling and nodding in the wings.

But the thing is done. I once asked a man in a Teheran government office if I would be allowed to make a trek over the Elburz Mountains to the Caspian. "But certainly," he replied. "You are our allies now, and under the terms of the alliance I will see if the Commander-in-Chief can be persuaded to lend you some ponies." I do not know how long these arrangements will last, in the somewhat brittle or spongy political milieu of Teheran; but in 1956 Persia has joined the West, and if her internal situation remains relatively stable, and if she gets the benefits she expects from the association, she may well remain with it. Even the Anglo-French assault on Port Said did not greatly shake the alliance; and when I stood that day in Sinai, wondering if the Russians would intervene, I remembered what the man said about the ponies, and hoped the Persians were still so obliging.

Anyway, it will be many a long year, thank goodness, before even so close and formal a link with Western ways corrupts the individuality of the Persian character. I was once in the Persian consulate in Baghdad, waiting for a few rampant lions to be stamped on my passport, when I happened to see upon a table an application for a Persian visa completed by a Dutch electrician. Either his knowledge of English was unusually limited, or his mastery of Persian tastes was profound, for the form, duly stamped and signed, was in the truest Persian tradition. These were four of the questions and answers:

"Q. Family condition (bachelor, married, widower)?
A. Yes.
Q. Are you connected with any political party?
A. Yes, Dwyer and Company Ltd., Baghdad.

Q. What is the actual object of your present trip to Persia?
A. Entry.
Q. Names of your minor dependents under the age of 16?
A. 33. Dwyer and Company Ltd., Baghdad."

In the old days the Persian monarchs often rewarded humor with dignity and high office; in the case of the Dutch electrician the Persian consul instantly approved his visa. Alliance or no alliance, that striding figure of the Isfahan bazaar, turban and spices and sheepskin boots, still exerts his timeless influence upon the conduct of the Persians.

THE PACT

THE INSTRUMENT by which the Persians took this momentous step was the Baghdad Pact, a military alliance with the West which cut across the established alignment of the Middle East with startling consequence. It is difficult to know precisely where the idea of this pact originated. In the days when it seemed to be a success, both the British and the Americans claimed credit for it, and the Iraqis and Turks, too, smiled with becoming modesty. Later, when it became rather less fashionable, the British blamed the American obsession with military alliances, the Americans mumbled about out-dated colonialist policies, and the Iraqis and Turks smiled apologetically, to show that they were only tools in the hands of their powerful and sometimes misguided friends.

Whatever its genesis, the pact was born with an agreement between the Iraqis and Turks; by 1956 Britain, Pakistan, and Persia had all acceded to it and the United States had given it a half-hearted blessing. The alliance, however, so infuriated the Egyptians that most of the Arab world was roused against it. So hostile was public opinion, thanks chiefly to the malignant competence of the Egyptian propagandists, that no other Arab government dared to join it. In the eyes of the extremists, it was a device to maintain Western (especially British) ascendancy in the Middle East. It compromised the sovereignty of the Arabs. It diverted the attention of the Iraqis from the common vendetta against Israel, the first duty of the Arabs. It dishonestly strengthened Iraq *vis à vis* both Egypt and Saudi Arabia. It was a slap in the face to Colonel Nasser. It was meant to divide and weaken the Arab world. In short, said the Egyptians and their advisers, speaking very loudly, it was intolerable.

Their views were not only misleading, but also parochial. The first thing to consider in forming a judgment on the alliance was the international situation in its widest implications, not simply the internal turmoil of the Arab world. Rightly or wrongly, in 1956 the Western strategists still considered it possible that one day Russia would try to extend her frontiers by the use of military force, and they had evolved a line of defense as a ring around

Russia and her allies. The hydrogen bomb was already an ac-
complished fact, and even more atrocious weapons were around
the corner, but the planning of the West was necessarily based
upon what the generals cheerfully called "conventional atomic
war"—that is to say, an ordinary war only enlivened by the use
of tactical atomic weapons. It was perfectly possible that the big
atomic bombs and their peers would, by the tacit consent of the
warring Powers, never be used at all. In this awkward situation a
string of old-style military positions, ensured by alliances, seemed a
sine qua non for Western security. The United States Strategic Air
Force had its atomic bomber bases strewn across the world, and
its great aircraft were ready, loaded with the ultimate deterrent;
but along the frontiers of the Eastern bloc it still seemed necessary
to have friendly armies on the ground, armed, trained, or rein-
forced by the West.

During the first postwar decade the weakest link in this chain of
defenses was the Middle East. It was not an obvious place for the
Russians to begin a new war, for all its beckoning oilfields, but it
was nevertheless frighteningly wide open to a straightforward military aggression. The Suez Canal base had been handed over to the
Egyptians by the British and nobody really had much faith in the
subsequent Anglo-Egyptian agreement on its reactivation. The
Cyprus base was awkward, inadequate, and stultified by internal
problems. The British forces still scattered about the mainland
were no more than driblets. The Arab armies were not only weak
and ill-equipped, but also of dubious political stability, and Israel,
much the most talented military nation in the Middle East, was
taboo because of Arab susceptibilities. No Western guarantees
bolstered this vulnerable region; it was simply a collection of
flabby, squabbling little Powers, not even allied with each other
except in the pursuance of petty and changeable ends.

This left a gap in the formal Western defensive system. Between
Turkey in the west and Malaya in the east there were no collective
security arrangements. The generals looked at the maps with their
logical eyes, and saw that none of the countries bordering Soviet
Central Asia was committed to the West, while some were wob-
bling dangerously between neutralism and worse. The Persians had
a long frontier with Russia and had already been badly scared by

Soviet intentions; the Iraqis were not adjacent to Russia, but felt exposed nevertheless because of internal difficulties and because of the vulnerability of Persia. It was not at all difficult to imagine a Russian army sweeping down from the Caucasus and Turkmen into the Tigris valley and the plains of Persia; at least, not at all difficult if you accepted the possibility that the Russians might be planning world domination by military force.

Thus, to close a gap, the pact came into being, to supplement NATO in Europe and the South East Asia Treaty Organization in the Far East. The Iraqis linked themselves by treaty first with the Turks, who were members of NATO, and then with Britain, Iran, and Pakistan. Each of these now received sizable quantities of American arms (only limited in the case of Iraq by the nebulous Western assurances that a balance of power would be maintained between the Israelis and the Arabs). All sorts of technical help was also provided. The whole of Western defense planning in the Middle East was accordingly based upon the treaties with Iraq and Persia, and the "northern tier" concept of strategy became paramount, replacing other ideas based upon possession of the lost stronghold of Suez.

It was, of course, the oil of the region that was of primary importance to the West. It lay in the fertile crescent and in the Arabian Peninsula, protected by a frame of high mountains which provided an obvious defense line for conventional war. In the north were the mountains of Kurdestan and Turkey. In the east the Zagros Mountains, through which we made that inspiriting journey from Abadan to Isfahan, connected the Turkish highlands with the Persian Gulf. The obvious snag to this was that if the Western armies manned these mountain chains, almost all Persia would be abandoned to the enemy. As it happened, the oilfields lay to the west of the Zagros chain, but all the rest of the country, including Teheran and the Palace of Marble and the Quivering Mosque and Qum, lay to the east. The Persians would have liked the primary defense line to run along the Elburz Mountains, south of the Caspian; but these were considered indefensible by the generals, and in military circles it was tacitly admitted, with a regretful shrug of epaulettes, that poor old Persia hadn't a hope.

So the plans were formulated. The mountains would be defended, with the help of the air power of the United States Sixth Fleet, American bomber forces based upon Saudi Arabia and Libya, and whatever anemic British force was currently available in the Mediterranean. Such was the military *raison d'être* of the Baghdad Pact. There were those who claimed that the strategy of it was totally out-dated, and that in any case only large Western forces on the ground could hope to stanch a Russian advance southwards from the Caucasus; but these were years in limbo, between the oil and the atomic ages, between the Bangalore torpedo and the H-bomb. The poor strategists were groping, and nobody offered any very practicable military alternatives.

Besides, the Pact was also a measure of political and economic defense. It was an attempt to bolster the region against Communist activities of all kinds, and of course to link as many countries as possible to the Western camp. If its origins were gauntly strategic, its economic and social branches later became at least as important. It was a channel for economic aid, for advice on defense against subversion, for cooperation of all kinds. You have only to examine the immense ramifications of NATO to realize how profoundly a parallel alliance could affect the affairs of the Middle East. Joining the Baghdad Pact was, in effect, declaring that on the whole you shared the values of the Western nations or at least that you were prepared to share their aspirations. It was a defense agreement, but it was a proclamation too; once across these borders, it said, and you are in the West.

The only two countries of our region that subscribed to this announcement were the ones most obviously threatened from the north. It is no secret that Britain tried to induce other Arab countries to join; but in any case their chronic instability, their constantly shifting aims and regimes, would have made their festooned and unfamiliar generals unconvincing members of a joint planning board. Jordan wavered for a month or two on the brink of the pact, before being pushed brutally off it by the Egyptians, Saudis, and Communists. Camille Shamoun, President of Lebanon, once told me frankly that he thought the majority of Lebanese approved of the pact. A few Syrians, with their eyes on the menacing mosaic of Damascene politics, were honest enough to commend it. But this was a region of violent nationalists at a period of particular passion, and not another country took the plunge. Despite all the Western investments in the Middle East, the ties of history and culture, the apparent danger of Communism to such shifty and precarious little states, only Iraq and Persia could be described as allies of the Western democracies.

This was the credit side of the Baghdad Pact. To its debit must be recorded primarily the violent antagonism of Egypt and the intrusion of Russia in Middle Eastern affairs. The Egyptians professed themselves convinced from the very start that the alliance was aimed against them, against Arab independence and against Arab unity. They saw it as an extension of the old device of dividing and ruling, and they violently objected to the strings that are inevitably attached, however lightly, to large-scale military aid from a foreign Power. This, at any rate, is what Colonel Nasser used to say. It was incompatible with his principles of "positive neutralism," it was "a prison intended to hold all the Arabs," it was an imperialist trick. My own conviction is that Egyptian opposition to the pact was based first upon a fundamental anti-Western bias— Nasser was convinced that the West, rather than Communism, was the chief barrier to the rise of Afro-Asia—and secondly upon the suspicion that with such powerful Western help Baghdad might emerge as the lodestar of the Middle East.

Whatever the motives, the Egyptians almost succeeded in sabotaging the pact. With their powerful radio propaganda, their Communist sympathizers, and their limitless Saudi funds, they stirred up passionate hostility to it throughout the Muslim Middle East. It became, in the minds of the masses everywhere, synonymous with foreign domination. Violent riots were provoked when the British sent a mission to Amman to discuss the advantages of membership; I found the road from the airport to the city barricaded, and when I asked why a man said unpleasantly: "Because the people will have nothing to do with murderers!" That hooded figure who bashed the Prime Minister of Persia on the head with a revolver butt was screaming Islamic pieties, but upon his shroud there were scrawled slogans of abuse against the Baghdad Pact. Never a riot in 1956, never a half-hearted schoolboy demonstration, never a tedious dogmatist in a railway carriage, failed to hurl the pact in the face of the unhappy West. Most of the newspapers of the Arab world vilified it consistently; and no wonder, for not infrequently the comment was supplied by the local Saudi Arabian embassy, with a fifty-dinar note pinned to the copy. The subject became obsessive and inescapable, and so successful was the Egyptian-Saudi-Communist campaign that when a British Foreign Secretary visited Egypt (to be sure, he was perhaps the most ineffective Foreign Secretary in all the illustrious history of that office) one Egyptian cartoonist portrayed him diffidently presenting to the airport customs a pair of decrepit old boots labelled "Baghdad Pact."

This torrential opposition inevitably led to a division of the Arab world. In this context Persia could be considered an outsider anyway, but for the first time Iraq found herself isolated from her neighbors. She remained a member of the Arab League, now dominated as never before by Egypt, but she was treated as a pariah among the Arabs. A deep rift developed between Cairo and Baghdad. Diplomatic relations were all but severed. Iraqis were generally conspicuously absent from Egyptian national celebrations, and the Egyptian ambassador always seemed to be away on leave when there was a public festivity in Iraq. The Iraqi public itself, partly disturbed by this sense of isolation, was by no means unanimous in supporting the pact, and the Egyptian propagandists did their best to stir up internal dissension. Nasser used to accompany his abuse of the Iraqi government with fulsome praise of the Iraqi people, and there were ugly allegations of espionage and sabotage being directed from the Egyptian embassy in Baghdad. It was largely by the astute exploitation of this issue, coupled with the bold purchase of arms from Czechoslovakia and the nationalization of the Suez Canal, that Cairo gained its position of paramountcy in the autumn of 1956.

There were thus many Western critics (some of them among the most sincere and best informed) to suggest that the Baghdad Pact was nothing less than disastrous, in that it antagonized the most powerful indigenous forces of the area without presenting balancing advantages. It was no good claiming a success in Iraq, such people would say, if you totally ruined your position in Egypt. According to this view, the Baghdad Pact had cost the West the

friendship of the Arabs who really counted—the Egyptian revolutionaries and the men of progress everywhere. Colonel Nasser, a
fundamentally pro-Western statesman, had been so affronted by it
that he had turned nasty; and other Arab statesmen who would
like closer relations with the West had been scared off by the pact,
which made all Western associations suspect.

Furthermore, the critics used to say, the pact had given the Russians entry into the Middle East. The West had seemed to be deliberately dividing the Arab world; very well, the Russians would
come in on the side of progressive, nationalist, anti-Zionist, wholesome Nasserite unity. The Czech arms deal, it was suggested, was
the direct result of the Baghdad Pact. The alliance had opened
the door for infiltration in the non-member states, especially Syria.
It had forced the Egyptians further into the Eastern camp, and it
had enabled the Russians to synthesize the problems of the Middle
East with the wider issues of the cold war. In short, said the
Western critics and their newspapers, speaking more in sorrow
than in anger, it was a tragedy.

There is truth in these strictures, but for myself I think they are
based on a fundamental misconception: I do not believe in the
original pro-Western bias of Colonel Nasser. I think his campaigns
to rid the Middle East of British influence, and to denigrate the
West in general, only needed a pretext. If he opposed the Baghdad
Pact, it was not on any lofty grounds of Arab unity, but because
he was hostile to Western influence per se and because he distrusted
any combination which would increase the power of Iraq. The
Communists naturally opposed the alliance which was frankly
directed against Communist subversion; the Saudis objected to it
as a Hashemite device. From such mediocre motives, I believe,
stemmed this raging hostility to the Baghdad Pact, which inflamed
the Middle East for months on end, brought honest doubts to many
liberals, fostered riots and rebellions and constant vicious disputes,
and led more than one state almost to the edge of revolution.

I do not consider these adequate reasons for abandoning a policy
so carefully conceived. Certainly the Baghdad Pact implied that
Britain, at least, was backing the future of Iraq rather than the pre-

tensions of Egypt; and of course there was a risk implicit in such an engagement. In particular, there was the very real danger that Nuri Said would be replaced by somebody of entirely different views. But friendship is the most desirable basis for foreign policy, and the most consistent friends of the West in the Middle East have been the present ruling forces of Iraq, entrenched, old-fashioned, and unrepresentative though they may be. If there was foolishness in the British attitude, it was in neglecting to propagate more effectively the truth about the Pact in answer to the calumnies of Cairo Radio and the check books of Riyadh. For the rest, I believe the Baghdad Pact has stood the test of time and fortune, and in the wreckage of the Western position in the autumn of 1956, it alone remained relatively hopeful and undismayed.

KURDS AND YEZEDIS

IT IS EASIEST to understand why Iraq joined this controversial union if you cross into that Arab Kingdom from Persia
through one of the passes which pierce the northern mountains.
Though you will then be crossing a frontier, you will still be within
a racial unity, for the country on both sides of the line is dominated by a hardy and flamboyant race of mountaineers, the Kurds.
This warlike people has never been altogether assimilated by its
conquerors, whether Arab, Persian, or Turkish, and has always
been something of an anxiety to the Iraqi government in Baghdad.
Nowadays such worries are aggravated by Communist activities.
The Russians have long espoused the cause of Kurdish independence, and for years a virulent stream of propaganda has been urging
the Kurds of the Middle East to unite under Communist auspices
and form a Kurdish Republic. This was especially irritating to the
Iraqi, Persian, and Turkish governments, for most of the Kurds
live around the junction of those three countries. Kurdish rebels
from Iraq and Persia have been fostered fondly by the Russians,
and at least one prominent conspirator broadcasts over the Soviet
radio. Thus, though Iraq does not share a frontier with the Soviet
Union, in Iraqi Kurdestan you never feel far from Moscow, or at
least from that tide of discord that flows outward from the Kremlin; and though you may have a sneaking sympathy for the idea of
an independent Kurdish nation, you can well understand why
Baghdad feels the need for support against subversions.

Here in these northern mountains Middle East meets Central
Asia, and the presence of this delightful country within the borders
of Iraq has a profound bearing on the outlook of the state. If a
third of Egypt were inhabited by Kurds, who knows what healthy
moderation would not be imposed upon Colonel Nasser? There are
nearly 750,000 Kurds in Iraq. They are as virile and as hardy as
ever, though not so lawless, and they have defended their rights so
vigorously that to this day they remain totally distinct from the
Arab majority, and yet manage to have their representatives in the
highest offices of the kingdom. The most famous of all the Kurds
was Saladin, and a little of his temper lingers among them still.

The Baghdad government treats them with respectful caution. "Please be careful what you write," an official in Mosul said to me anxiously one day. "Politically this is still an inflammable region, you know, and I am easier to ignite than anyone." But it is difficult to keep your mind on political shibboleths among so genuinely colorful and hearty a people as the Kurds. One of the great pleasures of the Middle East is to encounter a tribe of Kurds on the move in the great plain that stretches northwards from Mosul and Erbil. If it is spring, the grasslands are thick with flowers, and haunted by gazelles and innumerable twitchy birds. In the distance the mountain barriers stand blue and purple and formidable, blocking the way to Ararat and Tabriz, with a fleck of snow on their summits and a cloudless sky above. Against this heavenly background the Kurdish nomads move triumphantly. Their herds of sheep and floppy-eared goats scramble and jostle in the sunshine and behind them the bold herdsmen lord it across the plain; they ride their stocky horses like avenging marauders, rifles across their backs, bandoliers across their chests, sheepskin jackets slung about them grandly. The women walk alongside, carrying the baggage; the children scamper or lag behind; the great herds eddy about and spill over the landscape; and the effect of the procession, glimpsed in so wide and airy a setting, is that of a community of unusually cheerful brigands crossing a steppe to commit an atrocity.

In the villages that cling to the hillsides the Kurds lose a little of this brigandish air, but they remain stoutly individualistic, and they manage to combine a leisurely grace with a certain manner of bravado. The men's costume is dashing in the extreme. The head is swathed in a huge, indeterminate turban, fringed with pieces of hanging material like the frayed and chewed tassels of a child's bathrobe cord. The waist, often sizable, is bound with a cummerbund of blinding colors. One of its purposes is to keep the stomach warm; another, to enable the wearer, if he is ever in a tight spot, to swarm down it from the windows of his captivity. The legs swagger in baggy trousers, with embroidered designs around the pockets. In the cummerbund there is likely to be a big knife; in the eyes an expression of voluntarily tamed ferocity. But the splendor of this livery is often tempered into sweetness by the presence of a small rose, tucked in the folds of the turban, or clutched in the hand of some swarthy and mustachioed tough. The Kurds love flowers, colors, and music; they play their plaintive melodies upon handsome wooden instruments like truncated clarinets, and they have produced a respectable poetic literature.

They are Muslims, and are now being taught to speak Arabic in their schools; but they remain in almost every other way totally distinct from their Arab compatriots. The Kurds are highlanders, the Arabs lowlanders, and they distrust each other with an intensity that is easy to sense if you ever place an Arab and a Kurd side by side in the back seat of your car. This gulf, and the status of the Kurds as citizens of a nation without a state (there are Kurds in Syria and the Lebanon too) gives Iraqi Kurdestan an air of intrigue and mystery that has a recognizably British element to it. The British have always had a soft spot for the various religious and racial minorities of Iraq; and just as in Persia they are accused of cherishing the southern tribes, and in the Sudan of plotting to remove the southern provinces altogether, so in Iraq people will sometimes suggest that the British used to manipulate the Kurds of the north as a political weapon or bargaining counter. In Erbil an Englishman who represented a tractor company was pointed out to me as a well-known agent; he had, in fact, been imprisoned during the pro-Nazi Rashid Ali rising in 1941, and his knowledge of the district was deep; but so gentle a soul was he, and so kindly did he order me a Coca-Cola, and so pleasantly did we sit together in his white-washed office, that I did not like to ask him if he was a spy.

In 1956 the hint of underlying danger in Kurdestan has faded a little, but you can still feel it potently enough in Sulaimaniya, the political capital of the region. Ten years ago the Governor of Sulaimaniya could only move about with a heavily armed escort. The real masters of the countryside were the great Kurdish tribal leaders who ruled affairs from their mountain strongholds, and had a swashbuckling opinion of the value of human existence. Nowadays things are more sedate. Nevertheless, it is still obscurely exciting to sit at a café in the main crossroads of the town, eating a sizzling kebab wrapped in bread and spiced with onions, and watching the crowds go by. They are so very different from the Arabs or the Persians. Their shuffle has a hint of complaint in it, and the grandees who occasionally pass by have a fine ruffianly pose. Sometimes, indeed, there are obvious symptoms of Kurdish dissatisfaction—a couple of recalcitrants marched off to prison through the streets, for example, to the accompaniment of subdued public mutterings—and the conversation of Kurds often turns to the prospect of Kurdish unity and the establishment of Kurdish frontiers. Sometimes this subdued yearning still erupts into public violence, as it did in the autumn for a week or two in 1956; but on the whole the Kurds have been well treated by the Baghdad government, and as the roads and schools and cinemas come to Kurdestan, so the celebrated bellicosity of the Kurds will be tempered into sweet reasonableness (or at least that is the theory).

Certainly they now live in relative harmony with the other peoples who inhabit pockets and crannies of their delectable countryside. Aqra, for instance, is an overwhelmingly Kurdish town, a place of mud-brick houses on a hillside, with tiers of high walls and narrow serpentine lanes, so that the town seems to have sprouted naturally, like a fungus, from the edge of the mountain. Yet in this Sherpa-like settlement there lives a small community of Chaldean Christians, one of the bewildering variety of religious groups— Nestorians, Chaldeans, Syrian Catholics, Armenian Catholics, Jacobeans, Gregorians, and other Monophysites—which have resulted at one time or another from the Councils of Ephesus and Chalcedon. A tangled mass of brown buildings on the hillside marks the Christian quarter. It is intersected by channels that are at once pathways, sewers, and places for the women to do their washing; if you walk up there from the Muslim part of the town it is strange to find the women, looking up smilingly from their work, unveiled except by that murky film of dust and mud that is a concomitant of oriental housewifery. I once went up there to call on the bishop, a gentle old man with a bushy white beard, whose welcoming figure I could see far above me as I climbed, leaning over the balustrade of his verandah. He was a scholarly man, educated in Rome, and was glad of an opportunity to exercise his French. He had a sizable library, tucked away there above the ramshackle town, and read to me rather laboriously from a volume in Aramaic. The

Kurds, he said, were ebullient neighbors, and his community was generally left in peace. Indeed, the only outcasts of Aqra seemed to be a covey of ragged gypsies living squalidly in caves outside the town. These people, I was told acidly, told fortunes, stole babies, made the local equivalent of clothespins, hung about people's front doors, and generally lowered the tone of the place, and something ought to be done about them.

Some of the other co-inhabitants, though not Muslims, are nevertheless Kurdish in origin. Such are the Yezidis, the strangest of the communities inhabiting these hills. They live also in Syria, Turkey, Persia, and Russia, but this is their home and their holy land. These agreeable eccentrics bear a sinister reputation among the ignorant, because they follow an unusually cloudy religion, concerned with the worship of the devil (or the propitiation, nobody quite knows which). They seem to believe that on the whole the most potent force in the universe is the devil, and that he must therefore be either appeased or glorified, or both. The purpose of religion must be to arrive at an understanding with the Evil One, rather than waste time flattering a deity whose good will is, so to speak, ex officio. The origins of this faith have long since been forgotten, and the Yezidis themselves are distinctly vague about it all. They have personalized the devil in the figure of a peacock (or perhaps several), kept in one of the shrines of Kurdestan and produced at times of festival for the performance of secret rites; and they put great store in mysticism, cabalistic signs, taboos, and rituals.

So many and so fervent are the dislikes of the Yezidis that in their villages one is haunted by the fear of committing some awful spiritual solecism. You must remember never to mention the word Satan, for it is anathema to the devil, and therefore most vigorously shunned by all Yezidis; if somebody does utter the name, the really convinced Yezidi must either instantly kill the transgressor, or commit suicide. Indeed, you must remember not to pronounce the sound "sh," which begins the Arabic word for Satan, at all. The Yezidis themselves will endure agonizing distortions of sense and grammar to avoid uttering this terrible consonant, and until recently even refused to learn reading or writing because of its presence in the alphabet. Then lettuces are strictly taboo; it is said that the Evil One once tried to hide inside a lettuce, but found its

wicked leaves insufficient to conceal him. Radishes are also unpopular, I am told. The color blue is something the Yezidis particularly
loathe, I forget why, and there are innumerable thresholds and
flagstones upon which it would be insufferably insulting to set foot,
and one or two totems which it would be grossly irreverent not to
touch with respect. The Yezidis take these prohibitions and
antipathies so seriously that many thousands of them have, over the
centuries, died for their strange faith; so it is only right for the
stranger to tread carefully.

They are a clean and friendly people, their women unveiled and
their men, if a little touchy about their beliefs, frank and honest.
I once spent a day pottering about a village called Baasheka, north
of Mosul, and remember the place and its inhabitants with affection. Christians and Yezidis live side by side there, and seem to
tolerate one another; but one cannot help feeling, as the Muslims
do, that a certain uncanny sense of paganism pervades the Yezidi
part of the town. On the hillside above it there are a number of
whitewashed shrines, with fluted conical towers like decorations on
a birthday cake. These are the tombs of Yezidi martyrs, slaughtered
by the Muslim conquerors in defending their right not to eat
lettuce; and peering inside one of them through its latticed doorway is rather like peering into the cell of some dotty but benevolent
wizard, so infinitely removed is the atmosphere of Yezidia from
anything else in the Middle East. The Yezidis are organized into
rigid social strata—emirs, sheikhs, qawwaks, fakirs, and the rest;
each must marry within its own group, qawwaks with qawwaks,
fakirs with fakirs, and there has thus arisen a hierarchy of hereditary importance and gravity. Some of these people are credited
with magical powers. Some are dignified by enormous black beards.
It was sometimes disconcerting to sit in a Baasheka coffee-shop,
watching the earnest games of dominoes and meditating upon the
quaint peacefulness of the persuasion, to feel the dark eyes of one
of those divines staring at you fixedly from beneath the most wildly
voluminous of turbans and from above the blackest, longest, and
most ominous of beards.

But there is much gaiety in Baasheka too. A cheerful little stream
runs down to the village from the hillside above, and in it the
women blithely do their laundry. Children sit in the shade playing

wooden pipes; horses graze; grasses wave beneath olive trees; the rivulet tinkles; the women sing as they dry their clothes on the rocks; it can be almost ludicrously idyllic. The Yezidis are odd and contradictory about their religion, but welcoming enough in every-day affairs, and if you wander up the stream the washing house-wives will smile and make jokes (which, being expressed in a corrupt form of medieval Kurdish, may not be altogether intelligi-ble to you). Even here, though, the oddness of things Yezidi in-trudes. Where the stream emerges from the hillside there is a little grotto in the rocks, with a pool in it as clear as crystal, and so still that the movement of minute fishes casts shadows on the bottom. On the rock face above this pool, in the gloom of the grotto, there is a carving of some kind, and if you peer at it very hard, trying to grasp its form, there will slowly emerge from the stone the rough-hewn image of an animal. Nobody knows what it is, fact or fable, frog or alligator; but it peers back at you with a certain shady con-fidence, like the seal at the head of Mr. Thurber's bed.

Faced with such alien puzzles, the conquerors warily conduct their affairs on the edge of Kurdestan. It is only on the fringes of the mountain country, as you travel southwards towards Baghdad, that you will find the northern outposts of Arabism; great tribal chieftains from the desert, magnificent in their luxurious encamp-ments (there is oil in northern Iraq); or merchants trading in the cluttered covered bazaars, among the cross-legged tailors and the clamor of the smiths. Kurdestan is another frontier of the Arab world, almost as foreign in taste and temper as the country of those benign nudists at Juba; and the Arabs, who have left their mark eastward to India and westward to Spain, have not yet digested it. You may find the survival of such diversities pleasant to see; but for the Iraqi authorities Kurdestan still presents certain potential elements of—how did that kindly official phrase it?—combustion.

ON DEVELOPMENT

ASSIMILATION WILL COME, the Iraqis hope, as the effect of the great national oil revenues seeps through to the ordinary Kurds. High in the captivating mountains above Sulaimaniya, in a narrow gorge, near the Persian frontier, they are building a dam which will, they believe, so revolutionize agriculture in that part of Kurdestan that the inhabitants will become placid and well-heeled agriculturists, indistinguishable in outlook, if not in costume, from their Arab neighbors to the south. The land around Erbil is said to be potentially as rich as anywhere on earth, and the idea is that a series of barrages and channels will distribute water from the dam to convert all this country into a granary.

Dokan Dam is something of a gamble, and in this it is characteristic of the great development schemes being undertaken by the Iraqi government. It would be easier to devote the dam money to projects more immediately beneficial to the Kurdish peasantry, more obvious or more showy: houses, for example, grand roads, expensive public buildings, such as we have seen in Kuwait or Cairo. The Kurds, like some other sections of the Iraqi body politic, are sporadically on the brink of revolution, and it might be thought that a few economic sops of this kind would help to keep them quiet. The Iraqi government, though, has taken a longer view. Of all the oil states of the Middle East, with the solitary honorable exception of Bahrain, only Iraq is investing its revenues in what the Nilologists might call century storage. Advised by an enthusiastic and generally wise development board, the Iraqis are putting their money into a monumental program of basic development which will, with luck, turn the country into a kind of oriental Canada. They realize that their oil resources will one day be exhausted, and that anyway the heyday of oil may be passing; so they are burying their capital deep. In the meantime, this is a danger period. With crossed fingers and bated breath the Iraqi government (sitting permanently on several separate volcanoes) hopes it can keep the status quo until these policies pay off. Wise Iraqis foresee a nation of prosperity unique in the Middle East, founded upon the essentials of industry, agriculture, health, and education; but the poor man at the gate, clothed in rags and discontent, thinks more of his stomach than of posterity.

Many Iraqi skeptics, of course, suspect that the oil money is never going to benefit them at all, but is going the way of government funds across the border in Persia, or in the times of pashadom in Egypt. In this they are wrong. The astonishing thing about the Iraqi development plan is that it is, by and large, honest. Very little money filters into the pockets of the ministers and the administrators, and the funds earmarked for development are spent sensibly and without favor. From the start (that is to say, since the Iraqi share in the oil profits was raised to the 50-50 level) the plans have been given integrity by international interest. The World Bank sent a team to investigate possibilities. Lord Salter, the British economist, produced a comprehensive report. The development board itself includes, miraculously in so chauvinist a region, an American and an Englishman. Firms of many nationalities have won contracts, and it is common to find British consulting engineers working side by side (and fairly amicably) with French or German constructors. Indeed, what sharp practice is apparent is performed mainly by European contractors; the usual film of riff-raff sticks to the edges of the plan, and there are sometimes dark hints of unfair competition and corruption.

Another remarkable factor, unique in the Middle East, is the unlimited material promise of Iraq. For generations she has been in a state of semi-dereliction. Her medieval population of thirty-five million has dwindled to about five million. Her wide farmlands have, all too often, gone to waste. Health, education, techniques—all are in a condition of decay inherited from the stagnant years of Turkish rule, when Baghdad was allowed to become the shabbiest and least considered of all the provincial capitals. But Iraq still possesses the raw material of national wealth: two great rivers and three secondary ones; a population far too small for its territories; agricultural lands of wide resource; great reservoirs of oil. Poor Egypt, when she plans her High Dam, aspires only to maintain the present abysmal standard of living in the face of a rising population; but Iraq can look ahead to Scandinavian standards of comfort, and a position of influence and respect in the world. Only a decade or two, only a generation of social stability is needed.

The basis of the plan is the development of the valley of the Tigris and the Euphrates, the great trough running from the northern provinces to the Persian Gulf, which is the backbone of Iraq. You can grasp the significance of these great streams well enough from the map, where their twisty outlines draw a streak of green across the desert; but the best way to sense their supreme importance to Iraq is to travel by road across the desert from Syria. For more than thirty years a bus company, founded by two New Zealanders, has been running a service across these wastes, nowadays with enormous air-conditioned vehicles. The first part of the passage from Damascus is across open desert, and is exceedingly bumpy; the second part is along the road built by the British army during the war, and is exceedingly hot and long. There is no more arid, monotonous, and unfriendly desert in the Middle East than the Syrian desert, which separates Iraq from its western neighbors. Its colors are dull, its contours harsh, and until a few years ago the Bedouin who roam it were unpleasantly predatory. (In the early years of the bus service the New Zealanders had to pay them a subsidy, like the Masters of the Haj in the old days of pilgrimage.) Even in a foam-rubber seat, and with a box of chocolates, it seems that this wilderness lasts an eternity. But about a hundred miles west of Baghdad, when you are almost stunned into apathy, a miracle occurs. Suddenly you look through your window and find the landscape green. Abruptly, in a matter of moments, you pass from the desert to the sown, from waste land to the Fertile Crescent. You have crossed the wide Euphrates, and are in Mesopotamia, the land of the twin rivers. Without its two great streams, Iraq would be no more than the eastern edge of the Syrian desert.

As in most river development schemes, the Iraqi purpose is a triple one: to prevent floods, to provide water for irrigation, and to generate electricity. The engineers propose to do this by a series of dams and barrages throughout the lengths of the two great rivers, and on the three smaller ones (the Great Zab, the Lesser Zab, and the Dyalah) which flow into the Tigris from the east. Taming these streams, they think, may take anything up to fifty years and will probably cost at least nine hundred million dollars; but the economists believe that with proper irrigation and control Iraqi agriculture alone can produce an annual income of

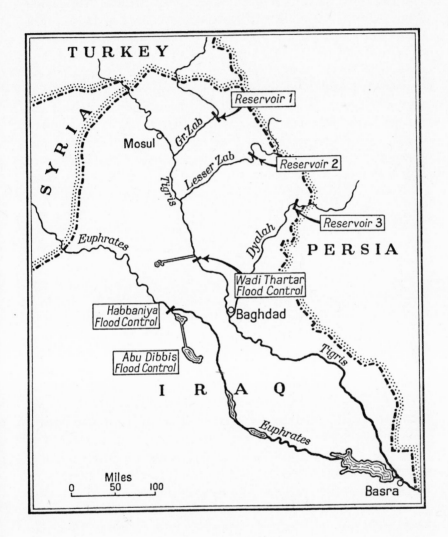

TURKEY

SYRIA

Mosul

Reservoir 1

Gr.Zab

Tigris

Lesser Zab

Reservoir 2

Euphrates

Dyalah

Reservoir 3

PERSIA

*Wadi Thartar
Flood Control*

Baghdad

*Habbaniya
Flood Control*

*Abu Dibbis
Flood Control*

I R A Q

Tigris

Euphrates

Miles

0   50   100

Basra

twelve million dollars—about three thousand dollars annually per capita. Even by 1959 the present investment will have earned handsome dividends. At the same time a startling variety of other projects has been approved, and some have been completed: an oil refinery, a bitumen refinery, a cotton mill, two cement plants, a sugar refinery, several big power stations, a rayon factory, a chemical plant, new roads and railway lines, new airports, six big hospitals, innumerable schools, new summer resorts, ski centers in the Kurdish mountains—the list is long and imaginative. In almost any other country of the Middle East one would take it with a pinch of salt. Five Year Plans are a dime a dozen in this part of the world, and generally fizzle out, or are shelved, or forgotten, or revised beyond recognition when a new regime erupts into authority. In Iraq it is, so far, different. The plan is being implemented now, with the help of able engineers from many parts of the world, and there is a good chance that one day it will be fulfilled.

Much of it, however, has waited upon flood control. The floods of Iraq are traditional and perennial scourges, and have severely handicapped agriculture in the southern part of the country. Iraqis grow up with the possibility of inundation always in their minds. Three-quarters of the population of Baghdad died in a combined flood and plague in 1831; and even as late as the spring of 1954 the capital was entirely encircled by flood waters. It will never happen again. Three barrages, two on the Euphrates and one on the Tigris, now divert the excess water into reservoirs, and only some unforeseeable catastrophe can swamp their capacity. The most spectacular of these works, and the most immediately effective of the Iraqi developments, is the barrage of Wadi Thartar, which has been built by British and German engineers beside the ancient capital of Samarra, where the son of Haroun el-Rashid once held court in splendor. From the air this place offers a spectacle of contrast which struck me as encouragingly allegorical. I chartered a small airplane to see the barrage and, as we circled over it to find a suitable landing-place in the surrounding desert, I caught a whirled glimpse of the whole scene. The old city of Samarra lies on the west bank of the river, and is dominated by a mosque with a great golden dome, a place of pilgrimage that stands above the crowded streets of the town like one of the great shrines of India. On the eastern outskirts of the town there stands an even more remarkable talisman—the spiral minaret, weird and crumbling, which is all that is left of the Friday Mosque, one of the most celebrated monuments of the Islamic world, big enough for the whole of the Caliph's army to pray in their ranks in its courtyard. Thus on the east bank the scene that was whisked dizzily past my window was antique and exotic, a golden dome, a twisted minaret, a tawny desert; but beside these wonders ran the broad stream of the Tigris, swift and silver, and thrown grandly across it was the barrage. It was as new and confident and clean as a skyscraper, a slab of masonry standing sentinel across the river, and so assured that it looked already natural to the scheme of things. The simple juxtaposition of old and new has become insufferably hackneyed in the Middle East (sheikhs stepping into Cadillacs beside couched camels); but two such remarkable products of different ages, the one a clutter of religious symbols, the other a masterly engineering work—two such alien products, side by side, now make the river bend at Samarra one of the most remarkable places in the Arab world.

The whole of the flow of the Tigris has been diverted to pass through the barrage. The structure itself was built upon dry ground, and the river was then blocked with an earth dam and forced to pass through its new channel. When I was there the water had already been diverted, and the flow of the Tigris was fully controlled by the gates of the barrage. To achieve this, perhaps the most notable single product of oil revenue in the Middle East, 35 Englishmen, 110 Germans, and 3,100 Iraqis worked at Samarra for two and a half years (though the oil publicists would put them the other way round).

The flood water is to be led away down the great channel to a depression in the desert called the Wadi Thartar. We flew along the line of this diversion. It is a ditch and a dyke forty-five miles long and sometimes so wide and deep that once my pilot took us tremulously down inside it, and we roared along between its banks. It was built by British engineers, who set up their construction camps in the desert for all the world like the pioneers of the American West, surrounded by excavators and tractors just as those rugged American adventurers slept in the circle of their covered wagons. The ditch took four years to dig, and cost about eighteen million dollars. In some places it is nearly five hundred feet wide and nearly fifty feet deep, and it presents such an obstacle to the Bedouin, who pass this way regularly with their flocks of sheep and loaded camels, that at one spot a ramp has been provided for them. In other ways, however, the Bedouin will gain from the Wadi Thartar; for the depression will, it is supposed, be turned into a lake by the successive influxes of floods, and the land about it will be green. Indeed, if all goes well, and all the water is not absorbed or evaporated, this will be the center of another irrigated region, and the wandering herdsmen will find themselves, all of a sudden, metamorphosed into farmers—or perhaps, as the cynics say, into serfs.

All this is, so the Iraqis hope, the precursor of a renaissance. The whole of the southern Mesopotamian valley, from Samarra to the sea, was once the home of a rich and creative civilization, based upon practical agronomy. Innumerable ruined cities remain there, beside the crumbled and tragic relics of abandoned irrigation systems. The great days of Iraq have always been in eras when its rulers knew how to use water properly; the air of dusty lethargy that seemed insuperable only a decade ago, when I first went to Iraq, was the heritage of Turkish apathy and corruption. The need for water control has never been quite so obvious or so crucial as it is in Egypt—even in the worst days of crooked government, Egyptian irrigation has never been seriously neglected; just as, in the country where there is now no danger of overcrowding, the Iraqi peasant is much less productive and less diligent than the Egyptian. (The obvious solution for many of the problems of the Middle East is the transference of Egyptian families and Palestinian refugees to the unexploited farmlands of Iraq.)

But the danger is, of course, that the present relatively capable administration of Iraq will not survive and that there will succeed it a period of turmoil and instability in which the rot will creep in again; or alternatively a society of Communist leanings, which might see to its irrigation dutifully enough, but would otherwise be a tragedy for the whole of the Arab world. Iraq is governed today, as is Persia, by a coalition of conservative forces. Its society is still feudal in basis, and in the cities there is a seething undercurrent of discontent, both social and political. Nuri Said, who sets the current tone of this remarkable country, and who guides it with Churchillian gusto and decision, can keep political order only by the strictest kind of repression. The press is carefully controlled, party politics is restricted. Communism is banned, diplomatic relations with Russia have been severed. To Nuri and his well-wishers, and to many a visiting foreigner, this is only prudence; but to the Iraqi progressive it is sheer despotism, and to the starry-eyed Western liberal it sometimes looks less benevolent than the classless society presided over by Colonel Nasser.

In particular the critics complain that Iraq's dazzling program of development is not accompanied by land reform. Most of the agricultural land of Iraq is still in the hands of a few rich men; not of the same style as the Turkish pashas who used to own Egypt, and who were notable for a certain voluptuous *savoir-faire*, but often bucolics of stubborn illiteracy. These people are heavily represented in Parliament, and still exert a traditional, and not wholly despicable, influence over their tenants. They thus form a dreadfully retarding force in Iraqi society (though the old-fashioned observer might claim that they stabilize it too). They do nothing to improve agricultural methods; they contribute little to the progress of health or education; they view innovations with distrust; but they own at least sixty percent of the cultivated land of Iraq. They are the more potent and entrenched because the Iraqi fellah has no such deep-rooted and instinctive attachment to his land as has his brother in Egypt. As often as not he has only settled to the agricultural life after centuries of nomadism, within the last century; his approach to the tilling of somebody else's soil is half-hearted, and he views with understandable apathy the improvement of techniques. At the same time these tenuous rural roots are another reason why the landlords oppose modernism; for if fresh land is irrigated elsewhere, they reason, their tenants are quite likely to pack their bags and follow the water. And indeed, there are farmlands in Iraq which have, for this very reason, recently fallen into disuse.

Nevertheless, something has been done to break the deadening rigidity of this system. Some state lands have been distributed to carefully selected settlers. New land brought under cultivation is to be divided among small farmers. These steps, besides altering the basis of ownership, will also presumably force old-school land-lords to modernize their methods and improve the conditions of their tenants, for labor will be at a premium in Iraq. Perhaps over the years, as the standard of living rises, as education reaches its warming fingers through the populace, as tuberculosis and under-nourishment and malaria and bilharzia decline, then the anomalies of the Iraqi society will disappear, and a new serenity will be achieved. Only a little time is necessary, and perhaps a few more concessions to human nature. (Tolerance is the salt of wisdom, as a devout Baghdadi remarked to me one day, ordering a whisky and soda.) The tide of oil will do the rest, God and the politicians willing.

THE RUSSIANS

IN THE MEANTIME, Iraq offers fertile soil for the sowers
of trouble, especially the Communists. It is a country of such
promise and latent resource that it invites jealousy and covetous-
ness, and with its combination of great wealth and restless poverty
it seems almost a copybook example of Communist opportunity.
In any case, the Russians, Czarist or Communist, have always kept
an eye upon Mesopotamia. Through the centuries the rulers of the
Russian Empires have looked greedily down the line of the two
rivers to the Persian Gulf, with its warm-water ports and its
passages to India. Peter the Great, in his supposed will, urged his
successors to extend the power of Russia down this portentous
route. At the end of the nineteenth century the Russians applied
to the Turkish government for a concession to build a railway to
Kuwait. Russian plans to acquire a Persian Gulf outlet were so
persistent and so menacing that in 1892 Lord Curzon announced,
in a Curzonism of authentic grandeur: "I should regard the concession of a port upon the Persian Gulf to Russia by any power
as a deliberate insult to Great Britain, as a wanton rupture of the
status quo, and as an international provocation to war; and I should
impeach the British minister, who was guilty of acquiescing to
such a surrender, as a traitor to his country." No quaking princi-
pality offered the Russians a concession, and no British Minister
dared run the gauntlet of impeachment by Lord Curzon, a terrible
prospect indeed.

In fact, the Russians did not acquire a solid foothold in the
Muslim Middle East, did not really rank as a Middle Eastern Power,
until the middle of the twentieth century; and their success in
achieving this at last was one of the reasons why we stood that
day in Sinai. Russian intentions had, of course, changed since 1892.
Warm-water ports were apparently no longer at a premium, and
there were no barriers to destroy on a conquering path to British
India. Instead there was oil, in a territory strategically placed and
racked by endless social and political disturbances. In Persia, indeed, the Russians tried to achieve their ends more or less by the
use of force: the Azerbaijan separatist movement in 1947 was an

armed insurrection directly supported by Moscow. Elsewhere, though, their methods were social and economic: they seem to have had little control over the local Communist Parties, which were generally weak anyway; and for several decades they groped their way rather ineffectively through the bewildering maze of the region. Except in Persia, in which the Bolsheviks had been active since the revolution, the post-war Russian exploitation of the Middle East was strangely dilatory.

This was possibly because Arab spokesmen and pro-Arab opinion had succeeded in convincing the world that Islam and Communism were incompatibles. It was simply not possible, they used to say, for a Muslim people to have truck with Communism. Islam was in principle a theocratic system, in which every human action was subject to divine regulation, and it would never be reconciled with atheism. There were other reasons, too, why the Russians fought shy of infiltrating the Middle East. The indigenous reformist or progressive movements were still feeble and uncoordinated; the feudal rulers were scarcely challenged; there were no technical alternatives to the presence of the Western oil companies; and the British were there in strength. Better to wait, the Kremlin perhaps told itself, until the natural fermentation develops.

Thus the entry of Communist Russia into the Middle East, Persia apart, was cautious and gradual. Until the end of the war there were few Soviet embassies in the region, and practically no Soviet trade with the Arabs. It was a rarity to see a Russian flag in the Suez Canal, a surprise to see a Communist magazine in a book shop, and an adventure to meet a real live Russian at a cocktail party or a coffee-shop. Soviet propaganda gave general support to the precepts of Arab nationalism, was ambivalent about the establishment of Israel, and merely did its usual best to foster confusion and dissension everywhere. It seemed puzzlingly lacking in purpose or decision.

The first effective infiltrations were aimed at minorities. In Iraq the Kurds were encouraged to accede to an independent Kurdestan, parallel to the proposed Azerbaijan Republic. Links were reestablished between the Orthodox Church in the Middle East and its Patriarchate in Moscow. The Armenians were encouraged to return to Armenia, and there were the early stirrings of such religio-political controversies as we experienced in Aleppo. Any restless minority could expect to find support from Moscow, if only in the interests of turmoil; though indeed nothing very much seemed to be achieved, as a glance at the roster of today's minorities will easily prove.

More direct political activity followed. Communist Parties were fostered in most of the Arab countries, though they did not soon achieve much eminence either in size or in quality. Sometimes alliances were established with other political groups. In Egypt the Wafd, the principal nationalist party of the time, allied itself for a time with the Communists; and both in Egypt and in Persia, so it is said, the extremist Islamic organizations established cynical and unnatural links with the Communist Parties. Among some of the Arab sophisticates Communism became sporadically fashionable. In Iraq, a country of primary emotions, it began to be a social force.

By the early 1950s the Russians were taking the Middle East more seriously. Large numbers of Arabists and Persian specialists were being trained in the universities of the Soviet Union, and diplomatists of high skill began to appear in the Russian embassies of the region. They included Muslims from the Asian territories of Russia, who concentrated on spreading propaganda about racial and religious autonomies in the Soviet Union. The idea of Russia as a great Muslim Power was carefully fostered—there are twenty-one million Muslims in Russia, more than there are in Egypt. The various issues of the time were increasingly exploited—the idea of a Middle East Defense Organization, for example, with Western participation; the future of the Sudan; the Israel impasse; social misery; the Anglo-Persian dispute; the rapacity of the oil companies, and the intermittent quarrels between Britain and the United States. The Russians, skillful fishers in troubled waters, were greasing their lines.

Soon enough, as they foresaw, their work was being done for them. The appalling problem of Israel threw into the arena a million discontented refugees, embittered still further the Arabs' relations with the West, and kept the whole place in a fervor of angry uncertainty. The Egyptian revolution gave new impetus to the forces of the left, whether or not they were sympathetic to

Communism as such. Feudalism was drastically weakened. Every-where reformist movements sprang up, there were hints of revolu-tion, the armies of discontent stirred themselves. And at the same time the positions of Britain, the only stabilizing force in the Middle East, were crumbling one by one, leaving the way open to chaos. This was no longer a Western sphere of influence, but a power vacuum of infinite possibilities.

It was now that the Russians became, for the first time, con-tenders for paramountcy in the region. Little by little they identi-fied themselves with the aspirations of the Arabs, and in particular with the virilities of Colonel Nasser's government. They espoused the causes of Arab unity and anti-Zionism, and adopted Nasser as their agent and ally (or perhaps their *poputchik*—one who works for them without knowing it). The Soviet line and Cairo's rabid politics became all but indistinguishable. As Cairo radio prodded its mischief-making across the Middle East, probably the most influential single political factor in the region, so Moscow radio supported its subversions and supplemented its abuse. When Nasser egged on the Jordanian refugees against Britain, Russia smiled encouragingly from the wings. When some new effrontery was offered the West, it often followed a talk with the Soviet am-bassador in Cairo. When the Arabs planned to take over the oil industry, the Russians offered to train their technicians. And when Nasser failed to get military equipment from the West free of any kind of obligation, the Russians instantly offered to rearm the Egyptian army. Within a few months there arrived from Eastern Europe hundreds of tanks and jet fighters, scores of modern jet bombers, artillery, half-tracks, destroyers, torpedo boats, sub-marines, and a corps of technicians and instructors.

The whole Communist bloc shared in this penetration. Egypt concluded a series of barter agreements with one Communist country after another, and for the first time a large proportion of her trade was directed towards Eastern peoples. A flood of Com-munist-made goods began to appear in Cairo. I went to a Chinese Communist trade exhibition—everything from oxygen masks to foundry presses—in which the notices were written in two languages, Chinese and Arabic; there was a grim symbolism in the fact that not even the scripts were intelligible to the Western visitor, so recently master of all Egypt's markets. So thoroughly did Egypt pledge her produce to these states, in return for arms and manufactured goods, that by the middle of 1956 it began to look as though Russia were gaining an economic stranglehold over her. When American aid was withdrawn from the High Dam scheme, the Russians promptly said they would finance it; indeed, they expressed themselves willing to finance practically anything, on the easiest possible terms. Russian ships became a commonplace at Port Said, loading cotton for Black Sea ports, and Colonel Nasser took to flying about in a fine Llyushin transport aircraft, a gift from the Kremlin.

One day in 1956 I picked up a newspaper in Cairo and scanned it at random for evidence of this Communist infiltration. It reported talks between the Soviet ambassador, the Hungarian Minister and the Egyption Minister of National Guidance, about ways of "promoting artistic relations." The Higher Council of Arts and Literature, it said, was selecting five Egyptian writers to send on a visit to Moscow. The Minister of Finance had been discussing trade relations with the Soviet Commercial Counsellor. An official committee was discussing the purchase of Soviet medical apparatus. The Czech Deputy Minister of Foreign Trade had arrived in Cairo. Communist China had agreed to supply Egypt with meat and poultry. The Egyptian Tourist Administration was to arrange travelling exhibitions in East Germany, and the East German government had offered to found a medical institute in Cairo and to train doctors in Germany. Plans were going ahead for the big atomic energy laboratory near the pyramids, to be financed, designed, and partly staffed by Russians. Trade talks with Rumania were being opened.

It was remarkable how swiftly all this changed the flavor of Cairo. The old Gezira Sporting Club, founded by the British officers as a pigeon-shooting club, suddenly swarmed with Communists and their graceless wives; around the corner the British still played their cricket, helped by the last of the Coptic Anglophiles, but the swimming pool was full of unfamiliar gutturals and dowdy Communist swimsuits, and often the Russian ambassador's black Zis car would sweep portentously past the squash courts. I once went to a reception at the Soviet embassy to meet Dmitri Shepilov, then the Soviet Foreign Secretary. He was a man of genial and imposing presence, and I found him basking in Egyptian adulation, rather as that horrible Nazi had been wallowing among the officers at Alexandria. There he stood, huge and beaming, with a drink in his hand and a red handkerchief protruding from the pocket of his smooth tropical suit; and all around him the Egyptians fawned and simpered, the women smiling voluptuously, the men in their white dinner jackets excited as much by the occasion as by the free vodka. I stood in a corner of the room with a benevolent American correspondent, and the crowd swept past us dizzily, a heavy breath of perfume, a clamor of Arabic, on its way to pay court.

Nor was it only in Egypt that the Russians now became respectable. They arranged another arms deal with the Syrians, now under joint command with the Egyptians, and Syrian officers came to Cairo for training on the new weapons. They established diplomatic relations with the Saudis and Yemenis. The new commander of the Jordanian army, successor to Glubb, told me darkly at a party one night that if Britain would not supply Jordan with more arms, the Russians always would. Emir Feisal of Saudi Arabia announced that the Arabs would "buy arms from the devil, if need be"—daring sentiments, coming from the Foreign Minister of a medieval autocracy. In Damascus the shops were flooded with Communist books and magazines, and portly Rumanian steel workers chased Miss Lollobrigida from the bookstalls. I once walked into the grandest hotel in Syria to find a Muslim ulema in robes of great magnificence sitting on a sofa in the lobby, surrounded by respectful courtiers. He was a Russian, and had come with a party of cultural magnificoes to present a Stalin Peace Prize to a well-known Syrian Islamic sage. ("But of course," say the apologists, "the two faiths are absolutely incompatible!") Russians, Czechs, Hungarians, and citizens of the obscurer satellites and autonomous republics became commonplace figures of the Middle East.

To achieve all this the Russians lulled many of the Arabs (though not all of them) into a mood of greedy gullibility. Nasser, it appears, genuinely did not understand the dangers of his arms deal.

Many other Arab leaders, wedded to neutralism and inflamed by anti-Westernism, could see no peril of Russian expansionism, either military or ideological. Russia was, like West Germany, free of the imperialist stigma; she could not be blamed for the establishment of Israel; she was scarcely known in the Middle East; and she managed to approach the Arabs in a man-to-man way very different from the somewhat hoity-toity attitudes so often exhibited by the West. Russian shows and exhibitions were very successful and often ended with a rousing sing-song of Arab patriotic songs, far beyond the capacity of Sadlers' Wells or the Comédie Française. Communist Parties were still officially banned in most countries of the Middle East; but in Egypt a clear line was drawn between Communism in Russia and Communism at home (reserved, where possible, for places like Kharga); in Syria the Communists flourished anyway, quite brazenly; and in Jordan the political scene was so chaotic that such ordinances were more hypothetical than real. Above all, Egypt's paranoic anti-Western policies, crystallized in opposition to the Baghdad Pact and the nationalization of the Suez Canal, had enabled the Russians to pose successfully as the champions of Arab progress.

So at our moment of history, November, 1956, Russia was a force in the Middle East, a new giant in the arena. Syria and Jordan were partly under her spell. Egypt had so mortgaged her assets to the Communist world that some people considered her already a Russian satellite. When the Israelis launched their offensive in Sinai, it was largely intended to destroy the power of the Russian-equipped Egyptian army; and the captured tanks that came lumbering by us, as we sipped our lemonade beside the road, were mostly Russian-built. The motives of the Western attack on Port Said were confused and multitudinous, but one of them was undoubtedly to smoke out a nest of Russian influence before all the eggs were hatched. Indeed, one of the more heartening episodes of the campaign was the spectacle of several hundred Russian technicians skipping away down to the Sudan, in awkward and uncomfortable conditions, while the going was good.

I do not myself believe that the Russians were very deeply entrenched in the Middle East. Naive and sometimes shameless though the Arabs often were, there was something that did not ring true about their growing association with Russia. It was opportunism, not ideology, that had given the Russians their entry to the Arab world, and before long they, too, would be having their difficulties with nationalism and xenophobia. Still, when we looked around us that morning at our Sinai horizons, the gloomy power of Moscow felt disconcertingly close.

DIVERSITIES

IRAQ has not for a moment succumbed to these Russian advances, partly because of her membership of the Baghdad Pact, partly because of the staunch (if ruthless) character of her leadership. But the dangers are always present, and are if anything sharpened by the resilient diversity of the country. Iraq's great rival Egypt is a nation of racial and geographical cohesion, and indeed may be suspected of inbreeding, so static and stagnant have become some segments of its society. Iraq, however, is more like a country of the New World in its patchwork texture. We have seen how distinct are the mountains of Kurdestan, and how largely inviolate the insularity of the Kurds and Yezidis; but even the southern part of the country, the alluvium of the two rivers, is remarkably heterogeneous both as to place and people.

There is, for example, the Arabian south. Iraq adjoins the Arabian Peninsula, and its southern outlet Basra is still the prototype of the Arab seaport. It has some splendid modern installations, and there are always two or three big steamers in port (though nothing like those futuristic tankers at Kuwait); but there are parts of Basra, dhow-yards and seamen's coffee-shops and cluttered minor quaysides, in which Sinbad could still find a familiar corner, if ever he came down from Baghdad again in search of gold and adventure. There is an oilfield outside Basra, in which an acquaintance of mine once saw a camel drinking crude oil out of a can; and there are thousands of acres of luscious date palms, the chief agricultural product of Iraq. Silent, muddy creeks intersect these date forests, and through them runs that same hot Shatt-el-Arab that washes the metallic shores of Abadan. It is a wonderful thing to wander through such a grove, deep, dark, and mysterious, blessed by cool shade, ornamented austerely by sudden dust-laden shafts of sunlight. "Honor your aunt, the palm," said Mohammed in legend; and so green and profound are these plantations that after a time the trees do begin to lose their woodenness and acquire a certain imperturbable kind confidence, quite like some unusually well-balanced maiden aunt with toffees in a tin. Like the camel, also exalted by the prophet, the date is a marvellous piece of design.

It contains almost every element of a balanced diet. The Arabs eat
it, ferment it to make alcohol, crush its stones to feed their cattle,
and use both fronds and trunk to build their houses. Some people
think eating dates prevents cancer; others say it prevents malaria.
Still others claim (perhaps on more scientific grounds) that it has
the highest caloric value of any natural, cultivated, or processed
food on earth. The date palm is all but indestructible, needs very
little attention, and bears fruit for two or three hundred years.
There are two hundred and fifty kinds, and they all grow happily
in Iraq. No wonder the date growers are a prosperous people, and
the headquarters of their association in Basra one of the most handsome buildings in Iraq. (And every single date that is exported
through that ancient seaport is already stoned, so carefully is the
fastidious Western market studied; if your dates have stones in
them, they do not come from Iraq.)

Then in the country to the north, the drab and dusty lowlands
of the two rivers, live the people who call themselves Mandaeans
or Sabians. There are about six thousand members of this obscure
cult, and they live in a series of derelict and fly-blown villages in
the region of Amarah, where they practice their traditional craft
of silversmithing (that is to say, etching pictures of camels on
ashtrays). They are a calm and handsome people, with big black
beards like the Yezidis, but their faith is unexpectedly complex.
I once asked a Sabian precisely what his beliefs were. He replied:
"Just the same as yours, except John the Baptist is our Jesus." This
was a monumental over-simplification, but it is true that the whole
of the Sabian faith revolves around the concept of baptism. So
dedicated are they to the necessity of total immersion, and so frequent and apparently trivial are the pretexts on which they will
submerge themselves in the Tigris, that they would feel readily at
home among the fervent hot gospellers of the American South,
who often share this hydrophilia. The very name means "baptists";
and in the early days of Islam there was a pagan sect which pru-
dently changed its own name to "Sabians" in the hope that it would
share in the toleration allowed by Mohammed to the People of the
Book—Jews, Christians, and Mandaeans. The present-day Sabians
seem to regard the rivers themselves as divine, and baptize themselves at least once every day. (The priests charge a small fee for

the ceremony, and this forms their stipend.) The marriage ceremony, indeed, includes several immersions; people who seem
likely to die are hastily dipped into the river, a process which often
decides the issue; and the cult huts of the sect are always built on
the very edge of the water, with the mud oozing up to their
entrances.

But the Sabians also have theories about the divine significance
of the universe, and in the past this has given them some intellectual
distinction. The planets, they believe, are administered by spirits
who are intermediaries with the Almighty. Sometimes they call the
planets their fathers and the elements their mothers, and they believe that holy spirits animate every atom of the physical world:
each raindrop has its own spirit. Even abstract arts, like music, have
their sacred affiliations—Orpheus is one of the gods of the Sabians.
This preoccupation with the relationship between things spiritual
and material produced, in the heyday of the Sabian civilization,
several eminent intellectuals—astronomers, mathematicians, physi-
cians, meteorologists, and mineralogists—and in the Middle Ages
there were one or two Sabian families which fostered successive
generations of distinguished thinkers. Nowadays they are a simple
people. Mumbo-jumbo astrology is more to their taste than astron-
omy, and their faith, once enriched by lofty ideas and deductions,
is now riddled with childish superstition. Still, it is odd to think
of them in their mud huts among the palm trees, invoking the help
of Orpheus each night as they bow towards the Pole Star.

Scarcely less esoteric are the Marsh Arabs, who live in the inaccessible fenlands between the two rivers. Just as the people of
East Anglia withdrew, under the pressure of hostility, into the low,
marshy country around the Wash, so the Marsh Arabs have been
driven into the secluded obscurity of this cozy country. There are
no roads at all in their territory, and the only way of moving
about is by boat. The reeds are anything up to fifteen feet tall, and
in shadowy avenues through their recesses the Marsh Arabs pole
their primitive boats and follow their elusive fancies. Theirs is a
civilization built upon the reed, as the Bedu's is founded upon the
camel and the date. They live in reed houses, sleep on reeds, weave
reeds into mats, twine reeds into ropes, and burn reeds on their fires.
Like the people of Sarawak, they build long guest houses for

moments of ceremonial hospitality, and they seem to live a fairly contented sort of life, disturbed from time to time only by the processes of law or the arrival of some eager anthropologist in waders. They keep water buffaloes, which ask for nothing better than a nice bog, and they catch a good many not very succulent fish; and their country is sometimes magically graced with multitudes of watery flowers. From the air these marshes do look undeniably uncomfortable; but at least they allow the Marsh Arabs uninterrupted privacy, and it is difficult indeed to catch a criminal who sneaks away with a boat and a few reed mats into these enigmatic waters.

In many parts of Iraq there are Christians, of diverse convictions, and in scattered ethnical pockets. Among the most important groups are the so-called Assyrians, many of whom live within sight of Nineveh but are not remotely descended from the people of the winged bulls. They are really Nestorians whose church was largely destroyed by the severities of Tamerlane, and who survived until the 1914 war chiefly in the highlands of Persia and Turkey. After the war they were saved from new persecutions by the British government and introduced into Iraq, over which Britain had acquired mandatory rights. They are thus the direct wards of the British, and have often been accused of subversive activities and of being puppets of an occupying Power. In the 1930s they were decimated in a series of terrible massacres. Nevertheless, the Assyrians have loyally served Britain in all her fluctuating relations with Iraq, and their devotion to things British is sometimes touching. Thousands of them formed, under British officers, a force called the Iraq Levies which was raised to protect British military installations in the country, and this remained proudly in being until 1955, when the British handed over their airfields to the Iraqis.

You may scoff at the Anglophilia of the Assyrians and their kind (for there are several such groups of British protégés in the Middle East). You may laugh at their penchant for English names and English manners, and think it unhealthy that one or two such communities should have been fostered with such especial care by the suzerain Power. Nevertheless, I shall always remember with sad affection the farewell parade of the Assyrians, when they marched for the last time under the British flag. It was at Habbaniy, the great air base west of Baghdad which was the center of British power in Iraq (and which in 1956 still provides useful services for what is left of the Royal Air Force). It was not, though, a sad ceremony. The agreement had been amicably concluded, and the British were leaving with handshakes and kind words. Three forces were on parade. First there was the Iraqi army, taking over the base; then the Royal Air Force, young, pink, and liable to heatstroke; and finally the Assyrians, an army of brown, stocky little men in puttees, looking very solemn. I found them infinitely poignant. They were not very impressive little men, nor very brilliant at their drill, nor expensively or glamorously equipped; but there was pride and pathos to their manner as they left the parade ground for the last time, heads very high, arms swinging earnestly, in that slightly exaggerated version of British drill manners common to colonial troops. Most of them had no trade but soldiering, no loyalty but to the British, no corporate pride except pride of service and devotion to their sad little community. Some of them, no doubt, found work with the Iraqi forces, despite racial and religious prejudices; the rest have presumably scattered into the shabby and drafty limbo reserved in the Middle East for unrespected minorities. The band played "Colonel Bogey" with gusto as these old friends and comrades of Britain marched bravely off the field into oblivion.

Even among the predominant Arabs of Iraq there are schisms and rivalries, as there are in many other parts of the Middle East; for about half the population subscribes to the Sunni sect, which recognizes as caliphs the leaders of Islam immediately following Mohammed, and the other half belong to the Shia sect, which passionately disagrees. (Mohammed is said to have prophesied that his following would split into seventy-three sects, of which one —unhappily he did not specify which—would be orthodox.) Indeed Iraq is the fountainhead of the Shia movement, which forms the principal bond (strategy apart) between this country and its neighbor Persia. For it was at Kerbala, in the southern plain, that Hussein, one of the great figures of the Shia faith, was martyred with a few companions in heroic circumstances. The holiest day of the Shia calendar commemorates the death of this militant saint, his brother Hassan, and his father Ali, son-in-law of the Prophet. Kerbala is therefore one of the supremely holy cities of the Shias, and to visit it is to sense a little of the fanaticism that still animates some aspects of Islam—and to feel, too, some of the power of this persistently compelling religion.

Kerbala is also a political danger spot: for so sacred is it to the Shias that many hundreds of pilgrims come to it over the mountains from Persia, and with them not a few agents and agitators. What is more, Shiism has so virile and touchy a following that there is always the danger of friction between its supporters and the Sunnis (as there always is, uncharacteristically, in Bahrain). Kerbala is therefore a heady and inflammable town. It is generally full of Persian pilgrims, their women in gaudy, trailing dresses, some of the pilgrims old men who have made the journey in order to die in one of the holy places of Iraq (some of them, in fact, already dead and conveyed on pilgrimage in coffins). These taut, intense people do not always look at you with kindliness. Sometimes, indeed, you may suddenly catch in the eye of a passing zealot an expression of such immediate and implacable loathing, such a burning desire to commit an atrocity upon your person, that you may feel tempted to leave for Baghdad at once. Of course there are friendly faces too, especially among the citizens of Kerbala, but it is difficult for a foreigner or a Christian to feel altogether at ease. You are not allowed to enter the most celebrated shrine of the place, the supposed tomb of Ali, so when I was there I walked into a neighboring house and asked if I might climb to its roof to see into the court-yard. The owner of the house was all smiles; but it turned out to be some sort of simple inn, catering to poor pilgrims from Persia, and as I walked up its narrow winding staircase I found myself passing a series of sparsely-furnished rooms—a bed and a prayer mat and a hard, cold floor. In each of these cells there was a pilgrim, and as I clumped my way up that steep staircase each turned his baleful eyes in my direction. I shall never forget the detestation that overcame the faces of those merciless old men when they observed a Christian on the stairs, nor the relief with which I at last escaped the gamut of their prejudice and emerged upon the roof, with the bright golden dome of the mosque in front of me, and the wide courtyard, crowded with pilgrims, spread before me like a chessboard.

Such a place, festering with violent emotions, must always be a powder keg and a breeding place of discontent. The Iraqi government much prefers you to have an official escort if you go prowling around in Kerbala, and my own companion during a tour of the bazaars was the local chief of police. He seemed to have the situation well in hand, and it was revealing to see how widely-flung was his intelligence service. Time and again some inconspicuous loiterer would reveal himself, by a signal or a mere flicker of his face, as a plain-clothes policeman; and many indeed were the merchants and craftsmen who seemed to have some permanent understanding with the police. The present regime in Iraq is not addicted to any wishy-washy domestic liberalism, and the wise citizen (unless he wants to be dragged off to some desert dungeon) does his best to please the authorities.

Such a confusion of peoples and regions—from Kurds to Marsh Arabs, from high mountains to date palms—makes for vitality in a state. It also inevitably makes for dissensions. The British understood the importance of minorities in governing an alien and predominantly suspicious country, and there is every sign that the Communists realize it too. Of all the prizes of the Middle East, Iraq is in many ways the most tempting, and the way to its control might well be through the rivalries and antipathies that still weaken its structure, and the hardly concealed contempt with which the ruling groups still regard some of their fellow citizens (though one cannot easily imagine the Sabians, for instance, collaborating with the Yezidis and the Nestorians to undermine the stability of the kingdom).

NEW IRAQ

RIGHT IN THE HEART of this variegated country lies the city of Baghdad, the driving force of the new Iraq. If Iraq is a country of many races, Baghdad remains uncompromisingly Arab. In the Middle Ages it was known to the Muslims as the City of Peace, and it is still one of the focal points of Arab consciousness, the only rival to Cairo as the capital of the Arab world. For at least a century Baghdad sheltered the greatest conglomeration of wealth and learning on earth; it was at once the Alexandria and the Manhattan of its time. To this day, of all the cities of Islam, it retains the most potent allure, and there are few simple citizens of the West who will not respond, if not with yearning, at least with wonder, to the old magic of its name.

The foreigner, though, is nearly always disappointed with his first sight of this legendary place. He has been surfeited with images of Baghdad as a caliphean boom city, a cross between Houston and the *Arabian Nights*, at once burgeoning with sky-scrapers and enriched with antique romance. Alas, few are the fairy battlements embellishing the modern skyline of Baghdad, and Rashid Street, its main business thoroughfare, must be one of the most insufferably dreary streets on earth. Endless are the evenings which stretch away, from the windows of hotel bed-rooms, down the shabby, peeling colonnades of this street. A pot-holed roadway, mean and grubby shops, whining beggars, a constant oozing, hooting traffic jam: "A fig for the caliphs!" says the new arrival, ordering a soporific whisky. "Boom city, my foot!"

But he is wrong, as new arrivals so often are. Baghdad is not only a city of vast and growing wealth; not only a political capital of great and increasing significance; not only a place of intrigue and suppressed discontent; it is also a capital of pervasive charm in which, for those who care to search, there still linger a few re-minders of Scheherazade and the despots of fable. Almost everyone who lives in Baghdad for long grows to like it, and the Baghdadis, an easy-going, arm-in-arm, slightly raffish kind of people, soon endear themselves to most foreigners. Cairo is bigger and brassier,

Beirut more sophisticated, Damascus lovelier, Amman more demure, Riyadh nearer the mores of the desert; but for me Baghdad
remains, in its sleazy old way, the most interesting and the most
hopeful of the Arab capitals.

This is partly because of the river. The Tigris flows grandly
through the very center of Baghdad, and often the quickest way to
get from one part of the town to another is to take a boat. There
are always a few boatmen hanging about at the ends of the alleys
which run down to the water, and courteous and flowery is the
competition with which they will entice your custom. The
cushioned upholstery of the craft, bleached by the sun, is carefully
rearranged; a plank is laid down for you; a wrinkled hand helps
you on board; and as he pushes you away from the bank with his
oar the boatman murmurs some reverent invocation under his
breath. The river is very wide and very solemn, swift-flowing and
sometimes turbulent, and it is often cluttered with dredgers, barges,
lighters or rafts; and sometimes one of those roofed river steamers
churns its prim way toward Basra. The Tigris has all the condescension of a great river, as if nothing could be so impertinent as
to interfere with the stately stream of its waters; but from the
middle of it, leaning among the cushions, you can see how dynamic
is the present condition of Baghdad, in which nothing is too sacred
for alteration, and hardly anything too difficult to try.

Downstream, for example, is a great new bridge, built by Germans, which is to link Rashid Street with the expanding northern
suburbs. There is the site of the new parliament building, a structure of dubious value in 1956 (for as it happens all political parties
are banned) but worthwhile as an ostentatious hostage to progress;
it is to be an enormous structure in vaguely caliphean style, all
pillars and Moorish arches. Nearby, perhaps as a sort of corrective,
is to be the new king's royal palace, with so much marble in it that
the Italian suppliers have a resident agent on the spot. Over the
rooftops you can see the handsome white block of a new bank,
clean, functional, and apparently incorruptible; it is only the first
of a series of banks going up in Baghdad's Wall Street, displacing
many a shuttered, tumbling money-changer's, and helping to eradicate the memory of those shrewd and subtle Jewish bankers who,
until the establishment of Israel, dominated the financial life of this

city. (Nearly all the Jews have left Iraq now, and their talents have
been badly missed.) Big new roads radiate from the heart of Baghdad. Comfortable new suburbs sprout in its shadow. The marvellous old bridge of boats upstream from the city is being swept
away, and you will no longer be able to look through its portals
and see its rusty pontoons wiggling snakily across the stream. Now
and then, if you peer between the houses on the bank, you may
glimpse a red double-decker bus crawling down Rashid Street, and
bask for a moment in the homeliness of these genial vehicles (especially if you have ever watched the big Mercedes buses go screaming with their streamlined trailers down the road to the Giza
pyramids).

Do not equate Baghdad with the raucous hustle of Kuwait.
Baghdad is still preeminently a dusty and crumbly city, instinct
with memories of the Turks, and here and there among the palm
trees on the river bank there are rows of fine old-fashioned houses,
with charming crooked balconies over the water, all ups and downs
and courtyards, date palms and wrought iron, with high rooms and
rickety guest chambers, and fountains in the gardens. Tucked away
among the demolitions many such places remain. It is true that the
Iraq development board has no preservation department, and that
if you ask for a picture postcard you will almost certainly be given
one of the Rafidan Bank or the Date Marketing Board; but try
though they may to be ruthless and unsentimental, tradition keeps
breaking through. Among the new splendors and mediocrities there
still run a myriad narrow streets, heavy with spiced oriental smells,
thronged with gowned Arabs, turbaned Kurds, bent-backed porters, donkeys, dogs, wasps, and ladies peering at life through the
thick, distorting curtains of the veil. Here are the Persian pilgrims
and the visitors from the desert, and here the wandering cabaret
girls, enough to "shake the saintship of an anchorite," pile into the
taxi for Teheran.

Especially in the great bazaars can you find some echoes of the
old Baghdad, and even fancy (if you are of an excessively romantic
turn of mind) the Commander of the Faithful wandering disguised among these rambunctious murky halls. The Baghdad *suks*
are less intimate than Jerusalem's, less businesslike than Aleppo's;
but they give an impression of boundless power. The big covered

bazaars ramble beside the river, dense with dust, particles of food, and heady vapors. Here is the draper's bazaar, and the alcoves are thick with bright fabrics and rolls of material, nylon slips hang in their scores on coathangers, coats are dull and frocks are flouncy and vivid, and the draper sits incongruously cross-legged on a wicker stool. Here is the bazaar of the perfumers, with the scents mysteriously bottled and an overpowering smell of cheap *eau de cologne* swirling through the arcades. Here are the food stalls (indigestible colors) and the leather bazaar (horse leathers and bandoliers), and the innumerable arcades of the shoemakers (ankle-straps, fluffy slippers, and enormous buckled sandals). But so hefty and muscular is the spirit of the Baghdad *suk*, and so redolent of masculine tastes, that most people remember it in terms of the Bazaar of the Coppersmiths. Brawny indeed are the backs of the smiths as they bend to their work in the heat, with their long handles crashing upon the metal in a ragged unison, and the clashing of metals, the hot sizzling of the coals, the glistening of sweat and molten iron, and the attendant boys, all thin legs and big black eyes, hovering on the outskirts with hammers or trays like acolytes at a rite. The Arab bazaar is a wonderful place, an oasis of kindliness, in which after a year or two of wandering the stranger finds himself curiously at home, whether he is in Shibam or Tripoli; and one of the best and most jovial, the most Chestertonian, is the coppersmiths' *suk* at Baghdad, a full-blooded, clanging, loose-limbed kind of a place.

But sharing tenements with the picturesque in Baghdad is its half-brother, the squalid. The city still has its gloomy complexes of mud huts, huddled together in misery like bedraggled peasants in a drizzle, the drains running open down their filthy streets, the old women caterwauling, the children's noses running: the usual excrescences of the Muslim Middle East, which we have seen everywhere, with small variations of refinement, from Syria to Muscat. The young men of Iraq, the disillusioned Sabians and ambitious Kurds, the half-educated peasants, the oil company apprentices, the sons of sheikhs, flock into Baghdad in search of office desks and starched collars, and the urban slums fester under

the weight of population. In Baghdad all the problems of the new
Iraq can be seen in distillation: the fight for time, the skepticism,
the struggle to convince the ordinary man that he is not forgotten,
the chronic suspicions of exploitation, imperialism, corruption. This
is a city, and a people, that does not believe in its own good fortune.

It is a volatile and zestful community, and who can wonder that
its squalor breeds discontent? With misery there comes, inevitably,
politics. I was once wandering through the purlieus of Kazimain,
another holy city of the Shias which lies on the outskirts of Baghdad. It was late at night; an after-dinner depression had taken me
there; all was dim and shuttered, except for the string of lights
around the door of the mosque and the sheen of its great golden
dome, high above. A stream of pilgrims still passed through those
venerated portals, touching the gateway for blessings as they
passed, and a few flashy Persian buses, made chiefly of glass and
chromium, brooded in the dusty square that lies in front of the
Golden Mosque. I left them behind me, and strolled into the
arabesque of narrow streets that surrounds the mosque. The street
lights softly shone about me. Hushed were the high, overhanging
windows and tilted wooden doors, and deep the shadows that
muffled the squares and alleyways. Beggars huddled in their
blankets on the cobblestones. Sometimes a muffled white figure
strode away down a back street, or opened a door with a clanking
of chains and wooden locks. The hum of the mosque, the perpetual
roar of the city, were far away that night.

"And why," said a distinctly vicious voice in English, "why, may
I ask, are you wandering through Kazimain in the middle of the
night?" A young man suddenly stood before me, dressed in
pyjamas, with a tweed jacket slung over his shoulders. "Do you
have an explanation, please?" "I was looking at its wonderful old
houses," I said, rather wishing I had foregone the last brandy, "and
—well, enjoying the old-world atmosphere of it all, you know."
There seemed to be no very convenient alley of escape, but it did
not matter; for the young man, far from assaulting me, pulled his
jacket around his shoulders and delivered what seemed to me an
excessively long sociological lecture, even as sociological lectures
go. Age had no wonder for such a young man of Baghdad, and
casements no romance. He saw only the disease and the wretched-

ness behind that antique façade. His theories were a little hazy, but his complaint boiled down to this: with all that oil in Iraq, with all that money, with all those high-faluting promises, why did Kazimain—and he flung his hand contemptuously out toward the street—still look like *this*? It was difficult to argue with him, for he turned out to be an extremely nice and earnest young man, and I could see how unconvincing he thought the appeals of the government ("Give us time, only give us time, and the oil will build you a new life!") Of all the emotions, impatience is perhaps the easiest to manipulate; and there are all too many people in Iraq to drop a suggestion, here and there, of embezzlement, to hint that the ruling conservatives are following the old, rapacious road of the pashas, and that the time is near for a convulsion to remove all vestiges of caliphism and feudalism from the society of Iraq.

So there are dark and turbulent currents running beneath the changing surface of the city. This is an autocracy, and the rash Communist or trouble-maker is swiftly whisked off from his coffee-shop to imprisonment in the desert. The press is ruthlessly controlled, the vestigial intelligentsia often disgruntled. Political parties are banned, but exist all the same, and I have occasionally been taken in cars to suburban villas where paunchy mediocrities have told me of their grievances. The differences between these shadow parties are insignificant, but the rivalry between them is intense, and their leaders are extremely catty about each other and ineffectively abusive about Nuri Said. There may be, tucked away in this limbo, some great Iraqi leader in embryo, but I have never met him. Except for Nuri, there seems to be no single leader of distinction. The brain-power of the Middle East remains in Cairo, and compared with that pulsing capital Baghdad still feels sadly provincial.

Sometimes the malcontents hurl their darts at the royal family, which lives in semi-British state in a series of cool palaces, with Rolls-Royces and Harrow accents. An audience with King Feisal (whom we last saw in his hand-me-downs at his cousin Hussein's wedding) is a pleasant experience, and is most easily arranged if you have an introduction to the powerful court chamberlain. The Iraqi court is efficiently run. The waiting room in which you will be deposited is spotless and richly furnished. A glass of lemonade will be pressed into your hand. Various other supplicants and de-

votees will make their salaams to you as you enter, and lower themselves carefully again upon their spindly chairs before continuing
their breathy undertone conversations. Outside the French windows two gorgeous lancers stand watch, their feet apart, their
pennanted lances crossed, as in regimental cap badges. When your
turn comes, and you hastily drain the sticky sediment at the bottom
of the lemonade, you are taken into a room rather like an executive
suite in a Hollywood comedy; and at its ample desk sits King
Feisal. He struck me as a pleasant and intelligent person, frank and
humorous, and gently Anglicized. Perhaps he is a little portly for
his early twenties, but at least he is trying to keep his fat down
(or so he told me), an ambition not apparently shared by his ex-
colleague Farouk. No scandal so far surrounds this young king;
he seems to bear himself well; if there is in his office and his manner
something that strikes you as out of tune, something alien to the
Arab milieu, it is undeniable that the existence of the Iraqi monarchy (founded in 1920) has given the country a stable element
dismally lacking in most of its neighbors.

Until a few years ago the real power of the Iraqi throne was
Crown Prince Abdulillah, a sallow but handsome man of ageless
appearance. When I was ushered on from the king to his uncle I
found myself on rather less congenial ground. Abdulillah talked
fluently and amusingly, and told me that he was planning to search
for any references to T. E. Lawrence in the papers of his celebrated
grandfather, King Feisal I. The conversation turned to the pictures
on the wall, a galaxy of chieftainship. "What a splendid costume
it is!" I said of a picture of Feisal I in Arab dress. "Do you ever
wear it yourself?" "Sometimes," said the Crown Prince. "You
would be surprised how comfortable it is." "And it does make one
look so fearfully dignified," I said lightly. This was not a success.
A chill seemed to settle upon our relationship, and the interview
soon ended. Crown Prince Abdulillah, it seems, needs no romantic
trappings to give him dignity.

It is difficult not to feel sympathy for the young Iraqi progressive, so sincere and so heedless, restlessly comparing the somewhat banal integrity of this royal regime with the flamboyant
blatancies of Colonel Nasser. Some people say the government has
erred in neglecting publicity, and in failing (until the last year or

two) to spend more money on things immediately apparent and welcome to ordinary people. I find it difficult to become very enamored of the Egyptian university student, who often seems to me to have some neurotic crack or flaw in his fiber; but his Iraqi equivalent is very attractive, and often surprisingly broad-minded. I went back to Kazimain another day to take some photographs of the mosque. Like the monuments of Kerbala, the Golden Mosque is forbidden to unbelievers, so I looked for some neighboring rooftop with a view into the courtyard. I had been told often enough that if a Christian stepped inside he risked facing a howling mob of the faithful, an encounter in which, it seemed to me, the odds were not worth accepting. I asked a youth, accordingly, if I might go to the roof of his house. We struck up a conversation, and after a few moments he volunteered to take me inside the courtyard of the mosque. "Don't be afraid," said he. "They are more bark than bite!" So in we went, through one of the great frowning gates, and I took my photographs at leisure. When, from time to time, some angry zealot approached us grumbling, my companion either charmed him into sickly smiles or chased him off with loud repartee. I was not absolutely sure about the rights or wrongs of this episode, for I have always been made uncomfortable by stories of clandestine entries into Muslim holy places, however daring the exploit and unimpeachable the motive. Still, the young man assured me that he himself was as devout a Shia as you would find, so I thanked him gratefully and departed with haste (for a pricking sensation at the back of my neck told me that the howling mob might at any moment emerge from the pillared recesses of the prayer hall).

Above all these cross-currents and dissensions, above the Sabians and the Assyrians, far above the King, stands Nuri Said, the grand old man of Iraq and the most distinguished statesman of the Middle East. It is Nuri's personality which has governed the destinies of the development board, his stature which keeps precarious order in Iraq, his vision which has to some extent reestablished Iraq as a counterpoise to Egypt in the uneasy equilibrium of the Arab world. Iraq still does not throw her weight (or her money) about as do

Egypt or Saudi Arabia. It is easy to feel, sometimes, that she shirks her responsibilities and evades troublesome issues. She is as viciously stubborn as her neighbors over the problem of Israel, and indeed never concluded an armistice with the Israelis after the 1948 war. But by and large Iraq's policies are, in the context of 1956, mature and sensible; whether or not you agree that it is right for an Arab Power to align itself deliberately with the Western alliance, you must at least agree that Iraq has done so with decision and courage. It is no light thing to incur the hostility of Egypt in the modern Middle East, especially if you are already half-estranged from Saudi Arabia by dynastic squabbles of the silliest and most pertinacious kind. Colonel Nasser himself has said that Egypt will "stand by the people of Iraq, whatever the government of that country does"—as open an incitement to revolution as the leader of one country ever gave to the inhabitants of another. Cairo radio, indeed, has often spoken frankly enough of the need to eradicate Nuri Pasha, and occasionally there sweeps through the Middle East a rumor that desire has been translated into action, and that the old lion has, in fact, been extinguished.

But he is a marvellously resilient politician. Nuri first entered the Arab stage when he deserted from the Turkish army in the First World War and joined in the Arab Revolt. Since then he has often shown stubbornness, sometimes foolishness, often a streak of despotism; but never, even in the wildest accusations of his bitterest enemies, cowardice. He has a Churchillian bigness to him. His ideas are often grandiose—for example, the scheme of a Greater Syria to include Iraq, Syria, Jordan, and Palestine. His presence is imposing, too. Often you may see him sweeping through Baghdad in his big black car, hunched in the back like a wise and fairly avuncular giant: off to inspect a new dam, squash some opposition, disentangle an imbroglio, or drop into Kurdestan by helicopter. Or you may see him among the welcoming dignitaries at the airport, waiting for some international celebrity to arrive. He keeps apart and aloof from his colleagues, stalking up and down in silence with his hands behind his back, upon his face an expression at once confident and disillusioned; and it is instructive to see how the chatter dies as he passes solemnly by, and how those lesser men follow his progress over their shoulders, as a girl talking to a dull young man will often prefer to survey the passing gowns.

Except for some high-class but powerless Lebanese, Nuri is the only statesman of the Arab world with whom the Powers, whether Communist or capitalist, can confidently deal; the only one whose convictions are clear and whose intentions are reasonably stable. Indeed, you can most easily gauge his caliber at an international conference. I saw him at his best at a meeting of the Baghdad Pact convened in the Palace of Roses outside the capital. Three foreign Prime Ministers were present, together with the British Foreign Secretary and the Chief of the Imperial General Staff (the saddest and most nostalgic of titles); and towards the end of the meeting the Commander of the United States Sixth Fleet was ushered into the assembly from an outer room, the very personification of brute strength and benevolence. But undoubtedly the most compelling presence in the room was Nuri's. He sat at the head of the long table, as representative of the host country, and he looked around him with a sort of paternal balefulness very impressive to observe (and disconcerting, I imagine, for those who disagreed with him). He is an old man now, and a little deaf; I shall always see him in my mind's eye, when he has long been laid with fulsome praise in his ornate mausoleum, sitting there among his rather insipid advisers, his hand cupped to his ear, his sharp eyes flickering, his shoulders crouched, now and then intervening in his rasping voice to suggest a modification of the agenda, insinuate a witticism, or tell somebody to shut the door.

The failings and virtues of the new Iraq are all Nuri's. It is a one-man country. Some say it is lacking in romantic imagination—that in its devotion to sensible progress it has ignored the trumpet-call of Arab unity. Some say it is too ready to abandon its Arab brethren in favor of association with the West. Some criticize its feudal leanings, some point with reason to its cultural sterility. Some suspect it of yearnings towards a Greater Syria backed by Western power and money. Some, on the other hand, are irritated by its persistent refusal to take up arms in the perpetual skirmishing of Middle Eastern affairs. Many of the complaints are justified, and the responsibility must be Nuri Said's. Nevertheless, when I stood among my Israelis in Sinai that day, I hoped our affairs would not estrange the Iraqis from the West: theirs was a country with many anxieties, but it bore upon its sturdy shoulders the hopes of wise Arabs and their friends.

ENVOI

THIS WAS OUR VIEW of the Muslim Middle East as we stood there, the colonel, the tank crews, and I, in the bitter sunshine of Sinai. This was the moment of purgation, when some of the misconceptions were to be cleared, some of the fictions destroyed, one or two of the malignant cankers pierced. Nothing would ever be quite the same again. With a laugh and a shrug of his shoulders the colonel threw his empty bottle into the desert and wiped his hands on his battle-dress trousers; and taking a cigarette from his breast pocket he propped himself against the wheel of a jeep and surveyed the prospect around him, from horizon to horizon, with an amused and cynical smile.

Events were soon to prove that the colonel, when he surveyed the surrounding scene with his air of contemptuous dismissal, was right. The Muslim Middle East, just as he said, would never be quite the same again. Indeed within a year, as a result of that peculiar November, much of the balance of power was altered and many of the old alignments shattered. The Suez Canal was to remain firmly in Nasser's hands; the British and French suffered their black period of ignominy; the Israelis forfeited much of the world's hard-earned sympathy. All the same, by the summer of 1957 prospects for the West in the Middle East did appear, on the whole, rather brighter. Nasser's hold over the Arab world was distinctly weakened, though he still seemed just as strong at home. The unholy alliance between Egypt and Saudi Arabia became little more than an improbable memory, and the Hashemite and Saudi dynasties, by a miraculous reversal of history, made the first tentative approaches to *rapprochement*. Nuri's position in Iraq was strengthened, little King Hussein sat rather more firmly in his throne, the restless rumbles of Arab discontent were momentarily hushed. At the same time, while old Britain withdrew her power a stage further, the United States more openly assumed her responsibilities in the Middle East (and high time too, in my own Anglo-American opinion). The Baghdad Pact was given a new meaning; the extent of Russian infiltration was at least made known to an oddly skeptical world. It would be an unconvincing rationalization, perhaps, to pretend that all these consequences were foreseen as we stood among the debris that November day: but they were all to be, within a matter of months, incidentals of our adventure.

At the moment, the colonel's eye took in the immediate scene. He saw his Muslim neighbors ravaged by perpetual strains and frenzies, exploited now by one Power, now by another; with no noble ideas to sustain them, no creative art to inspire them, no constancy of resolution, no simple loyalties, no unshakable faith, no skill, no sense of shame; with hardly a great man among them, and hardly a true artist, and scarcely a general of quality; laughable, pathetic, maddening, quarrelsome, covetous, dirty, ill-educated; valued as allies only because of their oil, tolerated as impudent enemies only because greater forces stood behind them watchfully. "After this little lot," said the colonel, "perhaps they'll learn to watch their manners."

Of course there was cause for his contempt: the Muslim Middle East was always vicious and generally chaotic, and its inhabitants sometimes seemed so totally hopeless as to be beyond reclaim. But the Arabs have a word, *baraka*, which they use to describe the illusive, indefinable quality of being at once blessed and benevolent —the quality that lives in silk, but not in nylon; in sherry, but not in gin. Squalid and depressing though the affairs of the Middle East might be, there were many places there, many people, many things still endowed with *baraka* in the autumn of 1956. There was the persistent and irrepressible humor of the Arabs, still a joy and a stimulant. There was the natural equality and hospitality of these strange peoples. The stately cadences of Arabic had *baraka* still, and so did the sweet voices of the muezzins at sunset; the wrinkled mordancy of the Cairo wits; the big new barrage at Samarra and the timeless mosque of the Omayyads in Damascus. There was blessing and benevolence buried somewhere in the concept of Arab unity. The cheerful Beirut bankers had a kind of *baraka*, and so did the man who winked an eye at me outside the hospital at Kharga. There was *baraka* to the Bedouin encampment above Aqaba, and the clowning workman in the Palace of Forty Pillars in Isfahan, and the Sultan of Muscat and Oman. Blessings haunted the fort at Buraimi; benevolence exuded from Colonel Boustead's drawing room at Mukalla, with the old men yelling on

the sofa. Often and again, for all the threadbare pettiness, the
violence and mediocrity of the Muslim Middle East, you would
find something good or noble or inspiriting embedded in the rubbish.

Ha! the colonel would say: but there was *baraka* to that tall
young god too, and the joy of incorruptibility in his eyes, as he
disappeared among the shadows towards the brothels.

INDEX